ZIONCHECK FOR PRESIDENT

ZIONCHECK FOR PRESIDENT

A TRUE STORY OF IDEALISM AND MADNESS IN AMERICAN POLITICS

PHIL CAMPBELL

NATION BOOKS • NEW YORK

ZIONCHECK FOR PRESIDENT
A TRUE STORY OF IDEALISM AND MADNESS IN AMERICAN POLITICS

Published by
Nation Books
An Imprint of Avalon Publishing Group Inc.
245 West 17th St., 11th Floor
New York, NY 10011

AVALON
publishing group incorporated

Copyright © 2005 by Phil Campbell

First printing October 2005

Nation Books is a co-publishing venture of the Nation Institute and Avalon Publishing Group Incorporated.

Library of Congress Cataloging-in-Publication Data is available.

ISBN: 1-56025-750-4
ISBN 13: 978-1-56025-750-9

9 8 7 6 5 4 3 2 1

Book design by Maria E. Torres

Printed in the United States
Distributed by Publishers Group West

Book Notes

The story is true. There are some asides to this assertion, however.

• *My housemate Doug's name, physical description, and occupation have been changed. A number of early incidents involving Doug were moved slightly in time to fit the book's narrative. "Theresa," our first volunteer coordinator, does not go by that name.*
• *Material about the Grant Cogswell campaign and other events in this book was supplemented by interviews from Grant, his volunteers, and some of my ex-housemates. The material relating to Marion Zioncheck came from a variety of historical sources. Numerous minor incidents involving the Grant Cogswell Campaign were shifted slightly in time (and occasionally in space) to accommodate the narrative structure of this book.*
• *I may or may not have lived on Twenty-third Avenue East.*
• *Grant Cogswell has given his full, if exceedingly nervous, cooperation for this book. One or two incidents, scenes, quotes, or actions involving Grant Cogswell were either fabricated or embellished to the point of falsity. This was done out of political loyalty rather than narrative necessity. If for any reason Grant needs to dismiss this book as "a malicious pack of lies," he'll be free to do so.*

"And you, you ridiculous people, you expect me to help you."
—Denis Johnson, *Jesus' Son*

———

This book is dedicated to my parents.
May they not believe a word of it.

Preface

August 1936

U.S. Representative Marion Anthony Zioncheck looked out his office window and down at the swelling, shifting throng that had gathered in his name and wondered if he was going mad. Thousands of people crowded the streets of downtown Seattle, cheering with a fierce, throaty conviction. They—Hooverville tramps holding communist tracts and wearing rags that were more mud than material; penniless Japanese flophouse managers from Skid Road; square-jawed sailors on leave in their windcheater jackets; hardbitten Scandinavian loggers; even a few sympathetic middle-aged rich women who were trying too hard to look like Jean Harlow—shouldered against each other, slid down the hilly sidewalks, climbed light poles, and carried on as if they had all just stumbled out of a bar.

"Hulet?" Zioncheck said. "Is the rumor true—is there another strike? Do they want me to give a speech?" But Hulet Wells—friend, roommate, and legislative aide—wasn't there, having abandoned him a few months before over a situation Zioncheck could only characterize as a lack of faith. The congressman felt a sadness when he recalled this. "Oh, forget you, then," he told the empty room.

His mind was on the crowd, anyway. The people were rising up. As he watched he ran a hand through his thinning hair and started humming an Irving Berlin tune that his wife Rubye had played on her old Victrola. He waltzed with himself around the room. Populism! Anarchy! More people kept pouring around the corner, completely blocking the car that was waiting for him. Rubye and her brother were in that car; he laughed at how angry they must be over the spontaneous mob.

Don't worry, my crazy lover, he thought. *Politics is always like this. If we ever stop fighting, the people have lost for sure.*

Zioncheck sat at his desk and thought about what would be on his agenda for his next term. He looked in his briefcase for a blank piece of paper. The first thing he must do, he thought, is demand the resignation of that son-of-a-bitch Hoover at the FBI, even if fighting him meant airing half of Washington's dirty secrets, from the Lindbergh baby to the way John Dillinger died. People are such cowards, always sipping at hypocrisy and smooth talk instead of swallowing the truth. He'd give them the truth! Next he would hire a couple more of his radical Seattle friends as his advisers *(Hulet, where are you? You and me, we were supposed to see this through to the very end.)* Then he'd lobby the President for expansion of the New Deal, so that no one in America ever went hungry again. And after that he would get the new FBI director to investigate the Negro lynchings in the South, and maybe the mistreatment of the Indians on their reservations, and then maybe after that he'd sock that no-good Texas Republican Tom Blanton in the face.

Zioncheck exploded in laughter at that last thought. He had been to jail too many times, and he probably didn't need to start another brawl on the House floor.

The cacophony outside was getting louder, and the downtown buildings were vibrating. Zioncheck grabbed the edges of his desk to steady himself, then ran to the window and tried to make sense of what he saw. Fog was enveloping everything, blurring his vision and trapping and choking him. Seattle weather. The shouting and the cheering now seemed to come from inside his head, echoes of a fantasy he had created for himself. *This all seems crazy but I'm not mad,* he told himself, pacing. *I just have to keep working that's all.*

Someone was outside his office rattling the locked door. "Marion! What are you doing in there!" It was his brother-in-law.

"Just a minute!"

Zioncheck looked down at his piece of paper, a sheet of congressional stationary. This would be his most important speech. "My only hope in life was to improve an unfair economic system that . . . ." As he wrote, hurrying, he wondered if he should change the verb tense. Americans only cared about the future.

A few moments later, Marion Zioncheck was rushing outside to meet his people.

1

Grant Cogswell was first captivated by the story of Marion Zioncheck in the mid-1990s, when he read about him in Skid Road, *a popular Seattle history book by Murray Morgan. The four-page profile of Zioncheck wastes little time in describing the turbulent events that turned Zioncheck from a young 1930s radical into an unlikely figure of international attention and then into a figure of tragic martyrdom. It is quite a story, though it is not hard to understand why America deliberately forgot it. Grant was so energized by the Zioncheck profile that he read it over the phone to his friend Bob Mould, former frontman for Hüsker Dü. Mould was awed, too. People's lives were so rich back then, he told Grant. What are you talking about? Grant said. Most people would envy your place in history, transforming music as you have. That's a form of revolution, too.*

November 1999

The crowds in downtown Seattle stretched far beyond my line of vision. I was barely awake but I had already spilled my coffee scrambling for my pen and reporter's notepad. I hadn't realized that the protests against the World Trade Organization were going to be this big. People were waving signs, marching, dancing, playing Rage Against the Machine, wearing strange costumes. Many of them had locked arms to form human barricades. All this activity and it wasn't even eight o'clock.

Three bearded men in expensive suits jostled past me. They had been given a tremendous push by a crowd of grungy student activists. I clicked my pen into writing mode and started asking questions.

"We are *French!*" they said. I followed them. The crowd, growing in size, strength, and weirdness, moved with us, a living organism with a collective will. The Frenchmen followed its contours like viruses trying to find an opening in a massive cell wall. Two burly cops materialized, ruining my metaphor. The Frenchmen, with the help of the Seattle Police Department, found a way to penetrate the crowd. I, meanwhile, was turned away at a service entrance of the Washington State Convention Center, where the conference was officially being held.

I walked around aimlessly, another uninformed journalist trying to make sense of so much organized chaos. Many of the protesters were white and in their twenties, and I could tell by their rhetoric that they had the same socially conscious anxiety that I did—the same indescribable panic of seeing so much materialistic excess in a posh department store, the same maddening frustration when yet another major American corporation was exposed for having put ten-year-olds in Thailand to work in sweatshop factories, the same thick outrage toward pollution along our country's *maquiladora* border. But I was new to the city and unfamiliar with West Coast liberalism, and I had not known that there were so many people who felt as I did, and (unlike me) had found a way to translate a desperate feeling into an action, asserting in the process that their protest would be part of a leaderless, semi-anarchical movement. Truly astonishing.

Hours passed. I had a conversation with a Norwegian delegate whom the activists had turned away. I exchanged brief words with some women dressed as sea turtles. I trailed filmmaker Michael Moore around for about an hour while he cracked jokes on a borrowed megaphone about how the WTO president, whose name also happened to be Michael Moore, was an evil twin. After a while I walked to a Burger King. As I paid for my food, I noticed some people staring at a television mounted on the far wall, watching the national news. They were airing live images of downtown Seattle. The police had decided to use force to disperse the crowd. I ran from the restaurant, notepad in hand, an inorganically grown french fry still hooked in my mouth.

Outside, the crowd roiled and gagged on smoke. The concussion grenades, pepper spray, and tear gas created an entirely new brand of disorder. I tried to be careful, but without the benefit of a gas mask—or even a black anarchist ski mask—I couldn't do much more than hold my breath and hope for the best. I stumbled around, clutching my eyes. Tears streamed as I fell and groped for my asthma inhaler.

Right then, my knees still rubbing the sidewalk, I saw Grant Cogswell, one of the few people I knew in Seattle. He emerged from the crippling vapors like a two-wheeled apparition. He was on his bike, moving through the bedlam with a surprising grace and speed. He was a mobile mirage, a blur of spokes and feet, a phantom with a white bicycle helmet, a glint of tiny glasses and fierce eyes. He flew right by me, his fingers glued to handlebars, his heavy, pale legs peddling ferociously. His face—what I caught of it—evinced a ruthless determination. Then he was gone.

The next morning, shortly after the Seattle mayor had declared part of the downtown area to be a "no-protest zone," Grant stood outside the Sheraton Hotel, where most of the trade officials had stayed, and shouted at anybody who even vaguely resembled a delegate. His one-man chorus went something like this: "We are not going to let you establish a government that does not honor the needs of the poor while it ignores the problems of the environment!" When I arrived at the same spot a half-hour later, Grant had disappeared. The police were still there, enforcing the mayor's zero-tolerance policy. I watched a young activist get tackled and arrested for carrying a stick with a plastic dove glued to the top; when his friends protested, they were handcuffed and shoved into a van.

When I did catch up with Grant, he was emitting short verbal ejaculations. "Will you look at this?" he shouted. "I am so stoked! I tell you, this is what it's all about! This is history! Right here!" Grant knew more about the WTO than I did, but he had been just as unprepared for the sheer *bigness* of what was taking place. He was so inspired by the protests, he later told me that he included imagery of it in his epic ode to the great Marion Zioncheck:

a circle gathered at Sixth and Pine
under the nervous eyes of police
and spoke onto the bare ground of the future:
I stood with them and I saw you,

there in your boyish madness and rage
shaking not from fear but love.
After that you stayed with me all year.
Everything you saw I see—

Grant and I stayed with the protests through the rest of the week, confronting police, fleeing tear gas, ducking into bars when the smoke got too heavy, and watching police helicopters buzz over our neighborhood of Capitol Hill until four in the morning. I yelled after Grant whenever I saw him. He would stop, recognize me, say hi, and veer off into another part of the crowd, hoping to get a better view, a better piece of the action, his bike helmet bobbing up and down in agreement with the anticorporate banners, the chanting people, the half-naked lesbians.

I couldn't say what separated him from everyone else who was out running around Seattle that week. He had played no role in organizing the event. He wasn't among the hundreds of protesters who had been arrested. He was no better than anybody else in articulating what the protests really meant. But he possessed something that the other protesters did not: Grant exuded joy. His entire body seemed to transmute the complications of global politics and environmental and social justice into understandable things: the romantic, the deeply personal, the human. Grant embodied ideas that I longed to comprehend. I could sense this about him before he explained his political theories, let me read his poetry, or showed me the bewildering tattoo on his arm.

I wanted that passion, that joy, that—*belief*.

And so it happened very simply: Grant Cogswell was thoroughly absorbed by the WTO protests, and I was thoroughly absorbed by Grant Cogswell.

June 2001

But however encouraging or stimulating the WTO protests may have been for Grant and countless other liberals, they did not help me. Less than two years after the protests, my own idealism was officially dead.

In a small conference room among the third-floor offices of the *Stranger*, a Seattle alternative weekly, words were being said that I had never thought would be directed at me. *It's not working out. You're not happy with us and we're not happy with you.* Within a few minutes I was out on the street. I had been promised a letter of recommendation to help me get another job, in some other city. Without having said a word in my own defense I knew that the meeting meant my career as a crusading journalist was over.

I got into my car, a grimy red Geo, switched on the ignition and pounded through the gears. The front tires skidded and hydroplaned on small puddles. A pedestrian glared as I swerved around him. The infamous, impotent Seattle glare usually made me laugh. Today I felt my own rage building.

I might have blamed *Stranger* news readers. Too many of them were West Coast lefties, the kind who looked at you with disgust for using the vegetarian spatula to turn over the meat at a cookout. It had taken me months to learn how not to get trapped in conversations with people who wanted to brag about something earnest that they had done, such as vacationing in Chiapas for no other reason than to listen to struggling Mexican peasants talk about their problems. The chesty self-righteousness of the majority of this bunch—a parade of liberals, progressives, socialists, and Marxists—often ballooned into the absurd.

Maybe the problem was Seattle itself. The city was not newsworthy. Most everyone had moved here from somewhere else, and they were all happy with that choice. City government was largely corruption-free. Officials rarely said anything provocative or daring. The police were polite and the murder rate was low. This was a far cry from Memphis, Tennessee, where I had last worked. Memphis—where racial tensions were always a front-page story, where the robbery and homicide statistics kept everyone on edge, where people filed for personal bankruptcy more than anyone anywhere, where undercover cops stole city money in order to blow it in Las Vegas—*that* was a real city. Seattle was a pristine little suburb set among some pretty mountain ranges and lakes. If it hadn't been for the WTO protests, I would have had no curiosity at all about the place.

I swerved around a bus and the Geo hit a pothole. I didn't see the yellow lights until they were red. I hit the gas and kept driving. I thought of all the car accidents that I had been in and did not care. I parked the car on a side street next to the house I rented. My new situation was still sinking in. From the moment I had been able to articulate my goals in life, I had spoken in terms of a mission, a *reason*. But now there was nothing.

The rest of the day was spent taking phone calls from friends, relatives, and colleagues from the paper who wanted to reassure themselves that my termination was my fault, not something random and capricious that might befall them, too. My girlfriend, who freelanced for the *Stranger,* dropped by, but she couldn't stay for long. I lay on the couch until I thought I heard my housemates start coming home, then I retreated to my room to sit on the bed and wait for nothing to happen.

Grant Cogswell was the last to call. A freelance music and

books critic who rarely dropped by the paper's offices, he always got the gossip thirdhand.

"I heard what happened," he said, frantic. "Are you leaving town?"

"Those motherfucking sons of bitches," I said. "They didn't even—"

"Answer my question!" Grant snapped. "Are you leaving Seattle?"

There was a lengthy pause. "No," I said. He could have at least asked me if I was OK. "I mean, I should leave, but I've got a girl-friend now, and I've got friends here, and I am not going to be forced to move anywhere else."

"Oh, thank God!" Grant said he would be out of town for a few days, but he would call me after he got back. There were things he wanted to talk to me about.

"Fine," I said, finger hovering over the disconnect button. "See you then."

Empty days passed. Yellow sunlight crept across dirty venetian blinds. A PlayStation 2 lay in front of a dying television set. Black footprints and bicycle tire marks streaked a wooden floor. I lay on the living-room couch, a decrepit old thing that looked and smelled like burnt toast. Unshaven and twenty-eight, I was the picture of contemporary unemployment. At this time of day, one-something in the afternoon, there was only one person I knew who was at home and not working. I grabbed my phone and dialed Grant. A recording. His flat, digitized voice warned me that his phone was being tapped. I was encouraged to leave a message.

"You're not being *bugged,* Grant," I said. This was the third time in four days that I had tried and failed to reach him. "God-dammit. Call me." As an afterthought, I added some lies about Grant's sexual proclivities, as well as a wandering discourse about what happened to small-penised men who didn't return their big-dicked friend's phone calls. I thanked the FBI agents who were listening, and I hung up.

Poverty loomed over me, as unappetizing as the third week's bowl of ramen noodles. My severance check was barely enough to pay off my credit card balance. I was given the option of taking individual health insurance, but the monthly premiums were prohibitive. The best I could do was visit my health care providers one last time, before my benefits ran out. Both my dentist and my optometrist had given me disapproving looks and a lecture when I told them I didn't know when I would return.

I did have one thing going for me—a fantastic rental situation. The landlady and I had a deal; she gave me a hefty rent discount and I managed the 3,000-square-foot house that I shared with six other tenants. It wasn't a tough job. I had to repair small things, like the showerhead or the kitchen sink's u-valve. I had to call the plumber or the electrician if something big broke and I had to find new tenants when the old ones moved out. Most of the time, I got by without doing much more than making sure my housemates paid their share of the bills.

I looked at the cable box clock. Still two more hours before a *Kids in the Hall* repeat. I stayed on the couch and stared at the ceiling. I could become an alcoholic. There were plenty of alcoholics in American history who had managed to make a pretty good name for themselves. Booze killed time, at least. My housemate Doug probably had some good hooch stashed in his room, but he and I hadn't been talking lately. There was always the unfinished bottle of tequila in the dining room.

Then again, I could just kill myself. Finding a gun in Seattle would probably not be hard, though finding a high-altitude bridge was easier. The only thing I'd have to overcome was the last moment of conscious action, when the fingers closed over the trigger, when the feet left the precipice. Then my worries would be over.

Was I talking to myself, or were the words only in my head? I looked around to make sure I was alone—I didn't want anyone to hear me; threatening suicide and not following through could look melodramatic.

The phone rang and I jumped. My cordless had fallen between the cushions of the couch. After I found it I picked it up.

"Yes," Grant said flatly. "I *am* being bugged." The FBI was undoubtedly curious about some of his recent anarchist-related activities.

He proposed that we take one of our usual walks around our neighborhood. A few minutes later, I was setting out to meet him at his apartment. Time was moving again.

Grant's apartment door had been left open. He was in the bathroom. I moved some books off his sofa and helped myself to a seat.

His living room was a collection of contradictory items and themes. A turquoise iMac sat inert in one corner; Grant barely knew how to use it. A grandfather clock imposed itself on another corner; it did not work. Some old, ragged Turkish rugs covered the hardwood floor. A light-colored chair resembling a grasshopper in avant-garde repose stood across from a beaten, hard, spotted sofa. The most prominent things on the walls were some African masks and a poster of the London subway system; on a hallway shelf sat black-and-white photos of his father and grandmother, who were both dead. The apartment did not get much sunlight, and Grant fought the darkness in the evenings with unfashionable brass floor lamps. He abhorred the idea of artificial light above his head, so even though there were ceiling fixtures, Grant made sure that there were never any bulbs in their sockets.

He emerged from the bathroom. Grant Cogswell was about five feet eleven, 180 pounds, with a frame that preferred beef over bones. He had a round head, thin lips, and compact ears, and he kept his thinning brown hair short. During the WTO, his bright, small hazel eyes had been intensified by a pair of tiny glasses, but recently he had purchased a pair of larger, thicker black frames, which made him look younger and more approachable. Once Grant showed me a picture of himself when he was a decade younger, when he looked like an angry Matt Damon. Now in his early thirties, Grant Cogswell bore a closer resemblance to Charlie Brown.

"Hey, how you doing?" Grant said.

"Oh, I'm OK," I said uneasily, unwilling to tell the truth. "How are you?"

"Awful," he said, and laughed. He put on his shoes and socks.

We walked along Fifteenth Avenue East toward Dick's Drive-In on Broadway, an unsavory outdoor burger joint that specialized in ice cream and some of the fastest red meat ever nuked. I spun my well-refined tale of woe about the *Stranger*. Grant listened respectfully, but I could tell he wasn't quite following me. He adored the *Stranger*, read it cover-to-cover every week as soon as it came out. And he loved crusades, so long as they were the right kind. In fact I worried briefly if losing my job at the *Stranger* would mean the end of our friendship, because there were some things about Seattle that Grant took very, very personally.

"They just gave you the wrong beat to cover," Grant said. "The police aren't the central issue in this town. You should have been covering gentrification and economic development." He seemed to be struggling to find words.

"So what about you?" I said, changing the subject. "What are you doing these days?"

It was obvious that Grant had something to say. He wasn't in one of his lighter moods, like the time he attacked my car windshield with a fresh pile of dog poop. But neither was he in one of his solitary moods, the kind that made me wonder how close *he* had ever come to killing himself.

He was tense. He looked like he wanted to go down to the docks and start a fight.

"I'm thinking of running for city council," Grant said. He paused to let this sink in. We both walked faster. "Richard McIver has *got* to go down," he fumed.

Richard McIver was a Seattle city councilmember and the chairman of the council transportation committee. Grant believed that McIver was ruining Seattle's chances of building effective mass transit. "He's worthless," Grant said. "Just awful. And what I can't believe is that nobody's stepping in to run against him. I tell you, if nobody else runs against him, *I will*. I've got no choice."

One of McIver's biggest mistakes, Grant said, was supporting Sound Transit, the multi-billion-dollar agency that was trying to build light rail in Seattle. To Grant, this was a catastrophic mistake. There were better solutions.

Grant stopped walking.

"If I get elected to city council, you know what I'm going to do?" he said, the words spilling from him like an outraged prophet. "I'm going to take McIver's seat on the Sound Transit board, and then I'm going to go to Sound Transit meetings in a polar bear suit."

I waited. He explained: "They're not going to want to deal with me, but I'm going to address the Sound Transit chair anyway. 'This place is a circus anyway,' I'll say. 'You're going to have to accept the fact that I'm dressed like a polar bear. You're going to have to talk to me like I am a polar bear, because I'm not taking this thing off until Sound Transit starts to act rationally and kills the light-rail plan.

"And time's running out," Grant said. "I gotta do it now or not at all."

2

Born Antoni Zajaczek in Poland in December of 1901, Marion Zioncheck and his family emigrated to the United States when he was a boy and settled into Seattle's Beacon Hill neighborhood. As a young man he changed his name to the more pronounceable Zioncheck.

He started his political career as an undergraduate at the University of Washington, where he challenged the excessive power of fraternities and athletics on campus. He organized non-Greek students into an independent coalition and then demanded an investigation into questionable athletic department expenses. His detractors decided to punish him for being so rebellious. They carried him outside in the middle of a cold winter night, shaved his head, took turns punching him, and tossed him into an icy lake. But Zioncheck refused to back down, and took his case to the city's daily newspapers. He won an instant reputation as a young iconoclast, while the jocks who had attacked him were suspended and expelled.

He was only in his twenties when he scored one of the most impressive political victories of his career, leading a successful recall election against Seattle Mayor Frank Edwards, who had dared to tinker with the city's utility company against the interests of the people. Soon after that, Zioncheck was announcing his ambitions to run for Congress. Though he ran a tough campaign, he received scant media attention—unless you count the time he visited the King County Jail to hand out cigars and ask inmates for their vote. When he won, it seemed to many that he had succeeded solely on the force of his personality.

This was 1932, the same year that FDR defeated Hoover. He was sworn in the year Prohibition was repealed.

Grant Cogswell was a punk rock fan who couldn't stand it if anybody danced too close to him in clubs. He was a taxi driver who despised automobiles. He often looked capable of kicking anybody's ass, even asses belonging to people much larger than him, yet his recurring back problems probably would have made that difficult. A true believer in the power of American democracy, Grant often dumped ridicule and contempt on the very by-products of that democracy, including (but not limited to) suburbs, corporations, and Top 40 music. A loner, he was one of the loneliest people I ever met.

When the WTO protests ended, Grant wrote about other left-wing protests for the *Stranger*. He caravaned with a group of demonstrators down to the 2000 Democratic National Convention in Los Angeles and spent all his time outside, where the speeches and rhetoric weren't marketed for mainstream digestion. In the spring of 2001, he took a bus ride across America with the Black Bloc, a group of anarchists in search of a protest in Quebec City. Back again in Seattle, he ran around downtown with a hundred anarchists who opposed the pro-globalist Asian Pacific Cities Summit. Grant considered getting laser eye surgery, so that the next time he was in a street demonstration he wouldn't have to worry about his glasses getting knocked off his face.

We had started hanging out together shortly after the WTO. Grant no longer drank, so we generally avoided bars, instead walking together around Capitol Hill, sitting in coffeehouses, reading and talking. We joked around, as friends will do, and we confided in each other about our problems, like Grant's ongoing battle with alcohol and depression, his conflicted feelings about his bisexuality, and my growing unease toward practically everything I could name. Especially politics. This was Seattle in 2000, and the left's ascendant argument was embodied in a third-party candidate named Ralph Nader, who believed that the entire American political system was so corrupt that it needed to be scrapped. There was a distinct sense that everything around me was unraveling; I was assured that this was a good thing.

Grant introduced me to the principles and aesthetics of anti-globalist rebellion. America was engaged in a class struggle and only the rich really knew about it, he said. The corporate marketplace consumed everything, so the only thing left to do was try to build democracy among the people around you—your neighbor, your co-worker, even your roommate—and hopefully those efforts would spread, eventually shifting the entire body politic. To live anywhere was to live in a city, and to live in a city was to embrace it completely, making you personally responsible for vigorous, conscientious political dissent, and for following the latest developments in local music, arts, literature, and culture.

"You've gotta get tapped in," Grant said, countless times. "Otherwise you'll never understand it." To Grant, *it* didn't just contain the streets we walked, or Seattle, or even the Pacific Northwest. *It* wasn't so much a single pronoun but a word weighted down by a million more words, each tinctured by observation, thought, criticism, and action. *It* was elusive. *It* was urgent, obsessive.

An image from that time: Grant, in a bleak, whisky-and-Pall-Mall bar, hanging out with me and other writers from the *Stranger*. The rest of us are toasting each other for no reason whatsoever, exchanging witticisms with hearty joviality and a sense of self-satisfaction. Grant sits nearby but apart from us, coiled and nettled, his old navy greatcoat draping over his shoulders and his hands in green fingerless gloves twisting around his coffee mug. Mostly he is silent, but when a stray comment interests him he pounces, moving forward in short declarative bursts to destroy any doubt about Ang Lee, Sonic Youth, or the inherent problems of mainstream politics. Among the members of this group he was safe; no one took offense at his brusque mannerisms because everyone harbored idiosyncrasies of their own. In wider circles his personality repelled as many as it attracted, but if you asked him he would insist that he was the one doing the dismissing.

At his urgings I bought a bicycle, so that I could absorb Seattle on a more personal level. I bought the Seattle books and albums he recommended and tagged along with him to clubs to see the best alternative rock bands the city had to offer. And I changed the way I perceived myself. Before I was just an underpaid skeptic, but now poverty was its own source of pride. Money only increased one's opportunities for hypocrisy. Seattle itself bored me, but the atmosphere of the city and Grant's perspective on it suffused everything with a sense of opportunity, of change, of enormous scale. We went to see *Fight Club* together and left the theater elated: The final scene in which Edward Norton blows up several major corporate skyscrapers provided a cartharsis that needed no explanation.

Grant's beliefs possessed him, absorbed him. His was a tightly bound, self-contained concentration of energy. His entire body, in fact, seemed enveloped in metaphysics and metaphor.

Which brings me to the story of his tattoo.

Grant moved to Seattle in May of 1994, the month after Kurt Cobain killed himself. He chose Seattle as his new home because his grandparents had once lived nearby, on Mercer Island on the other side of Lake Washington. Grant was nostalgic for the abstract things that reminded him of the Pacific Northwest, like the salty sea air that drifted in from Puget Sound. He was determined to get a fresh start, and vowed not to return to the sort of drinking that had nearly destroyed him two years before. To help him stay sober he sat in coffeehouses and worked on a novel that contained a lot of sex and a protagonist who was an urban planner. He kept to himself. Despite Cobain's death and Grant's social isolation, the city was fraught with possibility.

One day Grant saw an article in the morning paper that

intrigued him. A local cab driver named Dick Falkenbury had taken it upon himself to launch a grassroots political campaign. Falkenbury's goal was to extend the city's downtown monorail so that it would reach the whole city—perhaps even the entire metropolitan area—and in doing so to improve mass transit, which was in sorry shape. The downtown monorail was a useless tourist curio; it was one mile long and ended near the Space Needle, another useless structure built for the 1962 World's Fair that at least had earned its keep as an iconic image of the city. For Falkenbury, monorail wasn't just a plaything; it was an efficient peoplemover, a gorgeous piece of urban infrastructure that could shape the region's future by slowing suburban sprawl, reducing traffic congestion and lowering regional pollution levels.

The article excited Grant monorail made perfect sense, and it was inspiring to see a regular citizen like Falkenbury get involved. He thought about volunteering, but political activism seemed unrealistic, since he didn't know anyone in Seattle yet. He put the newspaper down and went about his solitary day.

Later that summer, Grant bumped into Falkenbury just as Grant was leaving Bumbershoot, the city's big music festival. The lumpy, amiable cab driver was standing just outside the festival gates, in the shadow of the old monorail, trying to gather enough signatures to get his monorail proposal placed on the November ballot. Grant, who was already fired up by an afternoon's worth of punk music, approached Falkenbury and asked him who he needed to call to volunteer.

"That would be me," Falkenbury said, loading up his beat-up van. Apparently, he had not had any luck expanding his campaign. The one-billion-dollar mass-transit proposal was a few months old and was still being run by just one person.

The two talked, and Grant was impressed with Falkenbury's ideas—the cabbie could out-talk anyone—but not with his campaign materials. Falkenbury was using a little card table with a plastic covering, accompanied by amateurish, hand-painted signs.

Grant thought the presentation was no better than a third grade
bake sale. Alone, Grant concluded, Falkenbury didn't stand a
chance.

Grant Cogswell became convinced with a revelatory certainty
that he could help Falkenbury. *This* would be where he made a difference. He joined the campaign.

They were an unlikely pair. Grant was twenty-seven, physically solid, hotheaded, blunt-spoken, occasionally brilliant, pos-
sessing a mind that reduced all issues to narrow fields of black
or white, epic or insignificant, poetic or contemptible. Falkenbury, on the other hand, was forty-two, physically oafish,
instantly likeable, easygoing, chatty, occasionally brilliant, pos-
sessing a mind that retained and regurgitated the most meaningless articles of trivia along the most circuitous of conversational
paths. Falkenbury drove the van and Grant sometimes rode
shotgun and sometimes got around on his bike.

They struggled to get the required number of signatures,
eighteen thousand, but because they didn't have the money to hire
a platoon of signature gatherers, they failed. By the time the filing
deadline arrived, they had gathered only ten thousand names. By
the end of 1994, they had to give up.

Depression, self-doubt, and bad luck haunted them both.
Falkenbury went on antidepressants as financial problems pressed
in. He was unable to keep up the mortgage payments on his two
houses, and he lost them both. He moved back in with his mother
on the north side of town. Grant fared little better. He gave up on
his novel, fell off the wagon, and was overwhelmed by memories of
relatives who had recently died. At one point Grant decided to try
politics again, throwing his energies behind a grassroots campaign
to prevent the government from taxing citizens to fund new stadiums for the Mariners and the Seahawks. He and other back-to-
basics populists fought hard, but big money won and the stadiums
were approved. Grant and Falkenbury contacted each other and
returned to the monorail campaign, more determined than ever.

Grant decided to address the problem of gathering signatures. Since they couldn't be everywhere at once, he invented a device that essentially gathered signatures for them. The self-service petition stand was a collapsible A-frame structure made out of cheap plywood and door hinges. The stands were placed on sidewalks in high-pedestrian areas all over town, with petitions stapled to them at eye level. Curious passersby read the petitions and signed them by the thousands. Grant and Falkenbury still had a lot of work to do, but this time it didn't involve personally selling their idea to every registered voter they could find. Instead, they drove all over the city each week monitoring their petition stands. As before, Falkenbury drove, rambling on good-naturedly about local history and the importance of good urban planning; Grant listened to Falkenbury and studied the contours of the city as it passed by.

Grant became obsessed with his political mission. One time he saw a local drunk, probably homeless, vandalizing one of his petition stands. Grant forgot all about his liberal concerns for the poor and for fellow alcoholics. He walked up behind the man, gave him a fierce push, screamed at him and threatened him with hospitalization if he ever touched another petition stand again. This seemed to do the trick, as the man, perhaps stunned that anybody in Seattle would act so aggressively, was not seen near any other petition stands.

It took until 1997 and required several changes in strategy and tactics, but they got the monorail proposal on the ballot. Falkenbury made the campaign entertaining, putting to work his growing reputation as a kook. He invited TV cameras to join him at the old monorail—to watch him race an automobile and the monorail. The car, of course, got stuck in traffic, but the monorail smoothly reached its destination. Falkenbury grinned for the cameras, the victor of a dumb, perfect stunt. TV news ate it up.

The election came, and they won.

Falkenbury celebrated by going home to tell his mother. Grant celebrated by visiting a neighborhood tattoo parlor called Lucky Devil and demanding a tattoo they had never given anyone before. About three inches high and almost as wide, the Seattle city logo is now etched on Grant's left bicep in blue-green ink, a stylized profile of Chief Seattle in the center of a small vortex of pointed half-circles, which, on closer inspection, are the outside parts of an *S*. The tattoo was the perfect bridge for Grant, connecting his self-styled punk persona to his passion for a rebellious form of grassroots politics. If anything qualified as being *it,* this did.

Grant told me this story in a coffeehouse (omitting the part about the homeless drunk, which he was ashamed of). I was seized with delight and started to shout and laugh.

Grant told me to shut up.

"Will you quiet down?" he said, snapping. When I protested, he said, "Don't you realize that this is a small town, that people *talk?*" His tone and gaze were so intense that I fell silent.

Later that evening, back in his apartment, Grant relaxed and showed me his tattoo. The logo didn't look like much on a government truck, but on a person's arm it was weirdly compelling. Grant had taken an obligatory symbol and turned it into something iconoclastic, subversive.

Grant also showed me a newspaper clipping of his monorail success from the *New York Times*. He and Falkenbury made the front page of the Sunday edition on December 7, 1997, the fifty-sixth anniversary of Pearl Harbor. The paper was already yellowing and brittle, but that didn't take away from its power. Grant's story was denied the most glamorous position of all, the space above the paper's fold, by breaking international events. A Russian military transport plane, carrying two jets in its giant belly, had smashed into an apartment complex in southern Siberia, killing dozens of people and making history as one of that country's biggest air disasters.

Times reporter Timothy Egan had this to say about Falkenbury and Cogswell:

> They were two men with no money, scorned by the political establishment and ignored by the press, whose campaign consisted of going around Seattle with a plywood sign that urged people to build a $1 billion mass-transit system. When the two won, gaining nearly 53 percent approval, it was perhaps the biggest political upset in the Pacific Northwest since a bartender was elected mayor of Portland 10 years ago.

Egan labeled them, too. Falkenbury was the visionary taxi driver. Grant, who did not yet drive a cab, was the energetic, part-time poet. A picture accompanies the article. Grant Cogswell and Dick Falkenbury both wear dark sweaters over white knit shirts, the only good clothes they own. Grant has on huge black sunglasses and a longshoreman's black hat. It looks like a promo shot for a rock band, but instead of false angst or hip indifference, their faces are radiant with victory.

If seeing Grant at the WTO had inspired my curiosity, then hearing the monorail story converted me. Grant didn't just talk about his political theories, he acted on them, in his own way, successfully and unapologetically. He looked at things with both an ideological fervor and a zealous pragmatism, a rare perspective in most people. Moreover, he was was someone who struggled through life honestly; he had his problems, but that didn't stop him from engaging in politics when he thought he had to.

Now Grant was saying that he could win a seat on the Seattle city council. And I thought so, too.

3

The best source on Zioncheck is Hulet Wells, his legislative aide and roommate. As a condition of his employment, Zioncheck made Wells leave the company of his wife and move in with him. Wells could not help but admire Zioncheck. "He could have had his choice of many beautiful women," he wrote in his unfinished memoir, "for he was the most eligible bachelor in the House [of Representatives], erect and broad shouldered, open-handed and friendly of manner, with good looks and ten thousand dollars a year . . . We became tenants . . . in a stupendous pile of buildings called the Westchester Apartments."

Wells saw Zioncheck at his best, from the early '30s through 1935, and his worst, in 1936, when Zioncheck didn't seem like Zioncheck at all but some dark alter ego.

I sat on the couch in our living room, a slim reporter's notebook in my lap. Grant hadn't asked me to help him in any specific way, but I was already consumed by the idea of his city council campaign. I had to get some ideas out. I turned to a fresh page and gazed at the wide, light blue lines. Then, like a child attempting to play the piano, I madly banged out some notes.

> Grant   =   *a friend . . . who's off his rocker*
>   =   *Temperamental, depressive . . .*
>   =   *City council? What the hell?*

I would have to learn to be less cynical.

My thoughts were interrupted by Emily, a housemate who, by the sound of it, was talking on her cordless phone as she came upstairs from her basement suite. I tried sinking lower in the couch to avoid her, but she saw me. She asked her friend if she could call her back and then she got my attention.

"Did you hear from the landlady, or the plumber?" she asked. Emily wasn't much taller than the couch I was lying on.

"Oh, hi, Emily," I said. "Yeah, I called the plumber, and they're coming tomorrow, but I'm not really confident we can fix this right away. It's such a strange problem and it could be anything. The landlady even recommended that we might try a specialist called an 'odor detector.' We might have to do that."

"It really stinks down there," she said, "especially whenever you guys flush the toilet upstairs."

"Yeah, I know. Listen, I'm sorry it's been taking me so long to get to this. There's been so much going on lately—"

"It's OK." Just as quickly as she had appeared, she left, darting into the kitchen to call back her friend.

I looked down at my notes and crossed out the list I had made. I tried again, this time moving with deliberate restraint.

- *Grant's political leanings mirror my own*
- *He has a track record as a successful activist*
- *Populists have real cachet in Seattle.*
- *Grant knows Seattle—has a 'vision'*

I grew more excited with every pro that I wrote down. Not only that, I thought, but since Grant and I were both writers, it went without saying that we'd be good at communicating our ideas. Grant was probably a good public speaker (*Question: Is he?* another note materialized, off to the side) and I know all about talking up reporters. *He could beat McIver . . .*

We could beat McIver. He would need my help. I knew it. I suspected Grant did, too.

Lying there on the couch, I closed my eyes and tried to understand why I was so feverish. Up until that point, I had not cared a whit about Seattle's grossly inadequate mass transit system.

The first time I ever argued with somebody about politics was in high school. By senior year I considered myself a budding political mind, reading *Time, Newsweek,* and *U.S. News and World Report* and scorning the ability of my hometown newspaper, the *Blade,* to cover national and world affairs. Gawky, eager, and unpopular, I did not run for student government but I did persuade the senior class president to give me some important committee assignments; I was also the president of the school's Model United Nations.

I had just seen a segment on *60 Minutes* about the U.S. Army's Bradley Fighting Vehicle, an overpriced machine that was so vulnerable to attack that soldiers felt safer walking next to it than riding in it. In the cafeteria the next day I made a passing comment about how inefficient the military was.

"What do you mean, the military is inefficient?" asked Matt Angle. Angle was a budding Ohio conservative who was thinking of becoming an engineer.

"Did you see the story last night on *60 Minutes?* About the Bradley Fighting Vehicle?"

"No—so?"

"So the Bradley's a waste of money, and so are a bunch of other weapons programs. We're wasting money on that when we could be—"

"Which other programs?" Angle demanded.

It went downhill for me from there. I hated debating people outside of Model U.N., where I could pretend to be someone else after conducting prodigious amounts of research. I had no talent articulating my larger points, which in this case was that *any* political institution that got billions of dollars a year would inevitably become bloated and wasteful, particularly the military, which in my opinion should have started dismantling itself the moment the

Berlin Wall had fallen the year before. Wasn't it obvious that the world was becoming a peaceful, civilized place?

Matt, however, was relentless, sticking to the original, technical point of my assertion. He pushed and needled me on my knowledge of the efficacy of various weapons systems and U.S. military bases throughout Europe and the world, and before long I realized that not only did I stand to lose an argument that I had not wanted to have, I stood to lose the cocky, carefree attitude that was helping me survive high school.

"Well what about the poor?" I said, desperate now. The poor were a constant topic at the Jesuit school we attended.

"What *about* them?" he countered.

I burst into tears.

Later that year I did a week-long class project in the office of our local congresswoman, Marcy Kaptur, who was a working-class Democrat, the kind I admired most. Her office staff seemed to like me, and I was given some random, innocuous assignments. Near the end of the week the office manager decided to test my political mettle by asking me to find the 'positive side' to a government report on out-of-wedlock teenage birthrates in Ohio. I walked to the library and studied the report for an hour before I realized what I was being asked to do, and the revelation horrified me. *Why would I manipulate an official government report? They're asking me to twist this around for political gain!* That night I didn't get any sleep, beginning an ongoing battle with insomnia, and by morning I had vowed never to work for a politician or run for political office. My personal integrity, I decided, was far too important.

Politics was too alluring to leave completely, however; in fact, the more repellant it seemed, the more attractive it became. So in college I found comfort in journalism. Objectivity was the shield with which I protected myself, and it carried me through three daily newspaper internships. Then the doubt seeped back in. The fact that injustice of any kind—poverty, war, racism, wanton environmental destruction, etc.—existed at all filled the duller moments of my youth with coagulated angst. The only way to stifle this feeling was to wear it out, to go for a run to keep from vomiting. After graduating I switched from daily journalism to the alternative press because the alternative press did not hide from its biases. I moved to Memphis to be an investigative reporter.

I was happy at first. I wore my press credentials on a chain around my neck as conspicuously as a rookie priest wears his neck collar. I toured jails and rode in squad cars with police; I inspected public housing projects for lead paint; I drank with sources in hopes of getting scoops; I knew the court clerks by their first names; I reminded every public official I could find of the state's open-records laws, and when they refused to listen I twice persuaded my newspaper to file lawsuits against them. Yet it seemed like everything I wrote inspired more shoulder shrugging than earth shaking, and I was eventually enveloped in a deep, unmistakable sense of impotence. The cocky priest diminished into the sort of existential Catholic Graham Greene would have understood. Insomnia returned, more powerfully than ever. My girlfriend at the time grew sullen with my 4 A.M. pacing, and I looked like hell. At one point I developed a nasty case of eczema. I gnashed my teeth, paced, and talked to myself. *I am twenty-five years old and—I—haven't—done—anything—yet!* I thought I was losing my mind.

By the time I moved to Seattle, I wasn't looking for a new career opportunity, I was burnt out and looking for a place to hide. I had stopped caring about fighting for social causes and no longer craved the byline. Ego had fueled idealism, and somehow they were both gone. In fact I battled panic every morning I checked my voice mail. *Was someone calling to complain? Was this about a small story I didn't care about, or, worse, a fantastic tip that might actually lead somewhere?* I was indifferent to the same scoops that once sent me sprinting to city hall.

And then the WTO protests happened. Although I was elated

by them while they were happening, it became clear to me just how exceptionally complicated the issues were that liberal activism was trying to address, and that it was possible that nothing anywhere could be fixed because we were all hurtling at an impossible speed toward a destiny that absolutely nobody could fully predict or understand. That's when disillusionment and fear set in with all the subtlety of a car accident. I lost all sense of activism, of journalism, and of my own identity. Getting fired from the *Stranger* merely confirmed what I already knew to be true.

A noise startled me. Doug towered over me at the edge of the couch, a loaded Corona in his right hand, a lime slice balanced on the top of its neck. I really should have stayed in my room.

"Hi Doug," I said, greeting my housemate with a mixture of suspicion and dread.

Doug squeezed the lime slice into his bottle with his right fist and watched its juices mix with the alcohol. He took a swig and stared at me expectantly. Doug had a doughy, six-foot-three-inch body and a thick red mustache, which he licked from time to time with his tongue. He looked like a walrus whose territory was constantly threatened by smaller animals.

"Oh, hey, Phil," he said. "Did Emily tell you about her problem? There's a smell of raw sewage every morning in her bathroom. She gets it every time someone flushes the upstairs toilet." His sentences were soaked with overly polite, calculated pauses.

"Yes," I said. "We've been talking about it for more than a week now. I told her that I was on it."

"Well, if you need any help, just let me know. I went down there but didn't smell anything. I guess it only happens in the morning, when we flush the toilet upstairs."

I averted my eyes and looked out one of the far windows in the dining area. It was so smudged with dirt that I could barely see the hawthorn tree outside. Six months before, Doug had gathered up the courage to tell me that he could manage the house better than I could. Though caught off guard, I had rebuffed him, knowing that what he was really after was my rent discount. My mind hadn't changed.

"Yes, I guess you're right," I said.

"Oh, and the lawn—" he said.

"*Yes*. You're probably right."

"—you think you're going to mow it any time soon? It probably needs it."

"Yes. You—are—probably—*right*."

Doug stared at me for a moment while his fat fingers reached for a cigarette pack and plastic lighter in his denim jacket pocket. He made a sniffling sound and headed for the porch.

Through the front window, I could see Doug engaging in his usual smoking ritual. He played with the cigarette for a while, at one point sticking it behind his ear in the way an absent-minded desk clerk might store a pencil. Then he grabbed it back and lit it, taking desultory puffs. He stared out at traffic, oblivious to everything but the motion of the cars. He did not move for a long time.

A small, wild impulse seized me. Doug and I used to get along really well. I headed outside.

On seeing me, my housemate stirred slightly and flicked cigarette ash over the porch railing. He was peeved, I could tell, but did his best to mask it.

"What's up?" he said.

"Oh. Uh, nothing, I guess." I plopped down on the wicker couch that pressed against the house. "My life blows chunks."

He didn't seem to hear me or want to hear me, and I was forced to stare at traffic with him.

Front porches in Seattle are an anomaly. Backyard decks and patios were preferred, perhaps because there the guest list could be restricted. The few front stoops in the city were generally used for other, nonsocial purposes, like daydreaming or drinking or smoking alone. Doug was well suited for these activities, and he used the porch more than the rest of us. He roamed its gray cement as if searching for trespassers. Doug was from some small town in rural Washington—I could never remember which—and this made me think he would never be at home in a city.

"That was a really great party the other weekend, wasn't it?" he finally said, his eyes on some distant point down the block.

"Yeah, it was. Hey, where were you? I didn't see you after like nine o'clock."

"Upstairs. With my brother."

"Oh." So Doug had disappeared into his room to drink with only one other person. This was odd because he had contributed more money for the party than the rest of us.

The cars moved through the lights of Twenty-third Avenue like ships plying a river canal.

"The cops came three times," I said.

This seemed to rouse him. "Really? Awesome!"

"You didn't see them?" Of course he hadn't. "Yeah," I said, warming up to it. "Three *times*. The last time they were so mad they threatened to confiscate all the DJ's equipment."

"What the hell? Why?"

"Neighbor complaints. It was only eleven-thirty!"

"Fucking neighbors. Can't handle a little old party on a Saturday night."

"I guess it was because all the smokers were hanging out on the porch, and they couldn't deal with that," I said. "And the thing was, we had a city councilmember here. God, I totally didn't think of it. I should have sent him out there to talk to them! I wonder how they would have acted."

"*Awwwwww*," Doug marveled. "And we didn't even use my speakers. Those damn things would have woken up all of Bellevue!" Bellevue was the suburb to the east. Doug had told this joke many times before, but it was funny anyway. He always got excited about his speakers.

We settled into a quiet reverie, me fondly remembering the

party at its wildest, Doug perhaps imagining what it would have been like had he bothered to attend.

"I heard you went out to a club the other night," I said.

"Yeah."

"Good for you!" I said. "Who'd you see?"

"Oh, I don't remember. Some band I read about in the *Stranger*. I stood next to this guy in a wheelchair. It was kind of amazing that he was there. He couldn't see the stage. I talked to him for a little bit. He seemed pretty cool. Then I came home. I don't like to go out to drink. I never drive drunk."

"You didn't hit on any women?" I asked. Ever since he had broken up with his boyfriend, Doug had never talked about men, only women. I tried to play along.

"No," he said.

"I don't really get out to many shows these days," I said, "but I still have my favorite bars. There's the Jade Pagoda and—hey, you should try going to the Twilight Exit. That's within walking distance." I pointed south.

"Isn't that where all the—" He trailed off, as if I were supposed to know what he meant. I did. There was a street corner on Madison where a lot of poor black people loitered and police cruised by. A drug corner, one of a handful in the city.

"No," I said. "That's a block or so to the east, by that little grocery store."

"But why would you go by there?"

I considered my response, skipping political correctness to appeal to Doug's pragmatism. "Well, you know, you really aren't in much danger. For one, the cops are there all the time. For another, white people don't get mugged on street corners like that. If people got robbed there, people would stop coming to buy drugs."

"I guess so," Doug said. We both looked out towards the street. Then Doug said, "I once broke a guy's nose."

"What? Why?"

"He kicked my cat."

The air shifted. We were both uncomfortable.

Doug had finished his cigarette. He rocked back and forth on his heels, his heavy body swaying to an unknown rhythm. I studied the cracks on the porch railing. The house needed a paint job. It was like we were sitting in the shade of a two-story lump of green-gray earth, a blotted vein of exposed moss and minerals.

"So how's work?" Doug asked.

"Work?" I said. "You mean, you don't know?"

Doug gave a shrug.

"I got fired."

"Really? *A-a-a-a-a-hh, du-u-u-u-u-u-de,*" he said. "Jesus! I'm sorry." His words came out like dirty oil dripping out of an automobile. Doug usually ended his sentences on a downbeat, as if nothing could interest him. This time, his stressors slid in the other direction. Doug worked for a roofing contractor, and he didn't identify very strongly with the job. But he knew how important my reporting career had been to me.

He looked away. We both did. "Do you want a beer?" he asked.

"Sure, man. Thanks."

"Come on."

We went upstairs. Doug motioned for me to be careful because he didn't want to disturb the piranhas. If you opened the door to his room too fast, they'd lunge around in their tank as if their very lives were at stake. It would take close to a minute for the water to return to a placid, aquarium state. I trailed Doug inside with a tiptoed, exaggerated caution.

"What'd you feed them this week?" I said, pointing with the bottle of beer he'd given me. I could see the piranhas' lower rows of teeth, jagged saws that could tear through other fish, hamburger meat, even human flesh. Whenever those saws were so clearly visible, I had learned, they had just eaten.

"I think last night they ate one of the other fish. See? Only three of the other ones left."

"Huh. I wasn't counting."

"After you've seen them do it half a dozen times, it gets boring." We stared at the fish together. They were more mesmerizing than the traffic. Doug looked at me, suddenly feverish. "Hey, did I tell you what I'm gonna do next?"

"No." I breathed, still. "What?"

"I'm going to breed the piranhas."

"*Breed* them."

"Aw, yeah, dude! I mean, you know these things are illegal, right?"

I did. He had already bragged about how he had persuaded a pet store owner in an unnamed part of town to show him the store's "secret back room" where the "real" pets were kept.

"So this guy and I are friends now, right? He told me if I bred this pair of piranhas, I could sell them for at *least* fifty dollars a fish. All I gotta do is raise a whole bunch of them. I could make thousands!" At this Doug let out a crazy-cooter guffaw. He didn't slap his knee with his giant hand, though I had actually seen him do that before.

"I'm going to need a bigger tank, of course, and that's going to be the hardest part. Fish tanks are expensive. I might have to take a job on the weekends to pay for it."

"Doug, how big of a tank are we talking about?" I passed my empty bottle back to him. He went back to the refrigerator and got me another. I normally wouldn't have done this—expected another beer—because Doug's gifts of alcohol struck me as a form of reluctant charity, not altruism. But today we were getting along.

"I want a hundred-gallon tank."

"One *hundred* gallons? Jesus. How big is that?"

With his arms, Doug showed me. It was a wider span than his limbs could display.

"Are you sure the landlady's okay with this?" I said. His room was a mess, with an odd assortment of DVDs, gadgets, tools, and bicycle parts covering every available square foot of floor and shelf. Where would he put a giant fish tank? I tried to imagine what would happen to the room if the earthquake they called the 'Big One' hit Seattle.

"Listen, don't worry about that!" he snapped, suddenly touchy. "I've *talked* to her."

"All right. OK." We both knew this was a lie, but I let it pass. Since he had taken the trouble to lie to me, he was going to have to accept the blame if the landlady ever found out.

"Let's go downstairs. I need another smoke." He looked like he didn't want me in his room anymore. We returned to the porch.

I leaned on the railing overlooking the street. Doug went into his patient find-and-light-a-cigarette routine. When he had situated himself, he handed me a piece of paper from his pocket.

"What's this?" I said.

"I found it stuck in the mail slot."

It was a brochure, the amateurish kind I normally threw out without reading. Somebody was promoting a lawn mowing service. "*This* was on the porch?" I asked.

"Yeah."

"Fucking, passive-aggressive, fucking-ass neighbors," I said. "I hate this town. I mowed the goddamn lawn."

"Last month," Doug said.

"*Hey,*" I said. "This isn't entirely my problem. Anybody can mow the lawn. It's not my job to mow the lawn. Even SnowWolf can mow the lawn—why don't you get on his case sometime? He never does any chores. It took me three months to persuade the landlady to let me buy a new lawn mower because none of us wanted to use that crappy manual push mower that we used to have. So I got us a new mower, and it works, and anybody can mow the lawn now, not just me."

Doug was itching for an argument, I could tell, but despite his size he was even worse with conflict than I was. I held my ground, staring right at him so he knew I wasn't afraid of him.

"I'll do it if you want," he muttered. "It's no big deal."

"No," I said. "I don't want you to do it just because I want you to do it. I want people to pitch in and do things of their own free will around here."

"Nobody's going to do it then."

"Then I'll put up a sign-in sheet in the kitchen. People sign up for a particular time when they'll mow the lawn. We'll get it done. And fuck the neighbors. That sounds pretty fair to me, don't you think?"

Doug gave up with a shrug.

I turned to go back inside. As I opened the front door, I thanked Doug for the beer.

"Sure," he said. "Any time." Behind me I could hear my housemate throwing his empty into the glass-recycling bin. He hurled it so hard the glass shattered.

4

*According to the newspapers of the 1930s, Marion Zioncheck had
a sharp mind, a hot temper, a gleaming roadster (make and model
still something of a mystery), and a fervent belief in the power of
ordinary people to change government. He was also impossibly
arrogant, boasting, "I'm the best congressman this city ever had."*

My Geo was parked in its usual spot, on a side street not far from
the house. The car, a '95 Prizm, was baptized as a Seattle automobile in March of 2000, when city officials imploded the Kingdome,
the stadium for the Mariners and the Seahawks. As it collapsed,
the stadium breathed a giant, inverted mushroom cloud of debris.
Hundreds of gawkers hacked and gagged from the dust, and the
city was briefly enveloped in a thick brown fog. My car, by all
accounts an innocent bystander nearly a mile away, was coated
with a fine patina of Kingdome remains that I never bothered to
wash off.

A globalized bastard child of Chevrolet and Toyota, the Geo
excelled not in the way of luxury or of power but in the sexless category of reliability. Its light-blue interior was in pretty good shape,
except for a permanent grape jelly stain on the front seat that a
friend of mine had left after one particularly exciting commute.
Aside from the Kingdome dust, the car had been victimized only
once, during my first week in Seattle, when an old man with a
giant Caddy rear-ended it after I had braked for a school bus.
Insurance had paid for the repair, but the body shop had given it
an inferior paint job; large red paint patches flecked off the back
end as I drove.

I climbed in and gunned the engine—I was late for a meeting with Grant. I darted westward, toward the center of Capitol Hill, past half-million and million-dollar homes, well-maintained private gardens, and a Catholic church that had a difficult time packing them in on Sundays. Eight blocks later, I turned south on Fifteenth Avenue East.

Fifteenth was a retail corridor with a wine shop, a vegetarian health food store, a vitamin/health store, three Thai restaurants, and a china shop with a sign that lectured patrons about the dangers of unruly kids in delicate places. The neighborhood had its share of renters, but some of these apartments were actually mansions that had been subdivided and rented out as shared housing (Fourteenth Avenue East, in fact, had once been known as Millionaires' Row). The homeless people tended to be older, less aggressive, and more solitary than the street kids found elsewhere in Seattle, and quite a few young families promenaded past them during the day. The few outsiders who ventured onto this sleepy street were yuppies hoping to get a seat at the Coastal Kitchen, an overpriced restaurant that offered a different foreign cuisine menu every month. As a whole, Fifteenth had a respectable, bland air.

In the middle of this five-block stretch sat Victrola, an independent café. When it had opened the year before, Victrola was a small space with unadorned tables and chairs and a no-frills environment, a direct appeal to Seattle's deep-seated aversion to ostentation. Victrola was so successful that by mid-2001 its owners were buying out a pottery shop in the building next door, knocking out the adjoining wall, and doubling both the café's size and popularity.

Grant lived across the street from Victrola and was one of its first patrons. He had never supported the mild corporate ambience of the Starbucks down the street; his loyalty to Victrola grew so fierce that it soon wasn't enough for him to simply buy his coffee there. He turned the place into his own living room, going there two to three times a day, chatting up the owners and staying for hours to write poetry and freelance criticism. To reward his devotion, the owners named a sandwich after him. The Grant Cogswell was made of free-range roasted turkey breast, drunken goat cheese, greens, and roasted red pepper aioli.

I parked, then jaywalked across the street. The drivers glared, but stopped. On a tranquil weekday afternoon like this one, the street was quiet. The only noticeable garbage on the sidewalk were a few stray subscription cards to *Yoga International* and the *New Yorker*. Two Victrola patrons sat on metal chairs and chatted furtively; I guessed that they were law students.

Inside, Grant had already found a seat—a relief to me, because Grant never liked my table choices. They were in a cold spot or not shaded enough. Or the table light was too bright. Or the chairs weren't good for his back. He often made me get up and change seats with him, sometimes not once but twice.

He waved me over. Grant was wearing a T-shirt, khaki shorts, tall socks, and black boots—shit-kickers—and the new, thick framed spectacles that made him look younger. He looked like any other hipster resident of Capitol Hill, the kind that's ready to talk up his favorite album but dismisses politics as a fool's game best never played. The only difference today was that instead of carrying his usual small poetry notebook, where he was constantly jotting down thoughts about Seattle and Marion Zioncheck, he was looking down at a battered calendar/organizer. I couldn't remember seeing him with it before.

I asked Grant how he was doing.

"Awful," he said. I waited for him to laugh self-consciously, the way he normally did when he gave that response. He didn't.

He was restless. He complained of a stomachache and said he could feel a migraine coming on. The stomachache was worse than the migraine. Grant had called a press conference to announce his candidacy, but no one had come. He wasn't sure about his campaign manager, either. The guy was an old friend but he had no political experience and was a bit of an introvert.

"I'm beginning to think that you should be my campaign manager," Grant said. This gave me an immediate, euphoric knot in my own stomach. Then he looked away.

We sat together in silence. I tried to cheer him up. I reached into my front jeans pockets and produced a key, a copy of my car key. I held it aloft for a moment, hoping the sunlight would catch it, make it glimmer brightly. To my disappointment it remained a dingy old key. I slid it across the table.

"You're going to need this if you have something to do in Phinney Ridge or South Park," I said. "Your bike won't be able to take you everywhere. If you tried, you'd show up at every speech drenched in sweat."

"Oh my God!" Grant said, touched. "Thanks a lot." He fingered the key for a moment, then slipped it into his pocket.

He had already made me the first member of his steering committee, a group that would meet regularly to offer him advice and moral support as he slugged his way through the campaign. Having gained this esteemed position, and having given him access to my car, I didn't know what else to do.

Grant was too involved in his own problems to notice my fidgeting. He grumbled and seethed, something nuclear welling up inside him. He could run this race and win. He knew it. Yet nothing was happening. "The monorail people will support me," he blurted. "They have to. And I know four or five people off the top of my head who will give me the maximum contribution.

"Some of our friends don't think I can do this," he continued. "I just don't get it. Why the hell don't people understand that I know what I'm doing?" He didn't say this in a way that suggested he wanted an answer.

"Why don't," I said, tentatively, "we talk about the media?"

"OK."

"When you go out on the campaign trail, you're going to have to start answering questions from reporters, and they're not going to give you any time to think. They expect you to respond right away."

"Of course."

I started posing hypothetical questions—I was the reporter and he was the candidate.

"Why do you want to run for city council?"

Grant looked away, embarrassed.

"If we don't do something about our transportation mess, or if we build the wrong mass transit infrastructure now, we're going to be stuck with that decision for the next hundred years." This came out without enthusiasm.

"Why are you running against Richard McIver?"

"Because," he said, "Richard McIver is the chairman of the council's transportation committee, and he's done nothing to help this city's transit mess except create more problems. And he's tried to kill monorail twice."

"Why are you running against the only black city councilmember?"

Grant told me that he didn't want to do this. He said he already *knew* how to answer questions, and he thought my exercise was silly. He kept dropping his eyes down to the tabletop, only to raise them defiantly again. He started to call me "Bill" to make the experience less personal for him.

"Well, why don't—"

"I can't do this," Grant said. *"Bill.* I'm just going to end up yelling here."

"Then you yell at me!" I said. "I don't care. I can take it. So you feel free to yell. But you can *not* lose your temper out there, in public." My own ferociousness shocked me. I looked at my fingernails. Grant rifled through his organizer. "Things are going to pick up right away for this campaign," he said. "I'm not sure what happens first, but I know the Democrats begin meeting in a month or so for their endorsement meetings. That's going to be key. I'm going to need a logo, yard signs, remit envelopes—"

"You know," I said, "there are—there are some reporters who

might ask you some pretty tough questions, questions you may not want to answer."

"Listen—"

"How are you going to respond? What about the Mariners? They're having a pretty good season. Do you support them? You did a lot of work in the campaign to prevent the city from tearing down the Kingdome so they could have a new stadium."

This was too much.

"People aren't going to care about that!" Grant said. His hands seized the edge of the table. "That was years ago. Who cares? Nobody's going to ask me that. *Look*. The Mariners have their stadium now, and the Seahawks almost have theirs. And you know what? There were a lot of people out there who voted against the stadiums. *A lot*. More than half. We won, and they cheated. And I got death threats over that stupid campaign. It was a bogus deal that they pulled, and it ripped off taxpayers.

"And you know what? I *still* have a little resentment for the Mariners!"

Grant lunged forward. His hands were white, all balled up. He held onto the table as if he meant to break it in half.

I fled to the bathroom. I scrubbed my hands and wondered how I had become so fragile. I decided to tell Grant over email that I didn't think a reporter from the *Seattle Times* or *Post-Intelligencer* would be very impressed with that sort of reply. I took a few deep breaths and went back out.

Grant's girlfriend Tara had joined our table. The two were quietly adoring each other, and Grant seemed calmer. "We were just talking about how terrible my life's going to be for the next five months," he told her as I sat down.

I tried to decide if I should leave. I barely knew Tara; she and Grant had been dating only a short time. She was slender and shy and liked literature, especially Borges, and whenever I saw her and Grant at parties, they were occupied with each other, shunning the conversations that swirled around them.

"I probably won't get any sleep until this thing is over," Grant said. Tara gave me a look that mixed diffidence with apprehension. After a few moments I told Grant that he should call me whenever he needed my car, and I left. I wanted to say more, but did not dare.

That weekend, Grant went on a hiking trip with some friends and I threw a party on my front porch. About twenty or thirty people attended, and the front stoop was transformed into a place for beer, smoking, and conversation. A few of my more garrulous acquaintances tried inviting the neighbors passing by on the sidewalk to join us. They declined, and gave us looks that made it clear that they didn't appreciate the way we were carrying on.

The more I drank, the more I dreamed, the bolder I got. At some point the alcohol restored some of my old self-confidence. I shouted over the din: "I'm thinking about running Grant's city council campaign!"

It was throwing a racquetball against a garage door; it just bounced right back. To an excited chorus of "Do it!" I ran upstairs, snatched my phone, and called Grant. It sounded like one of those 1:30 A.M. bar calls to a potential girlfriend. But my words were clear. "Hey, motherfucker, I'm gonna be your campaign manager! Fire that other guy!" I waited for a reaction, but then I realized I had his voice mail. I repeated the same message after the beep and hung up.

An hour later, Grant returned from his camping trip. The first message he played back was from a different friend, who soberly told him that he thought that I would make a great campaign manager. The second message was mine saying the same thing, only louder. Grant felt this was a sign. He wasted no time calling me back. He caught me back on the porch, drinking.

"Let's do this!" I said.

"Oh, thank you," he said. I could hear his breath dropping out of him. "I love you."

A long pause. "We're gonna kick McIver's ass!" I screamed. The porch, ignited by my war cry, went mad with drunken cheers.

I was so elated that I didn't notice that Doug and my other housemates Ben and Cate had joined our party. Cate would later tell me that Doug's face curdled at the realization that I was taking over the porch—*his* porch—for something as frivolous as a social gathering. But she tried diverting his attention by pleading with him about his drinking, which seemed excessive to her. She told him that she was honestly concerned about him.

Doug was happy to have her attention, but he didn't want to talk about his drinking. "Isn't Phil a crappy house manager?" he asked Ben and Cate. "Don't you think I'd do a better job?"

5

Marion Zioncheck opposed racism at a time when few politicians would. He protested the mistreatment of Native Americans and the use of the National Guard in breaking strikes. He was against increased military spending, even though the Bremerton Naval Yard was a prominent part of his district. He spoke out against the Silver Shirts, the self-styled American sympathizers with Adolf Hitler. He may also have been the first politician to publicly criticize FBI Director J. Edgar Hoover, calling him "the great dictator" and "the master of fiction." It should come as no surprise that the paranoid Hoover had a file on Zioncheck.

Asked if America was on the verge of revolution, Zioncheck replied, "We are already there!"

To buck the system! To rebel against indifference! To prove that change was possible!

"Fifty-one percent," I said. "We will win with fifty-one percent of the vote." Being so confident was a wondrous revelation in itself. And just two weeks ago I had been ready to give up on everything—completely.

Grant laughed, liberated and terrified.

We stood on the edge of a Seattle beach after a poorly attended Democratic district meeting in late June and watched the sun go down over Puget Sound. Young lovers and old couples stretched out behind us on beach towels and cotton blankets while high school kids, failed dot-commers, and college students on break stood around bonfires and got drunk on cheap beer. The pessimistic skies of late spring had given way to the frothy innocence of summer. It was a new season of exuberance, and it was laden with import. Here was a place in America where progress was still possible. Seattle had not yet yielded to social numbness, materialist distraction, television-embalmed apathy or right-wing fundamentalist incoherence. The keen edge of liberalism still thrived here, forged by history and sharpened by protests like the WTO. Once found in its best officials, but now more often relegated to the hard sidewalks and streets of the city, the edges may have been blunted but they were by no means dull.

Here, liberalism could win. Grant and I could win.

We *had* to win.

We started from the very beginning, or at least with what we assumed to be the very beginning, of any modern-day campaign— we went back to Grant's apartment and dialed onto the Internet. He had a database of hundreds of email addresses that he had been indiscriminately collecting for months. Grant didn't even know who owned many of these addresses, though I recognized a few of them as belonging to acquaintances who had attended some of my house parties. Soon we were copying each address and pasting them into a special folder, our very own spam file.

Grant sat at the computer, but after a few minutes he remembered that he despised technology more than he despised do-nothing incumbents. He was soon complaining about how he didn't understand what I was doing, how his back was beginning to hurt, how things would go faster if I did it myself instead of trying to explain it all to him. He said, "You know, I'm not going to be able to do all of this small stuff. And once we get started you're not either. We have to find people to do this stuff for us."

"OK, OK," I said, taking his seat.

"And we've gotta get off-line in an hour. I'm waiting for a phone call from a Phoenix radio station. They want to talk to me about the feature I did in the *Stranger* about how awful Phoenix is. They want to attack what I wrote."

Again I said OK and settled further into the chair.

Grant's modem was a panting, croaking dial-up device that belonged in a landfill. It took a full minute and a half to dump each individual email account into the spam folder. Surely some corporation out there had devised a software program to make the average political candidate's spamming needs easier. Too bad we didn't have the time to look into it.

Behind me, Grant did some breathing exercises to calm himself down. Then he got up and put in a CD. A harsh female voice I didn't recognize came wailing through the speakers.

"Who are we listening to, PJ Harvey?"

"Oh my God, dude," Grant's voice came from somewhere behind and below me. He was on the floor, relaxing his back muscles. My question made him sit straight up. "Are you telling me you can't recognize Patti Smith?"

My face flushed.

Grant's hands covered his face in despair. We had gone over this before. My hair had never been cut in a mohawk, as Grant's had. I had listened to classic rock and Top 40 until I was nineteen. I still never knew what to buy at the record store. Grant had once told me that he would have hated me had we met in the '80s.

"Sometimes I can't believe you at all," he said. "Punk music saved me from the suburbs. Patti Smith saved me from the suburbs."

"Well, nothing 'saved' me from the suburbs," I said, reciting a now-tired story. "I just left them. I went to school in Chicago and then I realized that I wasn't a suburban moderate but an urban, politically correct Democrat, and before I knew it I wasn't even that, just a smart-ass alt-weekly reporter who didn't belong to anything. And I didn't listen to punk music. I listened to whatever was on the radio, until I met people like you who introduced me to other kinds of music—blues, bluegrass, Steve Earle, Modest Mouse—and I've got a shitty memory and we've talked about all of this before."

"Oh my God, dude." Then a pause. "Hey, what time is it?"

Grant told me to get off-line, which I did. A few minutes later, he was on the phone and on the radio with a DJ in Phoenix.

Grant had written an article for the *Stranger* saying that the city of Phoenix was so unbearably hot, so impossibly ugly, and so unsalvageably blighted that its residents were moving to Seattle in "huge numbers." Grant had no statistics to back his claims, having talked to only a handful of emigrés, among them his new girlfriend and a Victrola barrista. He had also made some fairly grand assertions, such as that Phoenix children who fell on the pavement in the summertime were hospitalized with third-degree burns. Though entertaining, the article lacked some basic journalistic fundamentals, such as proof.

Grant gripped the receiver. His lips were the only things moving, and they moved in obvious discomfort. The DJ must have been giving a very long, opinionated introduction.

"I talked to several people," Grant said. "What? I said *several*. No, there were other people I talked to besides the people I quoted. Yes, one of those people works at a coffeehouse. Now, wait. Hold on. That's classist. I know plenty of Starbucks barristas who are as smart or smarter than me and you—" I couldn't tell for sure, but I got the sense that he was forcing the DJ to a draw.

After a while, Grant hung up. "That guy was such an asshole," he said.

"How did you do that?" I said.

"Do what?"

"You shoved *back*. You countered the guy, whatever he said, for being classist—something by the way that I've never heard anyone accuse anybody of—and—and you didn't cave but shoved *back*."

"Sure. What else was I supposed to do?"

"I can never bring myself to do that, and I've been on talk radio half a dozen times. When somebody nails me on something I'm a deer in headlights. I totally lose my composure."

My admiration lightened Grant's mood considerably. He stood up and moved about the room and launched into a small sermon about the biggest problem with progressives today. "You've got to learn to get over that. The left has a real war on its hands. The radios, cable TV, it's all just a contest over who can shout the loudest. Don't get lost in the details or they'll trample all over you." For Grant, nearly everything had political overtones, even this article, since one of his points was that progressive cities like Portland and Seattle were stricter about urban planning than many of the more conservative cities found in the Southwest. Of *course* Phoenix was hellish—their zoning guidelines and transportation infrastructures had been corrupted by the whims of real estate developers.

I sat back down at the computer and got to work on our mass email. Two monotonous hours later, I had it; a roster of potential volunteers and contributors, separated by commas and devoid of any discriminating political information. Grant and I then spent an hour composing a message for our unsuspecting audience. Grant wrote the letter in his convoluted prose, I edited it into recognizable political rhetoric, and Grant criticized my version and changed a word here and there to better reflect his own personality.

>Friends,

>Over the past several years I have been involved with political campaigns over issues I felt were crucial to the future of this city and the region. When I was thirteen I took part in a letter-writing campaign to the Renton City Council to oppose plans for a skyscraper megaproject on the shore of Lake Washington. My first "campaign," seven years ago, was to petition the Department of Construction and Land Use to save two of the last Victorian houses in my Lower Queen Anne neighborhood from the wrecking ball.

>Soon after that, I joined a cab driver named Dick Falkenbury with his audacious dream of a Monorail transit system and together we wrote and filed Initiative 41. City officials scoffed, even

though Monorail technology is cheaper, safer,
and faster than light rail.
    >You're probably familiar with the rest of the
story. Despite open hostility and dismissal by the
mainstream media and city hall, we took the
Monorail issue to the ballot . . .

By the time we were done, it was 9 P.M. We hit the "send" key and
watched the modem crash. Our work didn't disappear, fortunately,
but it did provoke a considerable amount of swearing. I went back
on-line and sent it again and watched about five hundred pieces of
spam disappear into the digital ether. There, the real politics began:
I had to apologize to about twenty people that same night for
sending them an email they didn't want.

• • •

Our campaign against the automobile would require the services
of an automobile—mine. A major order of business was to trans-
form my ordinary Geo Prizm into the Grant Cogswell Campaign
Mobile. To do so, we packed the car full of official Grant Cogswell
Campaign political propaganda, including: Grant Cogswell Campaign posters, Grant Cogswell Campaign yard signs, Grant
Cogswell Campaign flyers and assorted literature, Grant Cogswell
Campaign remit envelopes, and Grant Cogswell Campaign T-
shirts. We also threw in two hammers, some masking tape, a staple
gun, and, occasionally, for good measure, some empty paper cups,
courtesy of Victrola, so that the official campaign mobile took on
the aroma of old coffee.
    All of these items, including the coffee cups, were stowed in the
back seat, although Grant thought that the trunk was acceptable,
so long as nothing was carelessly folded or bent. The front two
seats of the Cogswell Mobile were to be kept clean, so that the
candidate and his campaign manager could get around in relative

personal comfort. The gas tank was always more than a quarter full, to assure us that we would reach our scheduled destination without unnecessary delay. The air conditioner was never turned on, as this might have dried out the candidate's skin. The manually powered windows were the preferred form of circulating air.

The radio was to be off at all times. Music may have been fine for Grant the critic, but it was much too distracting for Grant the city council candidate. He had to stay focused, especially when we were driving to a place where he would have to give his stump speech. We filled the air instead with the urgent soundwaves of our own voices, creating for ourselves a constant chatter of campaign-related news. When there was little news to discuss, we simply recycled and re-analyzed the same news, like two over-caffeinated CNN commentators. In this way, we produced and perpetuated the never-ending sense that things were constantly happening, that progress was constantly being made, even when it wasn't. This was fine because, quite frankly, nothing else could have been more interesting.

I flipped the trip odometer on the Grant Cogswell Mobile to zero. I wanted to see how far our ideals and ambitions would take us.

We decided to rely on email to stay in contact when we weren't in the Geo together. We would also use cell phones. Grant had handed me some old black mobile phones that he had briefly used a few years before. They were colossal by contemporary standards, and I was embarrassed to use them. Grant, who detested waste, was not swayed by my argument that we shouldn't look cheap on the campaign trail. But the salesman at the cell phone store I visited was on my side, claiming with an air of disdain that he couldn't forgo policy to resurrect such old phones. I walked out of the store with a pair of brand-new Nokias.

We would have no campaign headquarters. Cash-poor and overwhelmed by minutiae, we decided to divide the headquarters into three distinct places: Victrola, my house, and Grant's apartment. Victrola was for our mid-morning conferences and our late-night debriefings. Grant's apartment would be for fund-raising and filling out political questionnaires. He settled into his own office/headquarters with little trouble. I didn't see him spending too much time trying to set up a system; he kept his iMac in the corner of his living room and scattered various files all over the place. The system only broke down when certain pieces of paper were left under other pieces of paper or stray socks for too long. Grant had a solution for this problem: He would swear profusely, hand me the once-lost document, and beg me to fix the situation as quickly as possible.

My house—specifically, my room—would be the primary location for media and constituency contacts, databasing and number crunching. My room was like the inside of someone's mouth, claustrophobic and the color of stained teeth. The desk, dresser, and futon filled most of it, offering only three square feet for pacing. Luckily, soon after the campaign began, one of my housemates decided to move out. As soon as he gave his thirty-day notice, I claimed his room, which was almost twice the size of mine. Even better than the floor space, this room had a sunroom separated from the main room by French doors. A private office!

My old room was only twenty feet away from my new one, but I could not move all my stuff by myself; my futon was unwieldy and I had an enormous dresser that my father had built for me the year before. I hadn't given any thought to how I was going to move these things. I was just anxious to get back to work on the campaign.

I was hauling a stack of books across the landing when I noticed Doug staring at me from the open door of his room. The beer bottle in his hand was full, and he had a cigarette balanced in the ridge of his ear. It was obvious where he intended to go.

"Hey man, can you help me out?" I asked.

"You moving next door, huh, into Rick's room," Doug said. It was only eight o'clock at night, but his sentences were already slurred.

"That's right, man. All this additional space! Can you help me lift my dresser?"

Doug set his beer down and removed all the contents of his pockets. Cigarette pack, wallet, keys. He placed the cigarette that was on his ear on the cigarette pack on the floor. He was doing this with an air of someone who would not be hurried. "Now what do you need?" he asked.

"This," I said, pointing. "And the futon mattress."

"You can get that mattress, can't you?" Doug asked, perplexed.

"No. I can't get my arms around it."

"Here," he said, and hoisted the mattress over his shoulders. "Where do you want it?"

In less than ten minutes Doug was picking up his beer, wallet, keys, and cigarettes. I thanked him, he asked me why I was in such a rush.

"The campaign's just heating up and I need to get back to work. Haven't even set up my computer yet."

"How's that going?" He was aware of the campaign because I had already taken over the dining room table downstairs, filling it with large stacks of papers and an election map.

"Hellish," I said with gusto, as if hell were a fun place, a place where one wanted to be. "*Already*. And I have *no* idea what's going on. I'm really operating in the dark. There's all this little stuff, like statistics—" I trailed off. Doug didn't know anything about political campaigns. He didn't know anything about current events, local or otherwise. He didn't read. He didn't vote. He didn't care.

"So I guess you're not going to be able to get to cleaning the basement anytime soon, then, huh?" he said.

I didn't need this now. "Is that Modest Mouse you're playing?" I said. It sounded like the *Lonesome Crowded West* coming out of his speakers. He'd borrowed it more than a month ago.

"Uh-huh. I suppose you want it back, huh?"

Grant had introduced me to both the band and the album, which he thought captured the mood of Seattle and the Pacific

Northwest better than any rock album around. I was still listening to it—the moody harmonies, the unexpected change-ups, the contradictory lyrics—to try to understand what he meant.

"Yeah, kind of," I said. "Can you get it back to me sometime?"

Doug disappeared into his room.

"No," I called after him. "—I mean, *sometime*. Not now. If you still want to listen to it, listen to it."

Too late. He gave me back my CD.

We stood a few feet apart. The second-floor landing was suddenly very confining.

"Thanks," I said.

• • •

Time was not on our side. We had eleven weeks until the September 18 primary, and eighteen weeks until the November 6 general election. Our strengths—a clear message delivered by a passionate messenger and his savvy sidekick—were easy to discern, but we were just coming to terms with our weaknesses, which were legion.

Grant had no seed money. He owned his apartment but had no job—in fact he was $1,000 deep in credit card debt. And although Grant was looking forward to collecting around $200,000 from a trust-inheritance he couldn't expect to receive it until the following year, well after the election. Which meant that we would have to raise tens of thousands of dollars. His one positive financial advantage was that he wouldn't have to worry about paying me; I would lose my unemployment benefits if he tried.

Grant was largely unknown in political circles. Having abstained from grassroots politics for a couple of years, he had not cultivated any important allies. And Grant wasn't especially well known as a journalist either, since he only wrote occasional news pieces for the *Stranger,* and only when the topic seriously piqued his interest. His most relevant article was a fanciful what-if piece, in which he had proposed spending millions of dollars to rebuild the Pioneer Square Underground, a historic subterranean area that city officials had covered over a hundred years ago and that was now only shown to tourists. I was not convinced that this article or his stories on Seattle anarchists were going to benefit him in any significant way.

The whole *Stranger* connection, of course, raised another issue: How would the mainstream media treat Grant? (And, less importantly, how would the *Stranger* treat me?) If Grant were pigeonholed as an "alt-weekly music critic," he wouldn't stand a chance anywhere north, south, east or west of Capitol Hill. There had to be some way to downplay his *Stranger* ties without offending the paper in the process. This would not be easy because Grant had made quite a few enemies as a critic. Just the year before, for example, he had written the following about a book reading: "O. Casey Corr is one of the writers for *The Seattle Times* editorial page, so you know his account of the McCaw cellular phone empire, *Money From Thin Air,* will be a thoughtful, hard-hitting critique of corporate power and new money. And I have a twelve-inch dick. Use of cell phones during this event is encouraged." When I questioned him about this passage, Grant said that it was funny when he wrote it.

Race was another consideration: Richard McIver was the only African-American—in fact the only minority—on the city council. He held the only historically "black" seat on the council. In liberal Seattle this was an unusual conundrum. Politically, Grant was to the left of the centrist McIver, but Grant was also not black. How far should we go with the rhetoric? What rhetoric should we even *use*? One couldn't exactly point out that Seattle had never produced a great black city councilmember. Sam Smith, the first black politician to hold that seat, had been a shill for downtown business interests, demanding a curfew on unruly blacks in 1967 when rioting seemed imminent. John Manning, Smith's successor, was arrested and convicted for domestic violence against his wife while he sat on the council; McIver had been appointed to fill Manning's seat, even though he was not the the first choice of local black leaders. For the moment, Grant and I would have to wait and see on the race issue. We wouldn't avoid it, but we wouldn't bring it up, either.

Since Grant was challenging an incumbent, we couldn't bet on any major endorsements. McIver, in fact, had been securing the names of political heavyweights since January. I made a dozen exploratory phone calls for Grant and came back with nothing. I tried the major special interest groups, hoping for a sympathetic ear, but many of these organizations wouldn't even give us an audience. The King County Labor Council had endorsed McIver before the filing deadline to challenge him had even passed, despite the fact that his record on labor issues was at best mediocre. The Downtown Seattle Association, the most powerful special interest group in the city, didn't return my phone calls, even though they opposed many of McIver's mass transit policies.

Not even the people Grant had helped in past elections were pleased about his bid. He had volunteered on the campaigns of two sitting councilmembers, but neither would publicly endorse him. One councilmember, Judy Nicastro, offered "silent support," which amounted to a few bits of cheerful advice whenever we bumped into her around town. The other, former '60s radical Nick Licata, was more encouraging, allowing himself to be seen in public with Grant, and providing a few vital tips on potential contributors. But Licata did not want to ruin his working relationship with McIver, so a public statement on Grant's behalf was not forthcoming.

Grant was confident of one group of supporters: the monorail people.

Much had changed since Grant helped Falkenbury campaign for monorail in the '90s. The initiative they had passed was poorly worded and, as it turned out, unenforceable, which allowed city hall to ignore it for years. But another group of activists had emerged to take Grant and Falkenbury's place. These activists were more polished, more comfortable cutting deals with city officials and private contractors; some of them were lawyers. After numerous legal twists and political turns, monorail was finally being studied as a viable technology, and another voter initiative was to be presented in 2002, asking voters to (finally) fund and build the city's first monorail transit line.

The name of the new group of activists was "Rise Above It All." Grant went to one of their fund-raisers, sat with everybody else, and when the opportunity came, he gave a speech. Fiery and angry, the speech was well received, with applause all around. But after Grant spoke, he was approached by Peter Sherwin, the brusque, single-minded head of Rise Above It All. Sherwin offered him some unsolicited advice.

"Don't do this," he said.

They stared each other down. The two had never been close.

Sherwin listed the reasons why Grant shouldn't run. You got into the race too late, he said. You are not up to the emotional toll of a campaign. You don't have an organization behind you, and you don't have any money. Sherwin, never one to say anything delicately, wouldn't give Grant his endorsement. He'd barely let Grant use his name in public.

And then there was Dick Falkenbury. If Grant's former partner wouldn't back him, we were in very bad shape. The responsibility of asking Falkenbury for his endorsement fell to me.

I called him from my house. He was not encouraging. In fact he started cracking jokes about Grant's chances. "Yeah, Grant's got a great shot at winning—if Richard McIver gets hit by a train," Falkenbury bantered. "Or I suppose the old man could have a heart attack. How old is he, anyway, sixty-four?" He then launched into a rambling, happy-go-lucky tirade about incumbents and big money in Seattle.

Whenever I listened to Falkenbury, I felt like I was sitting in the back of his cab. His garrulous monologues drove the conversation with a sort of opinionated informality. Normally I liked this, but not now. If I let him keep talking, I couldn't guarantee what he subject he'd end up with—the *Nova* special he had just watched on PBS? The more unpleasant habits of German tourists?

"But I need you at a press conference backing Grant!" I said, cutting him off.

"Well, you see—" Falkenbury said, haltingly. "I'll think about it." Things looked bleak. So we filed a lawsuit.

One of the few equalizing tools of Seattle's electoral process is a thin pamphlet mailed to every registered voter in the city. It contains photos of each candidate with four hundred words describing his or her views and positions—a stump speech, essentially. A lot of voters relied on this pamphlet, since many never attended candidate forums or stayed on top of the news.

More than a decade earlier, the Seattle City Council had passed an ordinance forbidding candidates from mentioning their opponents in their personal statements. Ostensibly, this was to prevent mudslinging and to preserve politeness in a civil society, the "Seattle Way," as some people called it. Realistically, this rule prevented challengers from legitimately criticizing their incumbent opponents. While the incumbents were allowed to brag, manipulate, and lie about their résumés and voting records, the challenger had no way to question any of it.

It was hard to decide which was more inconceivable: that sitting city councilmembers were so brazen about restraining free speech, or that nobody in more than a decade had come forward to challenge the law.

I made some calls and arranged a meeting. Then Grant and I drove downtown to the American Civil Liberties Union, which was eager for a candidate to challenge the voter pamphlet law. The ACLU sent us to the forty-third floor of the Washington Mutual Tower, where we were shown to a conference room with a vaulting view of Puget Sound. Bluer than the water, however, were the dress shirts worn by our immaculate pro bono attorneys, eager to show what they could occasionally do for the sake of a good libertarian cause. Hands were shaken and motions were filed.

I sent out press releases to every media organization in town. What Seattle had here, I told the press, was a legitimate transportation activist who was being denied his First Amendment right to criticize his opponent.

The phone calls started immediately. We managed to squeeze everyone in.

"Some would say you're using this lawsuit to take advantage of the free media," KING-5 TV reporter Robert Mak asked. "How do you respond to that?" We were in a radio station, where Grant had just finished a talk radio interview. And now he was going to be on the noon and six o'clock news. The TV reporter had come to *us*.

Grant said, "Well, it's true that every candidate who's challenging an incumbent wants as much exposure as possible. But getting name recognition on Channel Five right now isn't going to help me in November, when people actually vote." I could see him curl his fingers lightly around the edges of the desk he was leaning against. His tattoo was covered by the sleeves of a brand-new suit. I exhaled with relief. He really did do better with questions from working journalists.

I drove the Grant Cogswell Mobile. Grant sat in the passenger seat, giddily fielding and making calls from his new campaign cell phone. We were off.

6

Seattle's geography may have influenced Marion Zioncheck from the beginning. For example, Beacon Hill, where he grew up, over-looks the skid road, later known as Skid Row. The skid road orig-inally referred to the place where freshly cut timber was rolled on skids down one of Seattle's steeper hills; it was a place of hard work and zealous individualism. But as the street grew older, changing names more than once, it became a magnet for leftist political radicalism, as well as such vices as prostitution. Today most people are familiar with Skid Row as a place of dereliction and alcohol abuse.

Self-starter, zealot, idealist, dissipate, drunk—Zioncheck embodied every incarnation of the great, terrible Skid Row. But one discovers such coincidences by turning history into a game, like listing all the bizarre similarities between the Lincoln and Kennedy assassinations. Sometimes it's significant, and sometimes it's just a weird fluke.

Our first official appearance would be among allies. Some fellow grassroots activists were gathering to discuss the latest develop-ments in local transit. "Let's take our bikes," Grant said. I protested because he was wearing khaki pants and a button-down shirt, but he scoffed at my concerns. So we donned our helmets and headed downtown, with him in the lead, moving at a delib-erate pace, his head turning to scan each intersection before crossing, his arms signaling well in advance of making turns. This wasn't at all the way I rode my bike, a cheap, heavy-framed machine with mountain tires unsuited for city streets. I liked riding in swift spurts through alleys, stop signs, and on crowded side-walks. Grant would have been appalled to learn this.

We rode south, then west and downhill, and the city raced by in colorful blurs—green-tree smudges, brown-brick smears, and yellow warning lights. Soon we came to Town Hall, a private audi-torium with high ceilings and white walls that paid vague homage to neoclassic architecture. We locked our bikes outside and, after unsticking our shirts from our backs, entered the building.

There was a small conference room at one end of the hall, and in it several middle-aged men were sitting around flipping through papers. Since nobody was introducing anybody to anyone else, I found a seat and waited for the meeting to begin. A few more people showed up, and I got a better sense of who was in atten-dance—lawyers, mostly. This gave me a thrill. I was attending a planning meeting to which journalists had not been invited! This is where history happens! Perhaps politics, not political reporting, really was where I needed to be.

The meeting was dominated by a few people. The issue at hand was light rail, the mass transit system that Grant and the other activists were trying to prevent from being built. I listened carefully before deciding that I had no idea what anybody was talking about; the technical minutiae were nearly impenetrable, and no one was slowing down to explain it. I stretched my arms and tried not to yawn.

Glancing to my right, I noticed Grant in the back of the room, slouching, squirming, saying nothing. His clunky glasses, which I had encouraged him to wear, now made him look like an awkward teenager. No one asked Grant for his opinion, or about the lawsuit we had filed, or about the campaign we had announced the day before. I tried to hide my panic.

"Don't you think you should have spoken up during that meeting?" I asked him afterward. It had never gotten more exciting than a school board budget subcommittee hearing, and from what I could tell nothing had been resolved. One lawyer had even stormed out when it became obvious that no one had any good ideas.

"No. Why?"

"Because you're running for city council?" I ventured.

"No," he said curtly. "Listen. Those people are going to support me. I already have their support. And they were talking about stuff that doesn't concern us directly." Grant got back on his bike, I got on mine, and we rode back to Capitol Hill. As I struggled uphill, I could only look at my foot pedals and think of what I was going to say to Grant in an email tonight, about how I thought political candidates should behave in public. The more I considered the issue, the more urgent it seemed.

Grant lived closer to downtown than I did, so we waved goodbye to each other and I continued on. Turning onto Twenty-third Avenue, I could see Doug from a distance, on the sidewalk playing with his remote-control car. A cigarette drooped from his puffy lips and a beer bottle was planted on the ground by his feet. His hands cradled the remote control.

I remembered the time Doug built that toy. He had started with the shell of a pink Barbie convertible that he had purchased at a garage sale for a dime, and had then spent about seven hundred dollars on five-inch-high rubber tires, a gasoline-powered motor, and a variety of other high-tech parts. The result was a shrill machine that could drown out a leaf blower. For several weeks after finishing the car, he stood on the sidewalk playing chicken with traffic. When I had asked him about the risk he was putting on such a large financial investment, he said, "It's only a toy."

One weekend Doug was replacing the Barbie plastic car shell with a new truck shell and tarting it up with acrylic paints, the next weekend he had come home bragging about the awesome BMX bike frame that he had 'stolen' for fifteen bucks at a garage sale. The remote-control car was forgotten while he spent four hundred dollars adding a seat, tires, handlebars, and other assorted parts to his new dirt bike. I then watched him work on it every night for two weeks his hands growing caked with oil and grease. But when the bike was finished, he realized he was too out of shape to use it, what with his beer drinking and cigarette smoking, so he parked it in his room and bought an old pickup truck, a gray, gas-guzzling behemoth with a white metal top. But when he couldn't get it in working condition after tinkering with it every evening for a month, he abandoned it on an upscale residential street, where indignant neighbors promptly had it towed.

A number of interests like this came and went. He was briefly consumed with a refurbished computer that our housemate Snow-Wolf had given him, using it to build a music collection through Napster, but he soon grew so disgusted with Napster that he threw the computer across his room. He would build a superior DVD collection instead. After he gave that up, the only thing he wanted to do was find, cook, and eat exotic meats like crocodile, kangaroo, dolphin. Then he was into gardening in the backyard. Then he could only talk about cooking Vietnamese food. He suspended that hobby for a while to get a pet crab, for which he built a small terrarium, but then switched to pet fish, for which he bought a fifty-gallon tank. Then the fish hobby evolved with a pair of piranhas, for which he bought an additional tank. He then decided that the piranhas were more interesting than his other fish, so he put all the fish together in one tank and watched the piranhas eat the other fish.

As I rode up to the house, I was curious about why he was playing with his remote-control car again. He had only just declared his new obsession—breeding piranhas for profit—and it wasn't like him to juggle more than one obsession at once.

I rode onto the sidewalk and stopped next to him. "How's it going?" I said, panting.

Doug gave a shrug. "I'm taking a break." Arms jerking, he maneuvered his black little machine out from underneath a moving Honda, nearly causing an accident.

"A break?" I said. "From what?"

"Upstairs," he said, his eyes on his toy. Then he added, "Riding your bike again, huh?"

"Yeah," I said. I went inside, before he could say something snide about the grass.

My new office was a narrow sunroom—a "solarium," as my landlady said in her classified ads. The wood floor was scuffed and faded and the off-white paint on the walls and ceiling was unevenly applied and cracking. The northern wall wasn't a wall at all but a flimsy partition, a reminder that the house was subdivided for renters. The sunroom used to run across the back of two bedrooms; exposed plywood now loosely separated my half of the sunroom from Doug's.

The house was on the edge of Capitol Hill, so there was a great deal to see from the sunroom's expansive windows. Below me and to the east was Madison Valley, a neighborhood that had the upper class good taste to obscure itself with evergreens. Farther east and slightly to the north shimmered the waters of Lake Washington, where sailboats dotted the surface like a scene from an impressionist painting. Directly east, beyond Lake Washington were the crisp peaks of the Cascade Mountains. At different times of the day, the clouds and the sunlight would interact with the surface terrain with kaleidoscopic unpredictability. The panorama would change hue and texture before my eyes, particularly in the evening, when late dusk blurred water, mountains and sky into one rich shade.

I frequently lost valuable campaign minutes staring out from this splendid perch, and I had to call forth all my energy to return to the work at hand. To do this, I adjusted my perspective so that I could see the landscape for what it really was: a political battle zone. That broad canopy of trees below wasn't just concealing yet another neighborhood of manicured gardens, tapas restaurants and a Starbucks central plaza. It was camouflaging a strategic village of undecided voters, caught in the cross fire of competing media opinions, candidate mailings, and man-on-the-street commentaries. I held the high ground, the PR soldier in an impregnable machine gun nest. I lobbed phone calls like hand grenades and media faxes like perfectly angled mortar shells, firing off emails as if my antiquated dial-up modem were a Gatling gun. Nothing but victory, I determined grimly, favorite coffee mug in hand, would dislodge me from this spot.

I tried to keep the sunroom as uncluttered as possible. The only things that mattered were the computer, the phone, the modem, a borrowed fax machine, and all relevant campaign documents. The only anomaly in this spartan set up was a dog-eared copy of Jonathan Raban's *Hunting Mr. Heartbreak,* an investigation of America by a British expatriate. Raban settled in Seattle in the early '90s, after falling in love with the city during his research for the book. Grant loved Raban's Seattle chapter, a section in which the writer explores the city's more permanent realities— the buildings, the sea air, the omnipresent gray of spring, fall, and winter. Everything in this "lumpy drab-colored marine city" is affectionately ripe for novelization, Raban said. I didn't have much use for this description, but I found myself rereading the Seattle chapter several times during the campaign. I wanted to "get tapped into the city," as Grant had frequently exhorted me to do.

I realized that I was out of coffee. My adrenaline buzz was dangerously close to wearing off. I headed for the kitchen to get a Coke out of the refrigerator.

The second floor landing was a flurry of activity. Doug was running back and forth from his room to the bathroom. Hanging from his right arm was a five-gallon bucket, the kind you might find in a janitor's closet. He had the lights on everywhere and the bathtub faucet running at full pressure. A trail of puddles marked the path he hurried along.

"The eggs!" he said. "Hatched! Last night! It's awesome! There must be eighty to a hundred baby piranhas in that tank!"

Doug set down his bucket, and we gingerly stepped into his room. I pushed my nose against the fifty-gallon tank. All I saw were the adult piranhas with their flat, ugly faces.

"Where are they?" I said. "Where are the little fuckers?"

"They're there. They're really small. Can't you see them?"

Pressing closer, I made out dozens of little black dots in the water. They looked like flecks of floating dirt.

"Oh," I said. "What's with the bucket?"

The problem with raising baby piranhas, apparently, is that the pH level of the water has to be kept within a very precise range. If it dips or rises outside that range, which it inevitably does in untended aquariums, the baby fish die.

"That means," Doug said, "until the fish get older, I have to keep changing the water in the tank."

"How often?"

"Once, sometimes twice a day."

We watched the activity in the tank. It was hard to believe that if all those little black dots matured they'd be capable of so much carnivorous mayhem. In their own way, piranhas were excellent anarchists.

"I'm really going to have to get a second job so I can buy that giant aquarium I was telling you about. I think they're going to hire me part-time at the pet store."

"You're gonna be really busy, then."

"Yeah," he said, happily.

Something occurred to me. "Hey, Doug?"

"Yeah?"

"Last night you were playing your music really, really loud."

"Oh, sorry."

"I banged on the door, but you didn't answer."

"Huh," he said, tensing. "I didn't hear you."

"You know the cut-off hour for noise is like ten or eleven. It says so on our leases."

"You haven't been home until late this past week."

"Well, I was home last night. And it was really distracting. What was that music, anyway? Butt rock?" Of course it had been butt rock, the only thing he ever played beside my Modest Mouse album. Of course Doug would have heard me knock, unless he had passed out from drinking. Of course he wasn't going to turn his music down. Not without a fight of some kind.

I made as if to leave, but added, as an afterthought, "By the way, the washing machine is broken."

"You're kidding me," he said.

"It broke last night, I think," I said. "Either me or SnowWolf did the last load, not that that matters—OK, it *was* me. Anyway, it was an old machine. I have to talk to the landlady about getting it fixed. Maybe she'll even give us a new one."

Doug lost all expression in his face. He let out a yelp and ran for the stairwell.

"What—" I said, stunned. Then I knew what he intended to do, and I yelped, too. "Hey! No, Doug!"

I gave chase. Our pounding feet on the wooden stairs boomed throughout the house. I caught up with him in the basement, where he had stopped, panting, in front of the washing machine.

In the light of the basement's exposed ceiling bulb, Doug's face was contorted with frustration and anger. "It can't be broken!" he said. "I can't afford—I can't have it be—*I'll* fix it!"

"I'm going to call the landlady," I said. "She'll fix it or have it replaced. She *has* to take care of it for us."

SnowWolf peered out from his basement lair, which was marked by a tiny door about four feet from where we stood. SnowWolf was short, with thick black hair and a thick black beard and a thick, stocky frame, and was wearing a black T-shirt that had an airbrushed mythological animal on it. It was 7:30 P.M., so he would have just woken up. It would soon be time for him to go to work, a graveyard shift at a dairy factory.

"What's going on?" he said. I was surprised that he had come out of his room at all.

"The washing machine's broken!" Doug yelled. "I've gotta fix it!"

"Ah," said SnowWolf, who turned around and disappeared into his room.

I left, too. Doug was too upset to be reasoned with. Two hours later, on a break from writing a press release, I looked down into the basement from the first floor landing. Washing machine parts were strewn all over the floor; I couldn't see Doug but I could hear him swearing.

After four hours of tinkering, cursing, and pleading, Doug couldn't get the washing machine to work. It was replaced in less than six days—an admirable response, I thought, on the landlady's part. But Doug didn't care. The broken washing machine was my fault, as was everything else that went wrong in the house. And, this time, Doug planned to do something about it.

He began by needling me. I had wanted to use the dining room as a place for our weekly campaign steering committee meetings. But when Grant and I and several volunteers sat at the big wooden table, Doug turned on the television in the living room and put an '80s horror flick in the VCR and cranked up the volume. We fled to the front porch, but the noise from the passing cars and trucks made brainstorming impossible. We were forced to move the meetings to a volunteer's apartment.

One night later that week, around midnight, he got drunk and turned his music up. When I went over to tell him to turn it down, he shouted over his music. "Ieeeeey!" he said. "I'd like your vote! I'm Grant Cogswell and I'm running for office! Ha! Ha! Monorail! Ha! I crack myself up sometimes, I tell you."

After he sobered up, Doug had an idea: He would challenge me for control of the house.

He began lobbying the other housemates, starting with Emily, who had been exceptionally patient when her bathroom started to reek of sewage every morning. Doug wanted to see just how strong that patience was. He made small comments to her about me, side comments, really, tangents of other conversations that he was hoping Emily would conclude for him. He tested her. He would find a way to bring my name up in casual conversation, then he would complain about the specific things I did as the house manager.

He would ask, "Why is Phil leaving notes on people's doors? Don't you think that's really unfair, ordering us around with notes on doors? I think it's really irresponsible." He pressed her on how rank the odor in her bathroom was, implying with his questions that she had on her hands a real emergency that I wasn't handling quickly enough, and that he, more than anyone else, cared about making sure that problem was taken care of.

But Emily wasn't interested in domestic warfare, so she played dumb, pretending that she hadn't noticed that Doug's voice had cracked a little in anticipation of her answer, as if he hadn't been watching her expectantly, his eyes lit with ulterior motive.

He worked on Ben and Cate next. They had moved out to Seattle from the Northeast right after college. To save money, they shared the second smallest room in the house. Doug loved Ben and Cate. He once offered to pay their phone bill, claiming he had to get rid of money that he didn't need. Doug would corner them in the kitchen as they fried tofu or cooked salmon and greens, and try to talk them up, joke with them. He'd wait for a sly opening to drop my name into the conversation. When he saw his chance, he would unleash a torrent of abuse against me. "All Phil fucking does is leave notes and expects you to communicate that way," he'd say. "I should be house manager. I'd be so much better." He'd shake his head regretfully and ask when the lawn was ever going to get mowed.

Ben and Cate thought they understood what Doug wanted. He wanted them to talk to the landlady, to tell her I did not have the consent of the governed. But they sidestepped the issue. They were planning on moving out of the house by the end of August, and they didn't see any point in raising a fuss.

Doug didn't bother with SnowWolf, for the same reason that nobody else did: SnowWolf was above commonplace issues like political intrigue, domestic squabbles, and house chores. He lived according to a script of his own writing, one that no one else was allowed to read.

One evening Doug knocked on my door. My girlfriend and I were getting ready for bed. "What is it?" I called out.

Doug peered in, his red mustache leading his face, a broad grin behind that. "*Heeeeey,* what's the landlady's phone number?"

I gave it to him.

He repeated it.

I said it again, articulating each number slowly. Then it occurred to me to ask him why he needed it. The only person who ever called the landlady was me; I was her liaison, and she didn't really want to hear from any of the other housemates. She only wanted their rent checks.

Doug repeated the number.

"Yes. That's it. Now what do you need it for?"

Doug repeated the same number back to me a third time. He wanted to see how long it would take before I got riled. Not long at all. "What do you need her number for?" I demanded.

"OK, thanks!" Then Doug shut the door and I heard the sound of hysterical laughter.

"What was that about?" my girlfriend asked. She didn't like Doug very much.

"I have no idea," I lied.

7

As a child, Marion Zioncheck was expected to help his family earn money to survive. He caught rats for local health officials during an influenza breakout, herded cattle, sold newspapers, and worked as a common laborer.

He was also a fisherman, catching salmon in the Duwamish Waterway and peddling them to nearby residents. Of course, in those days salmon were bountiful, and the rivers, estuaries, and creeks around Seattle weren't polluted or hemmed in by so many factories, highways, and strips of residential development.

When he was down on his luck in his late teens and early twenties Marion Zioncheck again toiled at a variety of jobs, in logging camps, boatyards, and, yes, fisheries.

I waited for Grant in the Geo outside his apartment and studied my notebook. My list of tasks pronounced themselves in a series of black entries, with dozens of blue arrows crisscrossing the page to arrange and re-arrange my priorities. *Get in touch with Brad about campaign T-shirts. Call Ben about our meeting with the elections commission downtown. Follow-up with Adam Weintraub about a candidate photo. Find a volunteer coordinator. Call the ACLU for a progress report. Call Anne about a fund-raiser. Call the King County Democrats and get the dates of their endorsement meetings. Ask all of my friends to volunteer or give money. Email Jen about using Victrola for our kickoff party . . .*

I suppressed a need to hyperventilate. By themselves, these were all menial tasks, barely requiring much thought. But there were so many of them on the list, extending four pages, and they all had to get done immediately. Moreover, almost all of these tasks required me to be upbeat, regardless of my mood.

Grant got in and I dropped my notebook. I switched on the ignition, the Grant Cogswell Mobile came to life, and I turned out of the parking lot and past Victrola. We were going downtown to talk to a graphic designer Grant knew.

"Watch out for that car!" Grant said.

"There was plenty of room," I said.

"No there wasn't. God your driving makes me nervous."

"OK. OK," I said, trying to sound soothing. "How am I getting there?"

Grant told me. He tugged at his paper coffee cup. He was drinking decaf.

"Do you remember that guy in my building yesterday morning?" he said. "The one who said something really weird to us as we left the lobby?"

"Yeah. It felt like we were being accosted by a crazy homeless guy. Was he OK? You knew him, right?"

"Yeah. We all know each other there. And, no, he's not all right. You will not be-*lieve* what he did after we left."

"What?"

"He lost it. He knocked on one of the neighbor's doors, and said to the woman who answered, 'Your husband's dead.' " Grant jabbed the air with his fingers, presumably as part of his imitation. "And she was like, 'No-o-o-o-o. I can see my husband. He's right there.' The husband was down the hall from her. But the guy said, 'No. He's hanging from a rope in my apartment—and you're my wife now.' "

I stopped for a pedestrian at a crosswalk. It took a long time for him and his pink fanny pack to waddle out of the way. Seattle etiquette dictated that he get to the opposite curb before I proceeded.

"That is fucked up," I said.

"Your husband's hanging in my apartment, and you're my wife

now," he said again. "The police came and took him to Harborview. They confiscated all of his guns, too."

"*Guns?* Plural? How many did he have?"

"I don't know. A few."

"People in Seattle don't own guns," I said.

"This guy did. They were worried he was going to hurt himself. Isn't that crazy?"

I agreed that that was crazy. I was tempted to tell Grant about Doug and his strange behavior, but decided against it. It seemed incidental, and Grant was tangled up in domestic problems of his own. He had gone several months without paying his share of his co op's monthly maintenance fee. This, he told me, was not usually a problem; one person he knew had gone a year and a half without paying. But somebody in his building had decided to take Grant's delinquency personally. Grant kept finding notes on the community board attacking him. He was hoping to put a stop to it but didn't yet know the identity of his enemy.

We drove in silence through Capitol Hill. I shot from worry to alarm in the time it took to get through the third stoplight. *That last conversation was depressing. Is Grant depressed now? I'm his campaign manager. Don't let him drag himself down. He can't afford to be in a bad mood, ever.*

So I brought up Stan Lippmann, an easy target for distraction and ridicule. A nuclear physicist and an attorney, Lippmann was running on a pro–mass transit plan, but he had a not-so-secret agenda to abolish rubella vaccinations. He was an odd non sequitur of a human being.

"That guy is such a freak," Grant joined in, giving no indication that he was depressed. "And his yard signs—have you *seen* his yard signs? They're so tiny you can barely read them. And they're placed about twenty yards off the shoulder of the road."

Soon we were talking about all the characters in our race. We were in a pack of four challengers to the incumbent. The primary was ten weeks away.

"Who the hell is this 'E. Heath Merriwether'? Where does the *E* go, after or before the 'Heath'? Is that a man or a woman even?"

"Heath's a he," Grant said. "He says he has a plan to get on the city council in five years."

"How does that work?" I snorted. "Good luck."

"He just keeps running until he wins on name recognition. He's twenty-nine. He seemed pretty cool about his plan."

"So he's not a threat? Are you sure? I saw he got six hundred dollars from Jeff Bezos from Amazon." That was the most that an individual could contribute to one campaign.

Grant whistled, surprised and opportunistic. "You think we could persuade old Jeff to give us some of that, after we knock his friend out of the primary?"

"I don't know. Maybe."

"I don't know anything about the other guy in the race. Wilson?"

"Jerome Wilson," I said. "I know him. He's connected to that small group of black activists who want an African-American heritage museum. Except he's not one of the original activists, so he doesn't have any cred. He just came along later, *after* the city nixed the plans, *after* it was obvious the activists weren't going to get what they wanted. That guy—I don't trust him. He comes in late, becomes the executive director, quote-unquote, of a defunct board, and *then* claims the city owes him tens of thousands of dollars for the work he did on a museum that the city said it wouldn't build, on a board the city no longer recognizes. And he's really, *really* persistent about it."

"Weird," Grant said. "I don't know him."

"Do you know Jeff Buckley?"

"Of course."

"The activist, not the dead Memphis singer. I know. I *love* that name. Jeff Buckley. I think an ex-girlfriend of mine did his autopsy. The singer's autopsy, I mean."

"Slow down," Grant ordered. I couldn't tell if he was talking about my driving or my chatter. "You're getting confused. I think the coffee's making you hyper." He quipped, "I should put you on a caffeine-free diet."

"Well, Jeff Buckley *the activist* is in the Green Party. And he's backing Wilson. I can't believe that."

"I can't either. He told me it was strategic. He wants Wilson to talk more about police accountability since nobody in the race is doing that."

"Yeah," I said, "but when's the Seattle Green Party going to back somebody who can actually win? Hey, wait. They'll endorse you officially, right? The Greens, I mean."

"They'd better," Grant said. He pointed. "This is it. Now find a place to park."

● ● ●

Back on the road, later that day. This time we were going to the distant neighborhood of West Seattle for an early meeting with some Democrats.

The Interstate 5 on-ramp on Capitol Hill was unlike almost every other driving situation in the city. The major rule about normal Seattle driving—predictable hesitation—didn't apply here. Everyone moved fast and without forgiveness. Among the SUVs, I always felt like I was trying to join a rugby game in the middle of a scrum against guys twice my size.

"*Hey*. Use your turn signal!" Grant said.

"We're fine," I said.

"What are you doing? Stay in this lane."

"I was gonna get in the HOV lane."

"No. Were getting off at the West Seattle Bridge. That's just up ahead. What are you doing? Careful!"

"OK!"

"Jesus!"

Sweat blotted my palms. I had never been given this many

orders in a month, much less in a day. My hand reflexively shot toward the radio, to bring some gratifying distraction to the situation, but then I stopped. Music irritated Grant.

I let a few cars pass by. Then I spoke.

"Uh, Grant?"

"Right. We should be—"

"I was thinking about—"

"—merging here soon."

"—about your platform."

"Here. Get in this lane."

"I'm already there!"

"Will you *reee*-lax?!"

I wiped my hands on my jeans. The bonus of campaign management was that nobody expected me to dress up.

"I understand," I continued, "what your platform is, but I think I need to go over the points with you again. I want to stay on message."

"Hit me."

"Your *platform*," I said. "Now I like talking to reporters, but there are a ton of things that I want to be able to say with confidence that I don't know enough about. I just want to make sure I get my facts straight."

"Go ahead."

This wasn't easy. I now understood how silly Grant felt whenever I tried to give him a mock interview. I hated the sound of my own voice.

"There are three or four things you're running on," I said. "The first, monorail. Of course you support that. You ran the first monorail campaign with Falkenbury—"

"His idea, my campaign," Grant said.

"Yeah," I said. Falkenbury didn't necessarily agree with that assessment, but I let it go. My mouth was dry, my water bottle was empty and my coffee was cold. "But the big problem right now isn't monorail, because that's on track. I mean, it's going up for another vote next year. So the main point of your platform involves your opposition to the countywide plan for light rail."

"Yes. Sound Transit," Grant said impatiently.

"Sound Transit is the agency that was created to build light rail, and it has completely screwed up. It's a billion dollars over budget, maybe two. It's going to divide the Rainier Valley—one of the only minority communities in Seattle—in half. It's—it's—"

"It's a street-level train that rides with traffic," he said. "That's the real problem. It's going to be slowed down by traffic. It'll get stopped dozens of times just trying to get downtown. And people say Portland's light rail is a good model, which would be true if people actually rode it. Portland's train doesn't do what its supposed to do—it doesn't take cars off the road. People admire Portland's light rail because it looks good, not because it works."

"You know what good advice I heard lately?" I said. "Never say 'light rail.' Always, always say, 'Sound Transit's light rail.' See, because people still want mass transit, and they think light rail is a good idea, but they don't trust Sound Transit. Some polls have shown that."

"That's a really good idea. Get out from behind that truck, will you? The fumes are giving me a headache."

"I can't. Too many cars coming up behind us."

"Well, slow down and let him get some distance in front of you."

"So anyway," I said.

"So," Grant interjected. "Sound Transit promised voters in the mid-'90s that they'd take cars off the road. And then they come out with a report that said they'd only get one out of every thousand cars off the road." He laughed. "That's nothing. They're over budget and they need all these deadline extensions to get done. *And* they're going to divide Rainier Valley in half."

"They're taking away three hundred properties in the Rainier Valley alone," I said, trying to regain control of my own speech. "It's a street-level train that stretches three-hundred-plus feet in length and weighs two hundred and fifty tons and they call it 'light' rail."

"Do you have any idea how long three-hundred feet is, how much it'll slow down traffic at intersections?" Grant asked.

"—But on the other hand, monorail—"

"Is above traffic so it won't get slowed down by cars. It can be built at one-fourth to one-third the price because it's easier to build. They can mass-manufacture most of the parts off-site and then just come in and throw it up."

"And that thing you said on the radio the other day about the columns?" I said.

"The stanchions," Grant said. He was bored, his monotonous drone like an engine on cruise control. "They don't have to be as wide as the stanchions they made for the old Seattle monorail. They can be much more slender, because technology's improved. They don't have to be solid blocks of cement. They can have a little trestling in the middle, to allow more light to get through. They could actually be pretty attractive."

"—And McIver's consistently been against monorail and *for* light rail," I said. "The incumbent tried at least once to kill monorail by preventing the ETC board from receiving a fifty thousand-dollar grant that would have kept it alive."

"You've got it."

"Sure. OK," I said. But I was flustered. "I'm going to have to write this all down at some point. I do a lot better taking notes. I don't know how to debate and this isn't easy."

"You'll get the hang of it," Grant said. "Keep going straight. Then turn left up ahead. Now, here. *Here!*"

• • •

We were now heading south into Rainier Valley, and stuck behind a city bus. Grant coughed, complained again about the exhaust fumes, and ordered me to change lanes, which I couldn't do.

"God this is giving me a headache," he said.

"I'm sorry," I said. "It'll be a while. There're about fifty cars coming at us." I added a couple sympathetic expletives.

There were only a few places in the city of Seattle that didn't seem like Seattle. Rainier Valley was one of them. After colossal Mt. Rainier dipped out of sight, assuming the clouds weren't obscuring it in the first place, there were no eye-candy vistas of mountains and lakes. What you got were fast-food restaurants and auto parts stores. One of the most racially diverse parts of the city, it was also one of the poorest.

I watched a small Korean boy drop a red kickball, which rolled into the street. A whole lane of traffic came to a stop. I couldn't say why. That kid wasn't going to be of voting age by November.

"If there was a light rail line right there, that little boy would be dead," I said. "Monorail rides *above* the street."

I imagined myself talking to a reporter. *Bill, just look at Rainier Valley. It's unconscionable that Rainier Valley is getting screwed in the way it is over light rail. You guys reported it in your own paper. In 1991, Seattle public officials demanded that the light-rail line accommodate the low-income people of Rainier Valley. So the proposed line was moved to do just that; they cooked the numbers and they moved the line to Martin Luther King Jr. Boulevard. But they put the train on the street, and what now? Three hundred properties taken, Bill, and the community divided in half. You know, Bill, Grant's opponent Richard McI—*

Grant interrupted my fantasized rant by saying, "If we build light rail, we've destroyed our chance to build effective mass transit for the next one hundred years."

"Uh-huh," I said, making a mental note to remember that line.

"Did you call Anne B—?" Grant asked.

I considered the question.

"She's on one of my lists of things to do," I said.

"So you didn't call her."

"Have you seen my lists?"

"No. What—"

"—because they're really long. There's too much to do. I worked seventeen hours yesterday!"

"*Exactly*. You have got to listen to me. That's *exactly* why we have to get volunteers. Neither one of us can possibly do everything that we need to get done. We can't do all this stuff."

"I know. I know. I'm sorry. I'm trying. I'm trying." I made a mental note to change the order on my list. No. 1: Call the ACLU. No. 2. Call Anne B—. No. 3. Take twenty-minute nap. No. 4 . . .

"I'm not falling asleep until two, three A.M. because there's so much to do," Grant said.

We were spiraling emotionally again. I could feel the downward pull in the Grant Cogswell Mobile.

"Grant," I said. "The rest of your platform? After transit, I mean?"

"What about it?"

"I gotta confess, I don't know that much about salmon. What are we going to do to save them, again?

"The biggest issue is Thornton Creek, which has been covered up for development. The neighborhood wants it daylighted—that means uncovered. The city's favoring developers over residents."

I did my best to keep up.

"But it's more than that," he said. "The city council doesn't care about local environmental issues. The only thing they've done is pass a resolution calling for a resolution calling for the Snake River Dam to be removed, but what good is that? The Snake River Dam is in eastern Washington. That's a state issue—"

"Ah," I said. "Sort of like how they protested the World Trade Organization with a resolution, or—"

"Or the proposed ban on circus animals. Useless. That's what I'm talking about. I'm talking about Thornton Creek, but it's bigger than that."

"Ah," I said. I could see us saving the salmon. What a noble fish! They journey thousands of miles, obsessed by one goal, to return to the place where they started. They undergo a massive physical transformation, from freshwater natives to salty ocean survivors, to attain that goal. Still, I'd have to research the Thornton Creek issue. I hoped I could find the time.

Animal imagery evoked another thought. "Grant, what about the polar bear suit?"

"Ha! I'm not going to talk about that until after I've won. Then I'm just going to do it."

"Whatever. Doesn't matter. Tell me about the polar bear suit, again. Please?"

Grant repeated his vow to dress up like a polar bear in order to make a mockery of Sound Transit meetings. I slapped the steering wheel with delight, and gave in to a vision of my own. A crowded Sound Transit board meeting. Lightning flashes outside. Grant sitting at a round table, an equal among elected officials. Except it's not Grant. It's the polar bear. A technocrat in a dull gray suit is talking about spending another billion dollars of taxpayer money that could have gone to help the poor. The polar bear howls. People run for cover. The polar bear picks up a scale model of a Sound Transit train and eats it. Behind the polar bear is me, the bear's aide. Except it's not me. It's a giant river otter. The river otter is hooting and dancing. It slaps the polar bear on the back. The two high-five each other. They walk out of the conference room into a bright, clear day, the only clouds in sight haloing Mt. Rainier. Television, radio, and print reporters swarm them. A front-page headline reads, "Bear Blocks Boondoggle." A parade starts, with ticker tape made of shredded Sound Transit documents. Meanwhile, on the other end of town—

"Slow down and pace yourself better, will you?" Grant said. "You've got these lights timed wrong."

8

Before running for Congress, Marion Zioncheck got his law degree at the University of Washington, and for a short while he provided legal services for those who had little or no money to pay for them. This being the Great Depression, there was an abundance of such clients to choose from.

Zioncheck kept himself from growing dispirited by staying focused and organized. He used all the connections and resources in his power to keep poverty-stricken families from being evicted. If a judge ordered eviction and the sheriff moved the family out onto the sidewalk, Zioncheck would call on his friends for help. One group of friends would break the locks on the doors and move the family right back into their old home, furniture and all; another friend working inside the city utilities would get the family's water turned back on. Zioncheck would then file a motion with the judge, and the courts would have to start the eviction process all over again.

But Zioncheck didn't always succeed, and his evicted clients were sometimes forced to move into Seattle's own Hooverville, a vast wood-and-cardboard shantytown to the south of downtown. That was one of the reasons Zioncheck became a politician. As a lawyer he could only help one family at a time, but a congressman, he could pass laws that helped millions of people at once.

I stood at the front door of Grant's apartment building at ten o'clock on a Tuesday morning and pressed the door buzzer for three full minutes before looking around in desperation. Grant had warned me a dozen times in the past about being too loud in the courtyard, but I was growing anxious and we were behind schedule so I cupped my hands and yelled in the direction of his bedroom window.

Nothing happened, so I considered my options. Grant's campaign cell phone was off and he wasn't answering his regular phone, which was attached to the downstairs buzzer. That left the last resort. I kneeled to search for some rocks. I had to get into the bushes along the walls of the building and feel around with my hands for a few small, dirty stones. Standing up, I took aim and hurled the stones at the candidate's bedroom window on the second floor. They made a satisfying clank on the glass before falling back into the bushes.

Grant opened the window and peered outside. He was bleary, shirtless, and unspectacled. His stout belly was so white it glowed.

"Will you quiet down?" he hissed. "I heard you five minutes ago!"

"Good morning, sunshine!" I said. "I need you to sign this—"

"Shhhhhhhh! Keep your voice down!"

Clenching, I said, "Should I wait for you at Victrola?"

"Yeah. Give me fifteen minutes."

Grant disappeared and Tara came to the window and waved. She had decided she liked me after we had run a small errand for Grant together. To fill the shy silence in the Geo, I had started singing along in a screechy off-key tone to some '80s pop songs that were on the radio, and she had concluded that I was quirky and amusing. Now Tara whispered down to me until Grant came back and slammed the window shut.

I walked over to Fifteenth Avenue and bought a bagel and both daily papers at the health food store. I then bought a cup of black coffee at Victrola and found a seat. There was nothing in the papers that interested me so I looked at my notebook and tried to make sense of my chaotic markings. In my peripheral vision I saw Grant enter the café. He chatted up the owners first, then got a decaf and joined me.

"I don't like this table," he said. "Let's sit over there." We moved and then got down to business.

July was going to go by fast, Grant said, but there was an extraordinary amount of work that had to get done before it was over. The lawsuit had given us some momentum, and we had to take advantage of it at once. We had to organize a strong base of volunteers and contributors before we approached the Democratic Party in August for the endorsement meetings. Grant also wanted the campaign to be at every summer neighborhood festival we could find, which amounted to quite a few throughout July and August. "We need volunteers passing out our literature at each of these festivals," he said.

"I've got a pretty heavy day," I complained. "I don't have time to call all those people—"

Someone called out Grant's name from across the café. He turned and waved and then turned back to rebuke me. I could already detect a slight change in Grant's behavior—his public façade was growing more expansive as his patience with me in private was growing thin.

"I *know*," he said. "We need more people to help us. Which reminds me, I've got someone who may be able to volunteer for us. Here. Write down this name and number." He handed me a piece of paper ripped out of his poetry notebook.

"I can't read your chicken scratch," I said. "You'll have to read it to me."

"I can't read your handwriting either," he retorted, but he did as I asked. The name he gave me was Theresa. She lived in the neighborhood. "She's worked on campaigns before and comes highly recommended," he said. "We should make her our volunteer coordinator."

After I wrote down her number we moved to the next item of discussion. "Our logo," he said. "I want to show you what we're doing."

He took out another piece of paper and handed it to me. It was a rough sketch in blue ink and jagged lines. A monorail, distinguishable from an ordinary train by its supporting columns, swept down a track, flying from the page's upper left side to its upper right side. Below the monorail Grant had written his name ("I'm not sure about the font yet") with the phrase "for Seattle City Council," in a smaller, semi-cursive style. It was quite an image, given that Grant hated corporate marketing so much that he ripped the logos off his clothes, even if it meant leaving a hole in the fabric.

I told him I was impressed. "I've had this inside my head for years," he said, warming up for the first time that morning.

We talked about some other things, including Grant's proposal that he read his Marion Zioncheck poem for reporters on the anniversary of Zioncheck's death. I protested, saying that no aspiring politician should write an epic poem, and Grant let the idea go without admitting I was right. Encouraged, I more strenuously objected to Grant's participation in the upcoming "Reclaim the Streets" protest, where anarchists and other activists were planning to confront police over an array of issues. Grant agreed; street protests would have to wait until after the campaign.

"Anything else?" Grant said.

"Media," I said. "I'm having lunch with James Bush of the *Seattle Weekly* today, and I'm calling the political reporters at the other papers, too. You know, I think that's going to be the easiest part of this campaign."

Victrola was filling up. I saw a number of unemployed friends in line for coffee. Grant said, "So we're meeting back here this afternoon? I need you to take me to North Seattle for Stan Emert's show."

"OK, yeah," I said. I flipped through my notebook and pointed. "Look at my list! I gotta be fifty places in the next four hours!"

"Tell me about it. I gotta start raising money today. Tara's looking up phone numbers for contributors as we speak."

I felt Grant's mood start to plummet—raising money was going to be his toughest job. I rushed in for moral support. "Cold calling?" I said. "Shit. Good luck. You want me to come by to help you with that? I may have some tips."

"Maybe," he said. "Don't forget this afternoon. I'll call you when I'm ready."

From my Geo I called Theresa, our potential volunteer coordinator. She said she could meet me in half an hour, so I moved my schedule around to accommodate her. I liked how politics was making me slick and articulate, my tongue sliding around in my mouth as if it had discovered a lubricant better than alcohol.

I was home and in five minutes I was heading out the door again, but Ben stopped me in the hallway.

He reminded me that he and Cate were moving out at the end of July, a month before their lease expired. I told him I knew this. He was wondering how long it would be before I found a replacement tenant. If someone filled the room as soon as he and Cate left, they wouldn't be responsible for August's rent.

"I'll do the best I can," I said, "But it's not going to be easy. The vacancy rate in Seattle is really, really high right now." The dot-commers were not only losing their jobs, they were abandoning their utopian city by the thousands. The landlady had instructed me to write a classified ad using phrases like 'move-in discount special' and 'first month's rent free,' something she would have found unthinkable the year before.

Ben persisted, asking, "How long do you think you'll need?" He and Cate really needed the money.

"I don't know! I don't know!" I said, backing away. "Look, I want to help you, Ben, but I'm really swamped right now, and nobody's calling me to look at your room. I'm not getting *any* calls, all right?" My cell phone rang. I waved at Ben and beat a hasty retreat.

Back at Victrola, in a different seat, I realized how anxious I had become. I wiped my sweaty hands onto my shorts and tried to regain control of my notes. Grant called twice as I rewrote my to-do list. I really could have used a Palm Pilot. Then Theresa came up to my table, introduced herself, and sat down.

She was a pale, terse woman with limp brown hair. Her every move was efficient and organized, and she had a classic Seattle civility about her, knowing the right pleasantries without appearing to be enjoying their exchange too greatly. She told me she had a three-year-old son and was hoping to find steady work soon.

"I'm afraid all I can offer you is three hundred dollars a week," I said. It was more than what Grant was paying me, which was nothing.

"That's fair," she said. "You guys are probably having a hard time raising money, aren't you?"

"We haven't even started! Grant's supposed to begin today." Realizing that I was being too pessimistic, I added, "But he's got a very good list of people and it's just a matter of going through the list and calling them."

"Oh, I'm sure you'll do really well," she said. "So where is your office?"

"Office?" I echoed. "Well, my house, and my car, and Grant's— I'm sorry, we don't really have an office."

"Then where am I supposed to work?" she asked, baffled.

I had to persuade Theresa that we didn't really need a campaign office, that such a concept was a throwback to a more difficult era in political history. She could work for us from her home.

I added, "I think you'd make a great volunteer coordinator. You come highly recommended."

At the mention of a campaign title, Theresa's face pinched with distaste. "No, no. I'm sorry," she said. "I already told Grant that I couldn't be the volunteer coordinator. It's too much work. I have too many things going on in my life right now. I have to find a new apartment. I have to find a job. I have my son—" She would do office work, she said. She didn't mind office work, even if there was no real office.

My mood began to slip. I felt like I was negotiating a business contract, not rallying a fellow soldier to battle. Where was the grassroots fervor in this conversation? What's more, we couldn't afford to pay someone three hundred a week if they only wanted to push papers around for us.

I noticed the time, however, and realized that I couldn't settle this issue now. I told Theresa that we'd be ecstatic to have her do office work, our conversation ended, and I rushed downtown to meet with James Bush, talking to Grant on my cell as I drove. I met Bush at his office, and together we walked downstairs to a nearby restaurant. I didn't know where I was eating, nor did I remember what I had ordered five seconds after I had ordered it, because Bush, a heavy-set, congenial fellow, started dispensing valuable advice and I was concentrating on every word.

"There are a lot of things you have to keep in mind," said Bush. His curiosity was clearly aroused by the sight of a fellow journalist trying his hand in campaign politics. "For one, it is possible for Grant to win on a single issue. It's been done before—Judy Nicastro won her seat a couple years ago on renter's rights."

"That's why our campaign is going to work!" I said. "Grant's transit ideas are just what this city needs!"

Bush gave an approving nod at my aggressive spin. "If you're running him as a populist, the thing you can do is make sure he looks like a populist. Make sure you have a crowd of volunteers surrounding Grant wherever he goes. An entourage."

An entourage! I saw it, and agreed.

Bush rested his chin on his hand. "Richard McIver's smart, witty, and likeable, but he's not going to have a lot of volunteers. He will have money, which you won't have. You're going to be Grant's legislative aide if he wins, right?"

"I hadn't thought about that," I said. "Sure. That might be interesting."

"You'd be making more than you did at the *Stranger*," he said. Maybe as much as 30 percent more.

I looked at Bush in disbelief. "Yes," I said. "I'm going to be his *top* political aide."

The check came. I made a limp pass for my wallet. "No, don't worry about it," Bush said, trying to keep the sympathy out of his voice. "Just try not to forget me when you've got a scoop—after you win, of course."

I rushed home, and with my energy still soaring, I called Beth Kaiman of the *Seattle Times* and Neil Modie of the *Seattle Post-Intelligencer* to pitch my candidate. Kaiman was polite but stiff, less interested in developing a potential source than in getting to the point, but Modie and I connected right away. I built up Grant's credentials and made some predictions. Grant was the challenger who would survive the primary. He was, in fact, the only one of the bunch who could take on McIver. Tossing in Grant's boilerplate speech, adding my own colloquialisms, I created a struggle of titanic proportions, one that would be both personal for the combatants and central to the city's future. When I finished, I took Modie's silence for rapt attention. We agreed to keep in touch and I hung up.

The only paper I dreaded was the *Stranger*. The editors had hoped I would take a letter of recommendation and skip town, yet here I was, not only living in the same neighborhood and dating one of their writers, but stepping smack into the middle of their regular news coverage. I felt like a dull-witted animal trapped on a busy highway during rush hour.

I emailed Dan Savage, the editor-in-chief, and pleaded Grant's case, pointing out Grant's loyalty and his positions. Savage had every reason to back Grant because he supported monorail almost as rabidly as Grant did. But as soon as I sent it I knew my email would never get a response. So, on the pretext of collecting my letter of recommendation, which I had written and Savage had promised to sign, I dropped by the weekly's offices.

The door to the editorial offices was ajar. Something wasn't right. The place looked deserted. There was no yelling. I stood near the door, wondering what to do.

He managed, somehow, to sneak up on me.

"Hey, Phil!" Josh Feit, my former editor, shouted, though he was just ten feet away. "I heard you're running Grant's campaign." His voice boomed. His voice always boomed. What I had learned to listen for was his tone; in this case, he was excited and loud, not angry and loud.

"Yeah, I know!" I said, shouting back. Then I remembered who I was talking to. The man who had gotten me fired was happy to see me. Pleasure evaporated into peevish discomfort.

I asked, "Is Dan around?"

"I think you just missed him." And then Josh left. I decided to come back another time.

I went home and sent a dozen emails. I called Theresa and left a message asking for help on a few phone calls that had to be made. I called some of the smaller unions in the city, trying to pick up at least one labor endorsement. I wrote a press release and then spent half an hour trying to figure out why our borrowed fax machine wasn't working. Grant called just as I trying in vain to open an electronic attachment our volunteer graphic designer had sent me.

"You're on your way to pick me up, right?" he said.

"Right," I said, pretending I had not forgotten. Ten minutes later he and I were northbound for Stan Emert's public-access cable talk show.

Emert—tall, businesslike—seemed to have a thorough grasp of issues, but he was a tepid interviewer whose soft questions barely penetrated Grant's stump speech, so the half hour session was sleep inducing. Grant was at his best when he was combative; he didn't have the kind of personality needed to fill in the spaces of a friendly talk-show format.

Emert liked Grant, though, and wanted to help our campaign. He gave Grant a one-hundred-dollar contribution and me a private piece of advice.

"So you're the campaign manager," he said. "Does Grant trust you?"

"Yes," I said, sensing an imminent, confidential moment.

"Good," Emert said. "Get him to stop wearing that suit. The color is hideous."

Twenty-five minutes later we were back in Grant's apartment, getting ready to make fund-raising cold calls.

Grant sat in an office chair in his living room, now wearing a T-shirt and shorts. He had avoided this all day. The phone looked diabolical. I sat on the couch, ready to provide advice and support, empathizing, but deeply relieved that this particular burden was not mine. We knew only a few rules about fund-raising, advice passed down to us by veteran politicos, the most important being that only the candidate can really raise money in a local election, because no one wants to hear a pitch from a volunteer.

Grant picked up the receiver and slammed it back down again. He swiveled around, towards me. "You know, I'm hungry, it's getting late, people don't want to pick up their phones at this time of night, and I don't see the point in this right now!"

"Just make three phone calls," I said soothingly. "Just three. Then we can eat. It's not that late. People won't mind."

He swiveled back around, hard, and confronted the phone again. Then he grabbed the phone list, and punched the first number with seven violent jabs. The caller picked up. Grant tripped over his own tongue as he gave his pitch. The caller wanted Grant to send campaign literature, which we hadn't prepared yet. Grant agreed, however, and hung up. Two more tries reached voice mail greetings. Grant hung up on those, as he had been advised to do.

He turned to me balefully. "There. Are you happy?"

I gave Grant a few words of encouragement and a short back rub, and then we went to get dinner on Fifteenth Avenue. After that we headed to Victrola, where we studied our to-do lists, crossing out the items that we had accomplished and adding new ones. From there I drove home and worked on a few office-related things on my list.

The phone rang. "Hello," I said guardedly, positive that Grant was calling me for what would be our seventeenth conversation that day. But it was my girlfriend.

"Hi," she said, her voice was both reassuring and foreign. "Remember me?"

"Of course! Hi!"

A weird pause followed.

"Well, should I come over?" she said.

"Uh—well—pea, there's really a lot of work left for me to do tonight."

"Honey, it's almost midnight."

"Yeah, but—" I started to tell her about everything that I had written in my notebook, but she didn't want to hear about it; she had worked hard, too. We said good-night. I felt a swell of guilt as I set the phone on the table.

I went downstairs, got a glass of water from the kitchen, and turned on the TV. I was tired after all. The President was on the news, insisting that he was above politics. Spectacular lies like that, delivered with perfect seriousness, were what separated the pros from the amateurs, I decided.

After a few minutes I muted CNN and tried to understand everything that had occurred that day. Campaign politics was a strange occupation. Nonstop, high-pressured, incremental, meaningless activity; people and ideas coming and going like images in an endless series of projected slides; a constant whirl of notes and phone calls and destinations and tactical decisions; volatile mood swings based on every unpredictable shift in the day's events; months of chaotic work in anticipation of a single night in which all of your efforts are either triumphantly legitimized or scornfully rejected. I could no longer tell if I was enjoying myself or not.

I heard some kind of commotion upstairs. Doug was blaring music and slamming doors. I turned up the TV to drown out his noise, but then he came downstairs to slam doors in the common area. I could tell now that this was leading somewhere, and that it involved me.

Doug walked in front of me, then walked away. I ignored him. He slammed a few doors, the same ones he had slammed before, then walked back to me again. I ignored him again. Finally he blew up.

"What do you do around here? Nothing!" He loomed over me. In the dark, all I saw was his chubby silhouette. "You just sit around, or you're gone on the campaign!"

I didn't know how I knew this, I just did: Doug wasn't angry at me, he was mad that Ben and Cate were moving back East, leaving him without any friends. He was letting off steam, in the only way he knew how.

"If you don't like the way I do things," I said, "then you have two choices: You can complain to the landlady, or you can move out!"

Unable to think of a rejoinder, Doug stormed off. Only after he had slammed the door to his room did I turn off the TV and go to bed.

9

"Possibly the greatest boozer of them all on the Hill was Democratic Congressman Marion Zioncheck from the state of Washington," wrote William "Fishbait" Miller, who for twenty-eight years worked as the Democratic doorkeeper for the House of Representatives before writing a tell-all memoir in the 1970s. "On the Hill, Zioncheck set new records in drinking that were hard to beat."

Zioncheck's affinity for alcohol was no delicate secret kept by congressional staff members. Zioncheck himself bragged about it, throwing countless raucous cocktail parties at his and Hulet Wells's apartment. He even claimed to have invented his own drink, which consisted primarily of honey and rum mixed to toxic potency. At least one newspaper pundit tried to challenge the true origins of the "Zioncheck Zipper," pointing out that a nineteenth-century army captain had made a similar drink, but nobody wanted to hear it. Marion Zioncheck was the stuff of a swelling legend.

"But—*wait* a minute!"

"Not now, Doug!" I said. I didn't know what he wanted and I didn't care.

I slammed the front door, sprinted across the yard, and nearly tripped on a large branch that had been obscured by the overgrown grass. Into my car and toward Fifteenth, leaving Doug to watch my retreating exhaust pipe from the front porch. I could only imagine all of the hexes and jinxes my housemate was now wishing upon me. Rubbing my tired eyes, I laughed to myself but stopped when I heard it come out all wrong.

Grant's kickoff party was being held at Victrola. I parked and walked over to the café; I had arrived ahead of Grant. "I'm coming," he said impatiently when I called. "I just have to get dressed."

It was late July. No one thought it strange that we had our kick-off party almost a month after we had kicked off the campaign because that sort of thing was fairly common. We took the extra time for the party because we first needed to build some momentum for the campaign, so that people would actually show up. The lawsuit, which was still in progress, had helped; now we had to formally present Grant to the public.

Theresa arrived and announced that she had a present: A mono-rail admirer she knew had given us a giant white banner as a campaign contribution. Six feet tall by eight feet wide, it had the Grant Cogswell logo—with Grant's monorail design flying across the top—emblazoned across it in blue. I ran to the health food store down the street to borrow a ladder from my housemate Ben, who was working at the cash register. With the consent of the Victrola owners and with a little help from some volunteers, I spread the banner across the café's façade.

It could not have been a more charming tableau. Draw the lens back for a wide shot, and you'd have the coffeehouse with its metal chairs on the sidewalk; our banner, fluttering and flickering in the evening air; the tiny barbershop next door with its striped pole and mustachioed proprietor; and a few curious pedestrians pausing to look on. Seattle, so often outside the cultural and socioeconomic norms of mainstream America, was just another Mayberry, USA, all caught up in the local boy's big plunge into the exotic world of politics.

About sixty people came—friends, neighbors, fellow activists, a couple reporters and a couple of political allies—with Grant showing up only slightly ahead of everyone else. The gathering was dotted with middle-aged and older people, but for the most part it was a jeans and Converse crowd. Dick Falkenbury, who had debated for two weeks whether or not he should endorse Grant, was the introductory speaker. Recounting old war stories involving his former partner, all of them cheery and upbeat, he ended his speech with a poignant choking sound. "You don't abandon your friends," he said. He then lumbered off, claiming that he was pressed for time.

Grant had been standing off to the side, taking slow breaths, hoping to focus his mind. He was wearing khaki pants and a button-down shirt, and had switched back to the smaller-framed wire spectacles he had worn in the past. Now he moved to the front of the room. His speech was new, but he had known the facts for months, if not years. He didn't use the microphone.

The WTO protests had given local activism an energy and a momentum that the city could not afford to lose, he said. Seattle needed more affordable housing, and it needed to protect the salmon. What's more, we needed to think more clearly about local mass-transit issues. Monorail was a good technology, he said, but Sound Transit's light rail plan was a costly mistake, and the city and county were toying with our future by supporting it over monorail.

A critic might have attributed the warble in his voice to inexperience, but to me Grant was striking chords of sincerity; the charisma that I had known in past conversations was finally showing, and I was reminded in that instant of the idealism that I never wanted to lose but often questioned, doubted, and picked at like a scab. "Mass transit *is* a social-justice issue," he said. I straightened up with pride, and when I looked around noticed that I wasn't the only person who was moved.

One of the veteran politicos in the crowd nudged me. There was a problem, he whispered. As the candidate, it would be beneath Grant to beg for volunteers and for money immediately after his speech. I would have to do that. I agreed, but reluctantly. I generally needed two or three hours preparing my thoughts in an enclosed space, like a bathroom or a car, before talking before groups of people.

I walked up to the mike. "Hi, I'm Grant's campaign manager, and I'm not as articulate as Grant." This statement fell, maimed and twitching, onto the café floor. People were paying attention, but not in the way I had hoped. "We need volunteers, and we need contributions. We can't do this on our own." I was strangely conscious of my neck. How thin and naked it was! I could imagine everyone watching my Adam's apple jerk up and down. I covered it with my hand and walked away.

An awkward silence fell throughout the café. My speech had killed the mood; the party was in danger of becoming a disaster. But nothing else had been planned; Grant and I and a few others were supposed to start mingling, recruiting, and soliciting with a relaxed ease. That no longer seemed possible. Fortunately, Maggi Fimia stepped up to the microphone. Fimia, a King County councilmember, was the only sitting elected official who openly endorsed our campaign. She told the crowd in a firm and motherly way to give to Grant Cogswell more money and more time than they had intended to give, chiefly because he and his top assistants would be putting in twelve- to sixteen-hour days, seven days a week. Her comfortable manner was the gift we needed. I exhaled, and the cursed moment passed. Dozens of people signed up to volunteer, and people gave what money they could. Not a glorious success, but it wasn't a failure, either, and there are times in politics when the latter is more important than the former.

As the days passed, we were pleased to see our efforts start to pay off. The media was paying attention:

> Of the challengers, Grant Cogswell—who writes for the *Stranger,* was a leader in the 1997 and 2000 monorail initiative campaigns and is a veteran of grass-roots politics—is waging the best-organized, most aggressive campaign.
> —The *Seattle Post-Intelligencer*

Grant Cogswell's message is clear. It blares.
He loves the Monorail. He talks about it at
forums and news conferences. His campaign
logo features a sleek drawing of it. His e-mails
lead with this header: HE SAID MONORAIL!
    In the race to unseat Seattle City Councilman
Richard McIver, Cogswell hasn't so much
emerged as he has bolted out of the block. From
the start, he has badgered McIver over his support for Sound Transit and promoted himself as
the white knight who saw it right all along:
Others may be mooning over monorail now, but
Cogswell helped write the first monorail initiative, which favored planning for its extension.
                                    —The *Seattle Times*

Josh at the *Stranger* rolled out his city council election coverage with
an article noting how Richard McIver was vulnerable on transportation issues, and that he had drawn "four count 'em—four" challengers. For such a partisan editor, it was an oddly neutral article.

"Oh, don't worry," he told me, the day after our kickoff party.
"We'll get behind Grant. We just want to see him manage on his
own for a while." I was in the *Stranger's* office again, this time to
drop off our official campaign photo of Grant. Josh and I stood at
arm's length from one another.

"And I didn't think you did a bad job with your speech!" he
added, loudly.

"Really?" I said.

Josh opened his mouth to argue with me on my behalf, but
couldn't think of anything to support his claim. We drifted away
from each other.

I drove downtown to the *Weekly's* offices to drop off Grant's
campaign photo. Walking through a conference room, I was
stopped by a male voice.

"Are you Phil Campbell?"

I said I was.

Seattle Weekly news editor George Howland introduced himself; we had never met before.

"You know, I can't believe the *Stranger* fired their best reporter," he said. I was flattered, we chatted, and he offered to let me fill in for one of his reporters when she took maternity leave later that year. "What are you doing now?" he asked.

"I'm running Grant Cogswell's campaign."

"You are?" Howland was incredulous. "Grant Cogswell? He has quite a temper, don't you think?"

"Oh, well, Grant's very—*passionate*." At least I knew how to talk when I wasn't standing in front of dozens of people.

" 'Passionate,' " echoed Howland, who had just written that Grant was the "monorail maniac," and not necessarily as a compliment. "Yes. I can see that," he said.

Howland's compliments cheered me up. My good mood lasted about as long as it took for me to walk back to my car, which is when Grant called. "Where's Theresa?" he asked without preamble.

I groaned. That was one problem I did not want to deal with. "I don't know," I replied.

"I've run out of people to call for contributions so I need those lists back from Theresa. Why is she taking so long?"

"I'll try to call her," I said, "but she hasn't been returning my messages."

"Tell her we have a check for her," he said.

"I tried that last time. She won't believe me now."

"*Find* her," Grant said. "We need to keep raising money because right now we don't have any. And I can't do it without that list."

I looked around wildly, as if the pedestrians at the crosswalk could help. "OK," I said. "I'll just go over there. Maybe she's home."

Even though Theresa had declined to be our volunteer coordinator, Grant and I were both trying to squeeze every ounce of work from her that we could, much of which technically qualifed as volunteer coordinating. *Oh, Theresa, could you call the people on our list tonight to get a few folks out to the 11th District Democrat meeting? Oh, Theresa, would you mind calling a dozen people or so for some literature distribution on Saturday?* If she had done everything we asked her to do, she would have been working sixteen-hour days.

Theresa lived in a co-op on Capitol Hill called PRAG. Originally run by a group of hippies who had come together in the 1970s, PRAG stood for "Provisional Revolution Against Government," though some had tried to update the name to "Professionals Rebelling Against Government." Most people just called it the PRAG house. In any event, PRAG was enormous, with an immense common living area, a giant kitchen, and a score of rooms spread out over three floors. I tracked her down in the attic.

"Here you are," she said, handing me a thick sheaf of papers.

I examined the lists. Theresa had used a typewriter, inserting the desired phone numbers with dazzling fastidiousness. I should have been impressed by this precision, but instead I was irritated. Was *this* why it had taken her so long? We were running a grassroots campaign with a style more akin to an emergency room than a boardroom; things had to get done fast and accurately, not neatly. And what did you do with someone who didn't share the same style, the same esprit de corps?

I took an involuntary step backward and almost fell down the stairs.

"You wanted them done right, didn't you?" she asked. "Now I'd prefer to have another hour with these, to clean up—"

"Oh, no. No!" I said, hastily shoving the papers into my orange messenger bag. "These are fine. They'll do just *fine!* Thanks!"

I later retold this story to Grant. "A *typewriter.* She used a *type-writer.* What I—"

"There's a parking spot," Grant said.

"—want to know is how much time she wasted lining up the text so perfectly."

"She hasn't been doing a very good job of calling those nursing homes for us, either," Grant said.

Despite the problems we were having with Theresa, we assembled a ragtag crew of reliable volunteers, raw recruits with plenty of energy but very little experience. Everyone seemed to come to us out of either a sense of personal loyalty or fascination with the grand political experiment in which we were engaged.

We had Kevin, an intern from the *Stranger*, who volunteered out of loyalty to me. Kevin made money on the side by freelancing fictitious orgasm letters for the porn mag *Just 18*.

We had database help from a Seattle University student named Bryan. His mother had died just before the campaign began. He needed the tedium of databases to work through his grief.

We had Jenny, who worked at the natural remedies store next to Victrola. Jenny kept telling us how thrilled she was to see Grant running for office, and she gave us our campaign contribution in the form of food for our kickoff party. Jenny was perpetually upbeat because a few years before she had beaten a malignant brain tumor.

And we had Tara, Grant's girlfriend, who was willing to help even though she increasingly looked like a cat that had been stunned and caged by the Ringling Brothers.

My own girlfriend avoided the campaign as best as she could.

The only real anomaly was our treasurer, a twenty-three-year-old whose name I kept forgetting. Whenever we had more financial papers for him to file with the city elections commission, which was often, we left them on the porch of his house, usually when he wasn't home. I saw him only twice during the entire campaign, and I suspect that it only happened because he had let his guard down.

I had no idea what motivated our treasurer, and that bothered me. I brought this up with Grant, but he told me to stop dwelling on irrelevant things and learn to be more focused.

"How many people are coming to help?" he asked, searching around the back seat for the suntan lotion.

"About five of us today, including you and me," I said.

"Good. Does everyone have a T-shirt?"

"I think so."

"You think so? Well, do we have more T-shirts in the car if somebody *forgot?*"

"Yes!" I said. "Yes, we do."

"Where? Because they're not back here!"

"In the trunk!" I shouted. "In the trunk!"

We got out and walked. Around us, the crowds were growing thicker. Children were tearing around and screaming, their parents docilely following. We were at a summer neighborhood festival called SeaFair. SeaFair festivals meant neighborhood children, and neighborhood children meant neighborhood parents, and neighborhood parents meant registered voters. Grant wanted to be at every neighborhood SeaFair event the city offered. Today we were at the seafood festival in the Ballard neighborhood.

The candidate and I walked to a local bank and compared the times on our cell phone clocks. This would be our rendezvous point, we agreed. We would meet up again at two; I would come back earlier to meet with the volunteers, who I now remembered— to Grant's immense irritation—were going to arrive later than he had wanted. We split up, each of us diving into different areas of the crowd.

Mobs of people all converging on one place at one time have always filled me with dread, as if I suspect the herd to stampede at any time. This time was different. In my blue uniform, using my blue poster sign as both billboard and shield, I held my ground, distributing the brochures that could help sway the campaign in our favor. I was having a good time—the job was easy, I didn't have to worry about anything else, and I was out of the house, out of the car, and in the warm sunshine. I chose a spot near a sausage vendor, where the smell of grilled meat kept me motivated.

"Hey! How's it going?" I asked Grant as he wandered by. Unlike me, he had decided to try moving with the crowd.

"Awful," he said. The heat was killing him. I watched as he melted off to somewhere else.

I went back to the bank to wait for our volunteers. They all showed up except for Kevin. I passed out stacks of brochures, dispensed some advice, and sent them to opposite ends of the festival. I then called Kevin, who was hung over. He apologized and promised to catch a bus right away.

Grant again came within my line of vision. I watched him for a few minutes. When single people passed him, he did all right. Sometimes he even got into brief conversations. But when the multitudes were spilling past, he had the look of someone being prodded with a hot poker. Moreover, his handoff was flaccid, uninspiring. I tried to tell him him but he did not appreciate my advice.

"It's fine. There's nothing wrong with it," he snapped. I walked back to the bank and waited for Kevin. When he arrived, he amiably dismissed his self-inflicted hangover with a quick laugh. I tried giving him advice on how to distribute literature and he laughed at that, too. I was partial to Kevin because he reminded me of a younger version of myself, at least the fantasy version of myself that never got flustered or depressed by anything.

"I think we've been here long enough," Grant said, approaching me. "And I've got a migraine coming on. Let's go."

We left, pausing only to ask Kevin and the other volunteers to stay for as long as they could. I dropped off Grant at his apartment and drove to Kinko's to pick up some copies I had ordered. Our campaign was barely a month old and despite the relaxing afternoon I felt like we were swimming the butterfly stroke in a swamp. Was *this* real progress? Where were all the opportunities to showcase Grant's populist passion? How could we fine-tune our message without the money to buy one lousy campaign poll? Why was campaign politics so dull? And when was I going to stop driving this car everywhere?

The next day, I was negotiating with one of our printing companies downtown when the phone rang. "You'd better get over here," Grant said. "Theresa just quit."

I arrived just in time to see, in the window of the neighborhood pizzeria, Theresa handing Grant all of her campaign files. The papers were all jumbled together, a clear *fuck you* from such a compulsively meticulous individual. I found out later that Theresa got a job working on Nick Licata's campaign. Unlike us, Licata offered a steady paycheck *and* a real campaign headquarters for office work.

My phone rang again. Kevin needed to make photocopies of some material I had given him. I was about to tell him to take it to Kinko's, but then I thought about the last time I had gone—the bill had been a hundred and thirty dollars, way too much.

"Can't you do it at the *Stranger?*" I said.

"Well, I guess so. How many copies do you think we need?"

"I don't know. About five hundred, maybe. Do *not* tell anyone that you're doing this, OK? Technically, we have to pay for absolutely everything we do. And since the *Stranger* is a newspaper that's covering the election—you see what I'm saying?"

Kevin promised to be surreptitious and to call me when he was done. Soon afterward, though, I panicked. What if the editors found him out? It seemed like a disastrous mistake, invading the line that separated journalism and politics. I got in my car and drove to the *Stranger*.

As soon as I walked into the editorial offices, I knew I had made another mistake. My presence could only make things worse, and why would anyone care if one of the interns used up a ream of paper? But someone saw me and said hi. Playing it cool, I asked if Savage was around. He still had my letter of recommendation. He was out in a meeting, so I sat on the couch and pretended to look interested in a magazine.

People came and went, some saying hi, some ignoring me, perhaps too embarrassed to talk to the fired employee who wouldn't
leave. I felt like Bartleby. Kevin was nowhere to be seen.

My girlfriend came in. I had forgotten that she had been inter-
viewing for a full-time writing job today. She sat down next to me
and took out a small slip of paper and wrote down a number—her
salary offer. It was a strangely familiar figure. Then I remembered
that that was the same starting salary I had received two years
before.

"Wow," I said quietly. "That's great, pea." My vision was
blurred, like when you're at a rave and the Ecstasy kicks in, except
without all the happy feelings. I decided to leave.

My car wasn't where I had parked it. It had been towed. The
rear end of the Geo must have encroached on the handicapped
spot, and the minister at the Lutheran church across the street had
taken offense. Or maybe the homeless people who received their
free meals outside the church had taken offense. Or some traffic
cop had taken offense. In any case, the Geo was gone, and it was
going to cost me more than a hundred dollars to get it back.

I walked home, about twenty blocks. My pace was slow and I
allowed myself to study some of the things I walked past. I was
most surprised by the gardens people were cultivating. Many of
them were attempting a natural, wild look, some to stunning
effect. It probably took an enormous amount of time to create a
garden that looked wild but wasn't. It was easy to typecast the
people who did them: Introverts with a relentless eye for detail.
Plenty of income for the house and for all the necessary tools. A
few shelves in the living room containing vegetarian cookbooks,
Eastern religious guides, and left-wing political screeds. People
with modest, selfish goals.

When I got home and entered the house, something didn't feel
right. I walked around the first floor trying to figure out what it
was, like a dog sensing an intruder. There were noises in the back
yard. At first I guessed that Doug was mowing the lawn, but then

I went to the back and looked out. Doug was there, with Emily. He was helping her replace the screen door to her basement entrance, something I should have done months ago. Doug looked up and saw me in the window. He gave me a big, triumphant, ugly grin.

10

Marion Zioncheck was a terror behind the wheel. According to the stories, which grew more fantastic with each passing week, Zioncheck believed himself immortal. He drove on the sidewalk. He drove with his foot on the gas but never on the brake. He drove while holding a bottle of absinthe (or, as the variant goes, with a flask of Zioncheck Zipper). In one story, Zioncheck outlined a theory on the timing of D.C. stop lights to a congressional aide he happened to be giving a ride: If he could catch all the green lights at thirty miles an hour, then surely at sixty miles an hour he could do the same. Zioncheck then tried to prove this. When he hit a red light, he drove through it anyway, complaining that somebody had rigged the system against him.

It was this belief, that somebody was out to get him, that may have led to his eventual downfall. "But while he lived," William "Fishbait" Miller wrote, "Zioncheck made a concerted effort to live life to the fullest."

"What is wrong with your car? It smells like oil's leaking all over the place." Grant waved at the air.

"I don't smell anything. Sorry."

"I do. It's giving me a migraine."

We were driving downtown near the Pike Place Market, a popular open-air farmer's market that had been saved from developers by preservationists thirty years before. The market, like the monorail, was a symbol of how the people's will could defeat city hall. It was also a traffic nuisance. Tourists in rented sedans, businesspeople in SUVs, restaurant employees in second hand VWs—these people were obstacles, and I swore at them.

"It's just terrible," Grant said, but I think he was still referring to my car.

"My nose is plugged from allergies. I can never smell anything. So you're probably right. But there's nothing I can do about it, because I don't have the time to take it to the shop."

"Tell me about it."

"Maybe we can just get out here and tell all these people to vote for you," I said, gesturing toward the crowded sidewalk. "If they hate the smelly cars and the congestion as much as we do, they'll love monorail. And it'll save us an hour."

"We don't have time," said the candidate. He shifted his weight in his seat.

"Jesus," he added. "I'm telling you, after we win this thing, we're all going to go down to Mexico. You, me, Tara, and your girlfriend, if you want to bring her. Just like Nick Licata took me and his aides there after we helped him win his city council race. We're all going to just sit on the beach and none of this is going to matter."

I tried to picture an isolated Mexican beach, but all I could see were the things that lay directly beyond the hood of the Geo—the road, the traffic, the Seattle Art Museum, and the garish exterior of a strip club.

"Let's go over what we have to do this afternoon," Grant said. "I have to give my videotaped speech for the voters guide—hey, turn *here*. If you don't turn now, we'll be stuck driving south all the way to the stadium."

The light turned yellow as I approached the intersection. With no other choice, I gunned it. Grant barked a short order before falling silent again.

Mention of the voters guide renewed my interest in our ACLU lawsuit. "Have you talked to our attorneys recently?" I said.

"No, why? Have you heard from them?"

"No. I was just curious." It had been four days since we last talked to our attorneys. In campaign time it seemed like a year.

"Call them and see what's going on," Grant said. "It'd be nice to get some more free media. There's nothing we can do to get in the paper this week?"

"I'm working on a couple things," I said. "I'm really, really excited about getting you written up by Jean Godden." Godden was the city's gossip columnist. Since there wasn't much actual gossip in Seattle, she wrote affectionately about people's dogs, their vanity license plates, and their stamp collections, like a woman cooing over her grandchildren. It helped that she was old enough to be a grandmother.

"I like Jean," Grant said. "I've talked to her a couple times. She's all right."

"I'm sure she's OK, but it's still just a gossip column. Anyway, I was talking to Tom Carr, who recently got his name mentioned in Jean's column, some ridiculous story about him and his son at a baseball game, and it ended with his boy getting a baseball, or something sentimental, and I asked Tom how the hell he got her to write about him."

"He called her?" Grant was deadpan. The candidate wasn't into games.

"Well, yeah, but more than once. He just kept throwing stories at her. He was totally shameless about it. Jean doesn't make anybody look stupid."

"So what are you going to tell her about me?" Grant didn't have a son who did adorable things, nor was he guilty of random acts of cuteness. And he no longer owned a dog.

"Well, if Tom Carr can get a mention, so can you. I don't feel bad about being a shill for dumb gossip if Carr's doing it. He used to handle cases involving the mob when he was a lawyer in New York. And *now* he's pimping for—"

"So—" Grant said.

"—I figure I'd tell her how you need to go to the bathroom every time I stop the car. Your bladder is *so* small."

"If she writes about that," Grant said, "then she's gotta write about the giant shit I heard City Councilmember Richard Conlin make in the bathroom in that church. He was *loud*."

"You keep bringing that up. You seem kinda fixated on that."

"I felt like I was in the stall with him, holding his hand."

We both laughed.

"Actually," I said, "I'm going to push the Grant Cogswell sandwich."

"Ah yes. The sandwich."

"The Grant Cogswell sandwich at Victrola. You live right across the street. You've been so loyal to that place they named a sandwich after you. That's perfect Jean Godden fodder."

"OK. The sandwich."

"I need details, though. How'd you come up with the ingredients? Did they assign them or did you pick them out yourself?"

"They asked me what I wanted in a sandwich, and I told them."

"And you chose these ingredients because—"

"—because I like them."

"Give me something. Even if it's dumb. It doesn't matter. Isn't there anything significant about the ingredients?"

"No. There's not. I just liked how it tasted."

"I'll figure something out. The other thing I wanted to know is—" I hesitated.

"What's that?"

"Well, we're doing all the right things in this campaign. We're not doing anything out of the ordinary. I know it's necessary, but it's boring as hell. And I don't want to wait around for you to put on that polar bear suit."

"I'm not going to talk about the polar bear suit until after we win," Grant said. "Then I'm just going to do it."

"Let's us do something fun," I said. "I don't know, some guerrilla prank or something. Just once. You know, something harmless but kind of punk rock. I was talking to a guy, a friend of mine who loves that kind of stuff. We were thinking about covering all the old monorail columns down on Fifth Avenue with chalk art about your campaign."

"OK," Grant said. "That'd be great."

"The chalk would wash off the next time it rained. It could get us a lot of attention."

"Hold on," Grant said. "How much time do we have before we have to be at city hall? All they're going to do is videotape my speech, right?"

"Yeah, it won't take long. And I think we have another hour and a half before we have to be there."

"Let's get lunch. I'm starving."

"Fuck yeah. Where should we eat?"

"Too bad we don't have time to go to the Continental," Grant said. "I could use some of that right about now. How about Olympia Pizza? They take my campaign checks."

"Sounds good to me."

"Slow down, will you? Don't hit the pedestrians."

We coasted through Capitol Hill, along Broadway to Pine Street. If there was one area we expected to get votes, it was from the people who lived around this intersection, the place where WTO protesters had been pushed by police wearing riot gear and using tear gas almost two years before. This was the densest area in the city and the heart of Seattle's youth culture, where struggling bar- tenders, musicians, students, video-store clerks, and yoga instruc- tors packed into tiny studios and one-bedroom apartments. Our real challenge was to make Grant's name known to the tens of thousands of people we didn't consider our neighbors.

On the I-5 overpass into downtown, I let my mind wander. I thought about being outside the car, walking to the library down- town on some idle Saturday afternoon, and about the vertigo I experienced every time I walked on the overpass separating Capitol Hill from downtown.

"I don't get this place," I said.

Grant didn't say anything.

"I moved here from the Midwest and the South. And I don't pretend to claim that southern hospitality is a great thing or that midwesterners are perfect, but at least the people there are outwardly friendly. The South especially. There's something cool about being invited to join in on a conversation at a bar, just because you were standing nearby and laughed at somebody's joke."

Grant agreed.

"That never happens here. Most of the time, I see somebody in a bar, and they're with somebody I know, but they won't even introduce me to the other people they're *with*. And those people won't introduce themselves to me on their own. They look uncomfortable but go right on talking as if I'm not there.

I went on. "People here are *weird*. You know those little plastic dividers at the grocery store? The ones you use at the check-out stand, to separate your groceries from the groceries of the person behind you? Around here, they're the most important thing in the whole store. They're a physical excuse *not* to interact with anybody. Last week this lady in line behind me snatched one of those dividers from in front of me and just *slammed* it down. I felt like I had a disease or something."

A bike messenger darted just ahead of my car as I turned left onto Fifth Avenue.   —

"And did I tell you about the time I was at that sandwich shop on Pike Street?" I asked.

"I don't—"

"I was by myself, and without thinking too much about it I took a table for myself that could have comfortably seated four. The place was empty, OK? So I sat down at a big table. Well, time went by and the place filled up around me. I thought about getting up and moving to a smaller table, because it seemed like the right thing to do, but then I noticed that there were these four people standing across from me, and they were staring at me. I got embarrassed and avoided looking at them. I'm like, 'What did I *do?*' "

"Listen, can we—" Grant said.

"I thought they were going to say something, but instead they took a really small table that was right behind me. They were all squeezed in together. And I wondered, 'Who wouldn't have the guts to ask someone like me to move?' But then I heard them all talking about me behind my back! They were saying, 'What's his deal? Why doesn't he just move?' So I had finished my sandwich but suddenly I didn't feel like leaving. I sat in my chair and read my papers for another ten minutes. When I finally got up, I put my coat on *reeal* slowly. That was when one of the guys said, to me, *finally,* 'Are you done there, bud?' He was twice my weight, but he didn't have the nerve to look me in the eye!"

"That sucks," Grant said.

"What the fuck is *wrong* with people here?"

"Well," Grant said, "At least this city hasn't screwed up things as badly as other cities have."

Then I remembered that I was talking to Grant Cogswell, the man with the Seattle logo tattooed on his arm. "Why do you love this place so much?" I asked, turning abruptly to face him.

"Hey! Watch the road."

I had quizzed Grant on this subject dozens of times before, but he had never answered me in a way that I understood.

"There are a lot of reasons," he said now. "The sea air, the gulls—there's an essence to this city that you could understand. You're gotta get tapped into it."

I shifted downward and we stopped at a light.

"I still remember," he said, warming up, "visiting my grandparents on Mercer Island and looking over and seeing the lights of Queen Anne's radio towers. I still know their rhythms." Grant made pulsing motions with his fingers. "No, wait," he said. "Like this." He changed the pattern minutely. He was enjoying the demonstration.

I didn't follow him. "I don't *get* this place," I declared emphatically.

Grant said, "Here's city hall."

"Parking is going to suck," I said.

"Look, can you just drop me off here?"

"Yeah, I'll find parking a million blocks away, then come join you."

"Good," he said, a little sharply. "Because I have to go to the bathroom and I need a few minutes alone to think before I do this."

"Let's get back to the things that still have to get done today." Grant said. His videotaped speech had gone well, but he was irritable. We were east of Seattle Center, not far from the old monorail. Heading north. After you passed the elegant Space Needle and the blobby, Frank Gehry–designed Experience Music Project, there wasn't much to look at.

We talked about a water-conservation proposal that a group of local environmentalists were pushing. They wanted the city to refuse to sell its surplus water to suburban real-estate developers. It was a fairly ambitious initiative that affected, among other things, regional sprawl, city/county relations, local salmon populations, and low-income housing. Grant supported the idea; he wanted to publicize his concerns that the city was trying to undermine the initiative, just like it had done with monorail.

"I think it's perfect," I said, "taking a stand against more underhanded city hall tomfoolery. It fits your outsider image. I think I can get a few reporters to show up."

"Good. When are we doing this?"

"I'm still trying to arrange the time. We can do it on the old monorail platform in Seattle Center. Probably in early afternoon or mid-morning, though. So the reporters can meet their deadlines."

"OK. Thank you."

"There's one thing, though."

"Oh, yeah? What's that?"

"There's all this stuff about this initiative that I don't understand, and I really feel kind of uncomfortable about it."

"What's not to understand? I told you what it's about."

"But it's complicated," I said. "I don't personally want to talk

to any reporters about it until I've had a chance to review everything and made up my own mind."

"But I told you what it's about."

"But I'm used to doing my own research and making up my
own mind on complicated issues."

"Why don't you just trust me?" Grant demanded.

"Because I don't trust anybody!" I said. I stopped short of
saying that I was beginning to question some of his other ideas,
including the 'daylighting' of Thornton Creek for the salmon.

"Fine," Grant said. "Do your research and make up your own
mind. But I like the press-conference idea. We need to do that."

I took a breath. "I'll put it on my list," I said.

"Do you have the new fliers? Oh tell me you didn't forget the
new fliers."

"No. I picked them up this morning, while you were still asleep.
How could I forget them when they've never been outside of the car?"

"Good. You gave me that look, and I thought—"

"Did I tell you? He gave us, for free, a whole box of fliers in
blue ink. Your blue. The metro blue we use on your posters and
the T-shirts. They look great. They're in the trunk, though. No.
Wait. I have the sample copy in my pocket."

Grant snatched the flier from my hand. It was a quarter-page
sheet—the staple of our campaign because they were so cheap to
produce. The Grant Cogswell campaign logo was on the back;
Grant flipped it over to read the message on the front.

"What the—"

"What?" I said. "What?!"

"It doesn't make any sense. Look at this! It says 'he' when it
should say 'Richard McIver.' How did that get changed?"

"Not everything fit. So I had to change it back to 'he.' So then
everything fit. But I don't understand your question. It's right."

"But it doesn't make sense! It makes it sound like Grant
Cogswell, not Richard McIver, did all these bad things on this
list."

"I don't think so. It's *right*."

"Let me ask you something," Grant said, each word a drop of acid. "Someone hands you something on the street, and you take it. And you take five seconds to read it, and you throw it out. Who cares if it's grammatically correct. They read the flier so fast they're not going to understand it unless everything's clearly spelled out. Listen. They'll see the list of all the bad things I've listed here, and they'll connect the 'he' with *me* because *my name* is on this thing in three different places, *not* Richard McIver's."

"But McIver's name is on the sentence preceding it! Of course 'he' is *him*, not you! If you actually read it, you'd understand what it meant!"

"It doesn't matter. Listen. You have got to think about this stuff more. You're not thinking this out. That's why I have to look over *everything*."

He wadded up the flier and threw it on the floorboard. "This is useless," he said.

"Well then we have a whole box of useless fliers in the trunk."

"Yes, we do."

The road was getting busier. The city was preparing to end its business affairs and shut down. For us the day was barely half over.

The silence was suffocating. I was waiting for Grant to tell me how to drive. I would be ready for him. Instead he asked, "Have you called Anne B—?"

"Yes," I said, snapping. "I did."

"What'd she say?"

"The dates we were throwing at each other weren't working out. We can't seem to get coordinated."

"Keep trying. I've gotta get some big contributors together. The money's not coming in fast enough."

"I know. I know. I'm trying."

"Try to relax, will you?"

"Well it's a little godammed hard to relax with you scrutinizing every godammed move I make, isn't it?"

Grant turned around, to look at the back seats. He was taking inventory.

"Where are the hammers? I don't see the hammers."

He was right. I had forgotten the hammers. I had taken them out of the car. They were sitting on the porch at home. I pulled over to the shoulder and burst into tears.

11

Seattle in the 1930s was still a frontier town, and Marion Zioncheck wasn't the only eccentric populist. There were dozens of people who worked in or influenced local public policy who today might be considered at best unelectable, at worst insane.

The most colorful was Vic Meyers, a prankish night club owner. In his unsuccessful bid for Seattle mayor, which the newspapers of the time had promoted as a joke, Meyers wore short-sleeve shirts to avoid being beholden to "vested interests," and he solemnly promised to accept all bribes. "Vic had more gag writers than a radio comedian," Murray Morgan wrote in Skid Road.

But Meyers was also a radical, and he scared centrists and conservatives alike when he was elected lieutenant governor based largely on name recognition. Governor Clarence Martin was afraid to leave the state, for fear that if he did Meyers would call an emergency session of the legislature and pass a slew of laws based on a socialist agenda. Martin finally decided to fly to Washington, D.C. to lobby Congress in 1938, when Meyers was on vacation in California. Morgan describes an extraordinary race between the governor and lieutenant governor to get back to Olympia first (the governor won, but only barely). It was moments like this that inspired U.S. Postmaster James Farley to say that there were "forty-seven states and the Soviet of Washington."

We didn't stop driving.

The well-meaning but high-strung campaign manager kept his hands on the wheel. His eyes twitched and turned red from stress, malnutrition, and lack of sleep. The grim, idealistic candidate never budged from the passenger seat. His mood simmered but did not explode.

The world outside the city lost all meaning. Seattle *was* the world, and as we drove it teetered on the verge of collapse. The evidence for its pending destruction was plainly there.

The first proof: In December of 1999 Mayor Paul Schell canceled the city's New Year's Eve at the base of the Space Needle celebration out of fear of a terrorist attack. Nothing happened, but the damage had already been done: Seattle had started the new millenium closed up like a nervous shut-in. The terrorists, whoever they were and whatever they wanted, were already winning.

Then the economy slid into a free fall, and thousands of unemployed tech workers began to flee the city they had once so greedily and smugly adopted. In early 2001 an earthquake shook the area, and though it lasted less than a minute and the damage to the city was not tremendous, it was an ominous reminder that the "Big One" was still coming.

Not much later some bars downtown tried to throw a block party to a Mardi Gras theme; a riot broke out instead. Police stood by as a young man was killed.

Shortly after that, Boeing, Seattle's oldest homegrown corporation, announced that it was moving its world headquarters to Chicago. Boeing officials were vague about why. It didn't really matter why. They could leave, so they did.

Some months later, a woman stood on the railing of a freeway bridge 160 feet over the Ship Canal and threatened to jump. There were few pleas of sympathy from commuters stalled by the incident— the woman was met instead with horns, catcalls, and obscenities for stopping traffic. She jumped. Though she survived, and though the pundits railed at the way that many motorists had behaved, everyone now knew all about Seattle's darker, crueler side.

Nothing was related but everything had the feeling of cause and effect. Mayor Schell was quoted saying, "I'm waiting for the locusts." It hardly mattered which crisis he was talking about. Not long afterward, an activist punched the mayor in the face at a family-oriented street fair; this activist thought he could do a better job than Schell, so after giving the mayor a black eye he filed to run against him from his jail cell.

I adjusted the Geo's sun visor and veered around a car that was trying to parallel park. The sun was like a weak table lamp. Grant was talking. "Mayor Schell doesn't have a chance," he said. "He might not even survive the primary."

"You're probably right," I said, picking up a pair of sunglass frames that magnetically attached to my glasses and putting them away with equal impulsiveness. "He doesn't look too good."

"He looks awful. Just awful," Grant said. "You should have seen him at that Democratic endorsement picnic I went to. They really destroyed him."

"Oh, yeah?" I said.

"He came late. *And* by himself. He stood around on the outside of the tent for a few minutes and nobody talked to him. Then he realized that they had already endorsed his opponent, and he looked ruined. His shoulders fell like *this*." Grant demonstrated. "And after a few moments he walked away."

It wasn't hard to imagine; Schell's gray suit, white head, stooped back and bloodshot eyes gave him the look of a wounded pigeon. We had run into him occasionally on the campaign trail. He wore the face of defeat; it was impossible not to like him.

"That woman who jumped—" I said. I imagined the height at which she stood. So far above the gray-green water. So ready to meet her own end.

"Jesus," Grant said. "I know. That was awful."

I agreed. There was nothing more to add. The newspapers weren't filled with the sort of detail I wanted anyway, like whether her clothes stank of fish when they pulled her out of the water, or what her suicide note had said and on what kind of paper she had used for it, assuming she had written one at all.

I felt sleepy. To stay awake I stabbed my wrist with my finger-nails. Grant might complain if I weren't more careful. The sun flickered between clouds. Grant was mentioning someone else now, Omari Tahir-Garrett, the activist who had punched the mayor in the face.

"Now there's someone who challenged reality," Grant said.

"Yeah," I said. "Garrett's a strange case, isn't he?"

In the early 1980s, James Cordell Garrett was one of several dozen visible and politically active African-Americans living in Seattle's predominantly black Central District. His concerns were his community's—police harassment, better job opportunities, and the lack of community centers and low-income housing. He was in his thirties and had the ambiguous reputation of being both reasonable and temperamental.

Black protest in the 1980s was reaching a crisis. Would the old tactics still work? Garrett and a number of other African-Americans believed that they needed to rethink their strategies. Intead of simply rising up against the latest bad idea coming out of city hall, it was proposed that they should try to get city hall to do something positive for the black community. This is how the notion of a tribute to local blacks was conceived. Alternately calling it an African-American museum and a black heritage center, the tribute would honor the struggle blacks had faced in the Pacific Northwest. Garrett and others started talking about their idea and it was well received by many in the black community. A petition was passed around and read aloud in city hall.

Seattle politicians, afraid of giving an outright no, gave a defi-nite maybe. A task force was formed and encouraged. This task force studied the issue and recommended that an abandoned ele-mentary school be used. It wasn't a perfect choice, since the building was not designed for such a purpose, but the old school was viewed as a good compromise, well before the word 'compro-mise' had even been mentioned.

City hall received the task force report and said—again—
maybe. Who knows whether local government planned to follow
through. Perhaps they did, but just as likely they wanted to stall
Garrett and his friends forever. Seattle isn't Memphis or Atlanta—
the eyes of the nation aren't drawn to it when racial controversies
flare. Garrett and his fellow activists might grow angry and frus-
trated, but there was little they could do, and everyone knew it.

Soon a rumor made the rounds: The school district was going
to sell the old elementary school; exactly the disappointing turn of
events that the black activists had expected. They were ready for
it. Instead of forming another protest to march on city hall, Garrett and three fellow activists broke into the school and declared a
sit-in. An old tactic would be used toward a new goal, and the men
readied themselves for confrontation.

But the city didn't respond. No starch-shirted police captain
shouted tough words through a bullhorn, no SWAT unit attacked,
and the media was only marginally interested. In fact the squatters
were able to come and go from the trespassed property as they
pleased. They washed themselves in buckets of water and received
food from supporters on the outside. They went without elec-
tricity, which meant no heat and no light. This didn't bother them.
What bothered them was that no one seemed to notice.

Time dragged. Garrett and his comrades vowed to keep up their
sit-in, but Garrett was growing impatient and strident. He now
insisted on being called Omari Tahir Garrett, saying that his legal
first name was a slave name. In 1988, with the sit-in entering its
third year, he left the school to attend a protest at the University of
Washington and, inspired by fury, grabbed a gun from a UW
police sergeant and pointed it at the officer's head. He was sen-
tenced to ninety-two days in jail—ninety days for the police incident and an extra two days for calling the judge "a stupid
European settler." It was a light sentence, but it passed without
much comment.

Things didn't look up for Garrett until 1993, when the city

abruptly agreed to give the black community its museum and cultural heritage center. Perhaps officials were stricken by a double
standard; while Garrett were staging one of the longest sit-ins in
civil rights history, a group of white homeless activists had been
winning decent concessions from short-term sit-ins in abandoned
buildings for at least three years (so charged up were *those*
activists, in fact, that several of them sealed their commitment to
activism and to each other by getting identical tattoos). In any
case, after eight years, Garrett and his friends claimed victory.

A board was created to organize the black cultural center. But
the board soon became divided, former squatters clashing with a
new group, African-Americans of moderate, business-minded per-
spectives. The board collapsed, and Garrett and his colleagues,
once heroes of civic resistance, were accused by fellow blacks of
being bombastic, misguided, and impractical. The city claimed
that the deal they had struck with the board was dead, since the
board itself was dead. Once again the project stalled.

Meanwhile, larger problems were plaguing Seattle's black community: The '90s were seeing slow and divisive change for the Central District. Middle-class whites were moving in while older blacks,
unable to keep up with increasing property tax payments, were
leaving. Resentment grew, and by the time the area's first Starbucks
opened on Twenty-third Avenue and Jackson Street, a major intersection in the Central District, it was greeted with a range of emotions—relief that the area's economic prospects were looking up,
but skepticism and apprehension about whether the changes would
benefit African-Americans. Garrett was one of the more outspoken
activists on these topics; his was the more cynical perspective.

In the spring of 2001, a black man in his car was stopped by
two police officers, not many blocks from the new Starbucks. He
tried to pull away but ended up dragging one of the officers with
him. The officer's partner shot and killed the man. The ensuing
outcry brought to the fore many of the issues about which African-
Americans had been complaining for years.

That's what led to Garrett punching Mayor Schell. Struggling in his re-election bid, Schell was attending a parade in the Central District. Garrett was there, too, carrying a megaphone, no doubt to talk to the crowd about an array of race-related problems. The mayor wandered, somewhat absentmindedly, near the spot where the police shooting had occurred just a couple months before. Garrett saw this and was seized with righteous anger. He wasn't a very big man, and he was in his fifties, but he still apparently remembered some of his high school football moves. He ran past the bodyguard and rushed the mayor with his megaphone. He was hauled away after landing the bruising blow.

"The thing about Garrett is, he's right," Grant said. He was speaking so softly that the Geo's four cylinders almost drowned him out. Grant added, "He sees things the way they are."

"What do you mean?" I said.

"Look at history," he said. "The power structure in this country hasn't changed. We still live in a race and class-divided society. Garrett sees things for what they are—and that is exactly why he's going mad."

I looked down the hood of the car and at the road's yellow median strips, a line created by man that was far too easy to cross. The car could just drift into oncoming traffic, if I let it, or, if I was brave enough, I could drive there myself, of my own free will.

"What about Richard Lee?" I said, steering into safer territory for both of us.

Grant laughed, and said, "What *about* Richard Lee?"

The public transformation of Richard Lee is shrouded in myth and conjecture. Not all of it is verifiably true, but as local legends go it's pretty entertaining.

In the early 1990s Richard Lee looked pretty much as he does now, with a dark, wide mustache and long, stringy hair pulled back in a ponytail. The hair was starting to thin in front, a problem he covered with a beret. He wore a pair of big, thick-framed glasses, out of which he peered with contemptuous vain-glory. It is rumored, too, that in those days he wore a white suit, à la Tom Wolfe, that always looked and smelled like it had been slept in for a week.

Lee ran his own public-access cable show, a program that addressed a variety of social, cultural, and political topics. This was a big move up from Lee's days as a film reviewer for the *Daily*, the student-run paper at the University of Washington. For once, he was in charge of his own material; he didn't have to listen to a college editor complain about how he overused his thesaurus and couldn't write a coherent sentence. Lee took his independence seriously, too, developing a unique directing and editing style. The close-up shot was patented Richard Lee: Viewers got so close to Lee's face that they could could count the hairs protruding from his nostrils, the pizza crust crumbs trapped in his mustache, the saliva trembling on his impassioned lips.

Lee didn't get much attention for his show until 1994, the year Kurt Cobain committed suicide. While Nirvana fans were packing the area around the Space Needle to hear Courtney Love read parts of Cobain's suicide note (at least one of whom was so upset that he carved Cobain's name on his arm), Lee started to grow troubled. Something about the singer's death bothered him. There were too many people who stood to gain financially from Cobain's death. Love stood at the top of the list, despite her public grief. Band members Dave Grohl and Krist Novoselic were up there, too. And then there were the big media conglomerates that owned all of Nirvana's contracts—who knew how much they could profit with a modern-day martyr? And you had to figure, somehow, that the Seattle Police Department had botched the investigation or had been compromised because—well, because they were cops, and you could never trust cops.

Greedy multi-national corporations, a ruthless spouse, two-timing bandmates, incompetent and maybe dirty cops—the more Lee thought about it, the more his suspicions felt like constants in an incontrovertible equation. He knew that he bore a tremendous burden. He had to expose the truth: Kurt Cobain had been murdered.

He tried approaching the print media. Lee collected as many police and medical records as he could and called the editor of the *Seattle Weekly*. His proposal: to sell the *Weekly* a freelance article that would break the Cobain story wide open. The editor was unconvinced, so he sent Lee to Carlton Smith for a second opinion. Smith was on his way to writing more than a dozen true-crime books; he had a pretty good idea of what constituted a homicide case and what did not.

Smith wasn't in a very good mood when Lee showed up at his apartment. He had his own problems to worry about, some of them personal, and he didn't care much about dead rock stars who had already made known suicide attempts. Murdered hookers were more his thing. Smith sat at the kitchen table and interrupted Lee's complicated narrative with hard questions. *Why wouldn't Cobain kill himself with a shotgun? So what if he was rich?*

Lee preferred to stand and keep Smith at a distance. Something about the conversation he was having didn't feel right. He didn't like the way Smith kept pressing him for more information, as if his theory could possibly be wrong. Or the way Smith suspiciously eyed the documents that he had brought with him. He couldn't help but wonder if he had made a mistake by coming out to talk to the crime writer, alone, in the privacy of Smith's apartment, without anybody he trusted knowing he was there. What if Smith had wanted to hinder his investigation? Mistrust grew.

As the story goes, Smith at that moment was peeling a fuji apple. Smith himself barely remembers the encounter with Lee, but he recently offered the theory that he may not have been peeling an apple at all. He may have been grating cheese. He can't recall what kind of cheese he was grating, but it hardly matters. The point is, Smith was casually wielding a sharp instrument, and that Lee started to fear what Smith would do with that instrument after he was done peeling his apple or grating his cheese. Lee fled Smith's apartment.

From that point on Smith became in Lee's mind a member of the ever-growing conspiracy that closed off truth like a toxic fog. For Lee, most of Seattle had lost touch with reality. But, even though his efforts with the *Weekly* had failed, he knew he had to keep going. He would have to find some other way to be heard.

Lee gave himself a makeover, trading in his white suit for a series of drab sweater-vests. He then changed the name and the focus of his cable-access television show. Originally called "Now See it Person to Person," he added a colon and the frank independent clause, "Kurt Cobain Was Murdered." With his hand-held videocamera, Lee set out to crack the Nirvana case. His modus operandi was elegantly simple, a radical departure from his days as a film reviewer. He would approach people directly, ask pointed questions, berate them if necessary. He would not let them walk away until they'd given the precise answer he wanted. And he would never allow himself to be intimidated by anyone—not by dirty cops, by thuggish security guards, or even by menacing strangers wielding instruments with pointy edges.

One of Lee's most notorious run-ins was with former Nirvana bassist Krist Novoselic. Lee first tried to reach Novoselic through the mail. When this failed, he wrote to Novoselic's mother, urging her to have Krist contact him over a very important matter. When this, too, failed, Lee set out to find Novoselic. He approached the musician outside a local club. Novoselic heard Lee out and replied, "You're pissing up a tree." Lee took this comment as a challenge and followed Novoselic to concerts, political fund-raisers, anywhere Novoselic made a public appearance—for six years. Part of the problem for Novoselic was that, as a civic-minded native of the Pacific Northwest, he couldn't bring himself to beat the crap out of Lee. He had friends, colleagues, police officers and bodyguards shoo him away instead. It never worked; Lee kept coming back.

Novoselic finally lost his temper and hired a lawyer, who filed for a restraining order.

(Lee's ambush of Courtney Love was less successful. Love, who is from Oregon but who is the exception to all rules, had no problem with being aggressive, and she responded to Lee's questioning succinctly: "I'm going to kill somebody. Get that fucking camera—One goddamn camera and I swear to God you're dead!")

Lee also challenged a variety of other public figures in Seattle, including Cobain biographer Charles Cross, various members of the Seattle City Council (some of whom weren't even in office when Cobain had died), the staff and officials of the King County Board of Elections, and all of the board members of the King County Health Department. He was arrested once or twice for disturbing the peace, but for the most part people responded to Lee by running away from him.

By the spring of 2001, Lee assessed his progress. It had been seven years since Cobain had been murdered, and yet he was no closer to justice. Though he was making some great television, no major media outlet had picked up his allegations of conspiracy and homicide. Neither the county medical examiner nor the Seattle Police Department had caved to his demands to reopen the case. Love and Grohl were gone, and Novoselic was suing him. The biggest problem was that he was an outsider, forever braying outside the walls of power. He could make people nervous, but was that really enough?

Then he had an epiphany. What if he were to gain legitimate access to all those private offices, city council chambers, and backrooms of power? What if people had no choice but to listen to him, instead of calling security or the cops like they usually did?

Richard Lee would run for mayor.

For posterity, Lee videotaped his run for office. One episode begins *in medias res* at a neighborhood supermarket. A homeless man trying to sell *Real Change* newspapers has apparently assaulted Lee, knocking down his petition materials and threatening to send him to the hospital if he bothered him or his newspaper customers again. Lee calls the police and shows how unafraid he is by complaining to officers and by holding the camera tightly to his face and giving smug commentary.

Another episode could very well enshrine Lee's status as a local legend. He was invited, by accident it was later insisted, to a mayoral forum sponsored by a local arts association. Lee wore a purple dress and took over the forum. He upstaged everyone, even Omari Tahir-Garrett, whose presence on the campaign trail (and outside of jail) was a spectacle in itself. Lee stood on a chair and demanded that people answer his questions about Kurt Cobain's death. Seen on tape, the incident seems like an explosion of repressed emotion, in which Lee finally realizes that he might never get justice, that the only thing left is a personal meltdown and a useless prank to draw attention back to himself.

"He wasn't wearing any underwear," Grant said, as I pulled into the parking lot across from his apartment.

"Really? How do you know? I heard that he was." I wiped my eyes. It had been another long day. "And besides, we weren't there."

"Yeah, but other people were. When he stood on the table, you could see his—*stuff*."

The punchline I had wanted to deliver was that Seattle was so polite a city that no one in the audience had had the guts to kick Lee out of the room for his shenanigans. Richard Lee's face was hairy and oily and unclean. Thinking of his other body parts did not evoke laughter.

Lee's madness was so unique that we didn't feel threatened by him, but he was a cautionary tale. We had so far managed to keep the media from lumping Grant with the fringe candidates who could be found in almost every local race, but we both knew that it really took only a few missteps to be ridiculed or, worse, ignored.

12

One of the most important early events to affect Marion Zioncheck's generation was the Seattle General Strike of 1919. The first of its kind in America, the strike involved hundreds of thousands of workers who wanted to show their support for city's dockworkers. For five days throughout the city, people refused to go to work, leaving the streets empty and the city without lights— the only services to continue running were the hospitals. It was one of the few genuine successes of one of the most radical leftist groups in America's history, the Industrial Workers of the World, or the Wobblies.

While impressive in scale, the strike was a colossal failure. Strike leaders had made no specific demands and therefore failed to win a single concession from anyone. Zioncheck was about eighteen when the strike occurred, and history doesn't record his thoughts about it. It's tempting to say that he supported labor's chutzpah but was embarrassed by its puny sting; Zioncheck would forever be torn between effective action and grand, useless gestures.

I posted my note on the living room wall.

Hey House,

So as you know, I've been working on Grant's campaign for a month or so, and there are two empty rooms that we need to fill. In other words, I've been unable to fulfill my duties as house manager for this month. Some of you have already pointed this out. Well, you're right. I just don't have the time right now to show the rooms to everybody who calls (there haven't been many). In fact I'm really stressed out and can barely think straight at the moment, so please be patient with me.

Would any of you be willing to take over the house management responsibilities for the next month? You wouldn't be doing it for free . . . You could have my $250 rent discount!

If so, please see me as soon as possible.

Thanks
Phil (your humble, struggling house manager)

I spent the rest of the morning in a meeting with Grant, but I was distracted. I had phrased my note poorly. I was sure Doug would misinterpret it. I wasn't going to cede my job to him, just loan it out for a while. I could see him grinning already, and it sickened me.

After meeting with one of our printers downtown, I rushed home and snatched the note with the intent of destroying it, but stopped when I realized that Doug might have seen it by now. He might have left for work late this morning. I returned the note to the wall and smoothed over the wrinkles I had made. I left the house and went back to my car, and while I drove I considered my options.

That evening, I went down into the basement and knocked on the door of Emily's suite.

"Oh, hey," she said. She was already out of her work clothes and in a pair of overalls and a T-shirt.

"Hey," I said, in chatty falsetto. "How's your bathroom? The stench is still gone, I hope?"

"It's better. Thanks."

"And all it took was a layer of caulk around the toilet. Can you believe it? Hey, I'm sorry it took so long for me to get to it.' "

"Well, it's better. I just hope it doesn't come back. Come on in, I'm on the phone." She darted off with her cordless.

Emily's suite was the largest private space in the house. I went through her kitchen and into her living room and found a place on her couch. My lower eyelids felt like they had developed an extra crease. I imagined myself from a third-person perspective, an underfed, overworked young politico who stared at everything with a spectral terror.

"So what's going on?" Emily asked. I was always surprised by her accent, how a native Virginian like her could make me think of Pittsburgh.

I tried to sound relaxed. "All the floor lamps in here really brighten your place up," I said. "It used to be so freaking cavernous in here—hey, Emily, did you see the note I posted near the front door?"

"No, I came in through the back. What'd it say?"

"Is there any chance you can take over the job of house manager this month? I'm getting my ass kicked on this political campaign. I'd give you my rent discount. Two-hundred fifty bucks—" I tried to linger on the sound of money.

"Well, that sounds OK, but I don't think I have the time to do all of it. But I can help out. Maybe Doug would do some of it."

"Doug?" I said, playing dumb. "Do you think he'd do a good job? He's so—so—I can't imagine him showing the house to people."

"Well, like I said, I don't think I'll have time to do all of it."

Having them share the job was better than nothing, I reasoned. "I'll ask him. That could work. God, *thank you*."

"No problem."

Back upstairs, in my room, I paced. I put in Modest Mouse's *Lonesome Crowded West* and turned on "Cowboy Dan," a song about an alcoholic cowboy who brandishes his gun because he feels trapped living in a city. But the sound was too chaotic so I turned it off and picked up Jonathan Raban's *Hunting Mr. Heartbreak*. I flipped through the chapter on Seattle and read at random:

> Seattle looked like a freehand sketch, from memory, of a sawmill owner's whirlwind vacation in Rome and Florence. Its antique skyscrapers were rude boxes, a dozen to fifteen stories high, fantastically candied over with patterned brick and terracotta moldings. Their facades dripped with friezes, gargoyles, pilasters, turrets, cornices, cartouches, balustrades, and arabesques. Every bank and office block was an exuberant *palazzo*.
>
> The whole thing was an exercise in conscious theater.

But concentrating on great writing was nearly impossible, so I put the book down. (Besides which, *Heartbreak* was starting to irritate me; I didn't like how Raban had created an alter ego named "Rainbird" to help him describe his love for the city. There was no point in creating an alter ego for such a benign idea, and Rainbird sounded like someone SnowWolf would know.) Instead I started writing a list of my anxieties:

• *Allowing one of your pesky idiosyncrasies slow you down by 4 minutes at 9:33 this morning: 3 votes*
• *Failing to extract the maximum political advantage from a social encounter with an influential citizen: 18 votes*
• *Failing to adequately tape poster signs to the wall at some poorly attended forum, so they all fell to the floor with a loud clatter during someone's speech: 19 votes*
• *Failing to have enough campaign flyers or remit envelopes*

on hand whenever we leave Capitol Hill: 54 votes
* *Allowing your ill-equipped personality to get in the*
way of this campaign: 1,301 fucking votes!!!!

I could never show a list like this to Grant, of course. He wouldn't
see the humor in it.

My life was overtaken by paper. I was drowning in all the little
scraps accumulating on my desk. Post-it notes, bits of loose-leaf
notebook paper, fragments of torn-off envelope backs, shreds of
paper towel—anything that was handy when I needed something to
write on. I needed a better system. At one point I borrowed one of
Grant's small black poetry notebooks, but it was too thick and it
felt inappropriate, so after a couple weeks I gave it back. I bought
a set of wider, thinner notebooks, something more akin to reporter's
pads, which felt more natural but didn't completely solve the
problem, mostly because I kept misplacing them and had to rely
once again on the same old Post it notes and napkins from Victrola.

But the paper was just a mild unpleasantry compared with the
new skills I had to master instantly. The most difficult of these new
tasks was psephology, or the arcane art of interpreting voter statistics. A database company in a neighboring suburb tracked
voters for every election, keeping stats on their address, age,
gender, voting frequency, and whether they voted at the polls or
mailed-in absentee ballots. This information was compared to how
issues and candidates fared in all of the city's thousand plus voting
precincts for every election.

It was a lot of data, and it came with confusing jargon. "I need
the lists of perfect voters for Wallingford, Fremont, and Capitol
Hill," Grant might tell me. But a "perfect" voter was not a senior
citizen who had been voting unfailingly since Truman defeated
Dewey—civic expectations in America were too low for anything
like that. A "perfect" voter was a citizen who had voted consistently in the last four elections. They were also called "four out of
fours," as opposed to imperfect voters, who were one-, two-, and

three out of fours. But perfect voters for which elections—primary, general, special, or all three? And did the category cover absentee voters, poll voters, or both? It turned out that there were many kinds of "perfect" voters. Grant left the number-crunching to me; my only real comfort was that he knew even less about it than I did.

Most of my new duties didn't require learning an entirely new language. Local campaigns weren't won by scientific theories as much as by personal interaction, and my interpersonal skills needed considerable readjusting. I had no idea, for example, that it was acceptable to be pushy with professionals whose services you were buying. I had always relied on waitresses, bartenders, phone-service reps, CD-store and bookstore clerks without getting too worked up if they didn't meet my expectations. I prided myself on this, because I sympathized with people in the service industry and I knew how my low blood pressure impressed my doctor. Yet now I was in charge of ordering people around on excruciating deadlines. And if any of these people failed, I had to demand changes in accordance with our schedule, not theirs.

Then there were volunteer and fund-raising parties. Before running a campaign, I assumed that these parties somehow ran themselves, without much planning. People came, they were energized, they gave money, they went home. I could not have been more wrong: These parties were all about obsessive image manipulation. Total, unassailable confidence had to be exuded at all times. The candidate had to be portrayed over and over again, by himself and by others, in the most sublimely nuanced terms. The candidate was the inevitable victor—unless you don't help. The city was a wonderful place to live—but would soon fall to ruin if the candidate weren't allowed to save it. Money and pleas for volunteer help had to be repeated endlessly, in an infinite variety of ways. One veteran politico I knew described it as both psychological seduction and torture. You had to get people used to what you were asking for to the point where they didn't wince, hesitate, or bolt for the door. You broke their will to resist, until they had given two, three, and four times in one night, yet you didn't let anyone leave feeling bad about the candidate. I understood these concepts and strategies intellectually, but goading myself into using them was another issue altogether. The seduce-and-torture model rattled my conviction that democracy was something in which individuals were free to make up their own minds.

And it still wasn't clear if we had a volunteer coordinator. After Theresa quit, we found Hal, an early monorail fan. Hal was a forty-year-old New Jerseyite, a friendly fellow with a penchant for obscene jokes. But he had worked for us for only a couple of weeks and his burnout was already apparent; his response time was growing slower, and I had noticed that he had started talking about how anxious he was to get back to finishing a second house he was building on his property in the Fremont neighborhood. Grant was getting pissed and I was getting frantic; if we didn't find someone who could devote all their time and energy to the campaign, the work would fall to me.

I paced in circles and ovals. My to-do list had twenty unfinished items on it, maybe thirty. The stress was so great that I had lost my sex drive. I had to tell my girlfriend "no" several times a week, because the only thing I could think about was the campaign— where was it going, why weren't we raising enough money, why had our media coverage slowed, why weren't things moving faster, and why wasn't I living up to the standards I had set for myself?

There was a knock, and Doug came in without waiting for a reply. In one hand was my crumpled note, in the other was a beer bottle, its brown glass catching the light from the opposite window.

I shouted, hiding irritation, lunging for the advantage, "Just the man I wanted to see. Hi! Listen, Doug. I'm just so overwhelmed I can't spend any time finding tenants for the house. Emily wants to do half the house management stuff, and since it's such a big job I think that it'd work out best if you both did it this month."

"Emily wants to do it?" His smile vanished.

"I just talked to her a minute ago."

"And so that means—"

"The rent discount gets split in half. A hundred and twenty-five bucks apiece. I admit it's not much money, since it is a lot of work—does that sound cool to you?"

"Yeah, sure," Doug said sourly. This was not the victory he had expected.

"I really appreciate this. It's one of those things that it's just gotten so—this campaign, I mean—"

The phone rang. I threw an index finger at Doug. *Just a sec, OK?* "Hello?"

"Hey, it's me. Are you ready to pick me up?" Grant said. His sentence did not sound like a question.

"Where are we going?"

"That candidate forum in North Seattle. Jesus, did you forget?"

"No, I'm just—OK. I'll come get you. Call you from the parking lot." I hung up.

I turned back to my housemate. "You know, Doug, I have to get going. Can we talk about this after I get back tonight?"

Doug turned and stormed off while I congratulated myself. Some political battles were easy.

I went into my sunroom/office and grabbed my most recent list and ran to the car and looked into the back seat from the passenger window. I had to make sure everything we needed was in the car: Grant Cogswell poster signs, Grant Cogswell campaign lit, remit envelopes, two rolls of tape, two staple guns—everything seemed accounted for, even the hammers.

Oh my God, Where's my pen, where's my fucking pen! I looked in the space between the seats, where I kept some for emergencies, but I had used them already and had not returned them.

Deep breaths, but not too many. I reached up to feel the top of my ear. Nothing, I then felt my lips. Bingo. A plastic ballpoint was lodged in my teeth. I put it in my right pants pocket, patting it twice so I would remember where it was.

The neighborhood blurred by as I drove. The city had become

a flat, computer-generated matrix to me now, maintaining the same physical borders but characterized by swaths of color-coded data. It was a game. If we mailed the right kind of data (targeted campaign brochures) to the right bits of data (voters), then we could turn the election in our favor. It was a necessary, cynical, depressing exercise.

Fifteenth Avenue was bustling. The unemployed, the homeless, the college students, and the harried mothers passed each other on the sidewalks without exchanging words or glances. I turned into the grocery store parking lot and called Grant.

"How are you?" I asked when he opened the car door.

"Shitty," he said. He had been fund-raising all day. As he sat down he said, "What's this?" and pointed to a cardboard box on the floorboard.

"Oh, yeah," I said, too surprised to pretend I had not forgotten about them, "The new lit. I picked them up this morning. There are several more boxes in the trunk."

"Let's see." Grant tore at the box.

The new campaign literature was a page long on thick brown recycled stock and folded three times. Our message was conveyed in both the layout and the paper choice: DIY environmentalist, tastefully and fiscally moderate Seattleite wants to be your next city councilmember.

"What the—"

I didn't see the mistake until he did. "Cogswell" wanted your vote. There was a big empty space where the candidate's first name should have been.

Grant's jaw tightened. My stomach twisted and I flinched. The mistake, technically, wasn't mine; it was the printer's. But we were desperate for new literature and it therefore *was* my fault for not scrutinizing it more closely before I left the print shop. It was my fault that I did not scream at the nice Asian man and his attractive daughter to fix the problem for us, for free, immediately.

I waited for Grant to shout. He didn't. Instead he clawed at the door handle and flung himself out of the Geo. He walked twenty feet away, where he looked liked he'd explode. He didn't. He pressed his lips together until they disappeared. He got back in the car and told me to get the literature replaced immediately. I assured him that I would.

Grant told me to drive and I did.

The next day was Sunday. We sat at Victrola to plan, to complain, to apologize to each other, to nurse some campaign wounds (both real and imagined), and to go over our agenda for the imminent committee meeting. The mood was about to turn ugly again when we were approached by a man who said hello as if he knew us.

"I'm sorry," I said. "But I'm bad with names. Who are you, again?"

His name was Wayne. He had a cheery disposition. "We met at the Rally in the Alley," he said, "about a month ago. My friend and I passed out some flyers for you."

"Ah, yes," I said. I had given him some of our flyers, but had later fretted to Grant about the decision because Wayne had been wearing a Che Guevara T-shirt, a sure turn-off for many potential voters.

Wayne told us he still wanted to volunteer. He had wanted to do more than pass out flyers, and he reminded me that he had given me his phone number. I told him that I had passed his number to our former employee Theresa, and he replied that she had called him once but had never bothered trying again.

Grant pounced on this information. "See!" he snapped at me. "Here's someone who's slipped through the cracks! We gotta get him involved." Turning to Wayne, he said, "We've got a steering committee in a few minutes. Why don't you come and join us?"

When we got to the apartment where the meeting was to be held, we realized something was wrong. Our gifted team of advisors was largely absent. Grant demanded answers. I told him I didn't know why no one had come. I had sent out the email reminder two days earlier, only one person had RSVP'd, and only three out of more than a dozen people were there.

We tried to get the meeting going. As usual, I facilitated. The first agenda item was the same first agenda item since the beginning of the campaign: race. How were we going to deal with the fact that Grant was white and McIver was black? Normally, this question produced about ten minutes of discussion, hand wringing, frank dismissals, and unpleasant sighs before it was tabled for the next meeting, but today there weren't enough people present to do even that, so I moved on to the next agenda item anyway.

Grant got mad. "Where's Hal, our volunteer coordinator? Why isn't he here?" He turned to me. "Call him," he said.

"I did," I said.

"Call him again!" Grant said, veins appearing.

"All right, calm down—"

Standing up, Grant shouted, "Why don't we just make Wayne our volunteer coordinator?"

"Me?" Wayne said. "I just got here!"

Wayne proved to be a true workhorse. First he shared responsibilities with Hal, then he took over the job completely, putting in ten to twelve hour days. He even apologized when he wanted to take an afternoon break. We paid him $300 a week, not a bad salary for a grassroots campaign. It came to about $3.60 an hour.

Time compressed itself, fracturing and spinning, until we lost almost total control. In mid-August I found myself in a volunteer's apartment, picking up a fresh new pen and notebook and reluctantly turning down a beer. We were throwing another volunteer and fund-raising party. Grant, I saw, was behind a table in the kitchen, ready to teach us the art of building yard signs.

"Listen to me," Grant said. "You have *got* to do this right." Grant was in another foul mood. The host volunteer, with my approval, had been playing Bruce Springsteen's *Nebraska* album when Grant arrived. Introverted, depressing, and slow, *Nebraska* wasn't the kind of music you used to pump up the troops. Ronald Reagan may have subverted "Born in the USA," but there wasn't much you could do to make a song like "Reason to Believe," with its ironic resignation and dead dogs on the highway, into a campaign anthem.

Grant held up a stick and a lathe as if he were going to slay a vampire. "You take the stick, here, and you lay the lathes across it flat. You have *got* to make sure the lathes are even across the sticks. Then you staple the lathes into the sticks, but I wish we had nails, because they're better. Why don't we have nails? You call these nails? They're terrible!"

In a few quick moves he had the lathes nailed to the sticks. "Make sure that it's sturdy," he said. He demonstrated by shaking the stick. It was sturdy. "Then you staple the yard sign into the lathes. You have got to make sure they're sturdy, too. Then you turn it over and staple a sign to the other side of the stick, across the lathes just like this.

"Jesus, these staples are terrible. They're not going into the sticks."

We were rushed and disorganized. Someone told me it was time for Grant to give a speech, and I urged him forward. Grant did his best, reaching within himself once again to call forth the idealism and spirit that had given the campaign its initial momentum. But he rambled off topic, repeated words needlessly, and—most uncharacteristically—never found the steady gaze that made his speaking so effective. Josh, the *Stranger* editor who always seemed to be around, told me afterward to tell Grant to keep his speeches shorter. I nodded without comment.

The party drifted onto the front porch. I overheard a woman telling Grant that she felt uncomfortable voting for him because he was running against the only black city councilmember in Seattle. I nudged Grant's shoulder to distract him from that dangerous conversation, and gamely asked, "So what are we going to do with all these yard signs, Grant?"

"You and Wayne are going to cover all of Seattle with them," he said.

There are two ways of putting up political yards signs. The first, the legal method, involves finding people in the city who support your candidate enough to declare that support on their lawn. The upside to this method is the candidate can actually boast having real, live voters backing him. The downside of this is that someone in the campaign has to spend endless hours delivering signs all over the city to people who may or may not live on a street where anybody will actually see them.

The illegal method is simpler. After you build your yard signs, you get a pickup truck, SUV, or station wagon. Then you get about eight of your favorite CDs, two large hammers, and two volunteers dressed in dark clothing. You pick these volunteers up after the sun has gone down. You fill the vehicle with the signs and a tank of gas. It doesn't matter where in the city you start, but you should plan your trip so you don't waste any time. Once on the road, you stop and hammer the signs in any location that has a high volume of automobile traffic, such as highway off-ramps and the shoulders of major arterials.

"I can't be out there doing this with you," Grant said, holding up a sign and testing it to see if it had been built correctly. He borrowed my staple gun when he saw that it hadn't. "It'd look bad." I agreed; illegal yard signing sounded like fun.

The next evening, I hid in my room to avoid Doug, who had been using Emily's cordless phone to talk to prospective tenants. He had been making a nuisance of himself, occupying the entire downstairs with his new swagger and boasts to strangers about the house and its amenities. Both he and Emily seemed sure that they were going to find new housemates soon.

When I emerged from my room, I was wearing dark blue jeans and a black T-shirt—it was, in fact, one of the shirts Grant had made to honor Marion Zioncheck. This was accidental but appropriate, given the late congressman's reputation with automobiles. It was warm outside, so I skipped the ski mask. I crept out of the house furtively, for practice. It was 11 P.M.

The campaign yard signs were piled in front of the porch. My girlfriend's 1984 Volvo wagon was parked on the side street. I got in the car and drove through my next-door neighbor's driveway and onto my front yard. As I looked up I saw Doug watching through the open window. So much for being furtive.

He apparently wasn't in a combative mood that night—he was waiting for me to leave. I went to work without acknowledging him. After I had piled about eighty signs into the back of the Volvo, I drove away.

My volunteers for the evening were Kevin and Wayne. After picking them up, I pulled off to the side of the road and began to instruct them on the proper procedure for hammering in yard signs. I followed Grant's instructions for giving instructions.

"This is the best way to do it," I said. "You take this stake here and you make a divot with it. That makes it a lot easier to pound a sign into the ground." I got on my knees and started making a divot with the stake and a hammer.

"See?" I said.

"I think that takes too long," Wayne said.

Kevin laughed. "We're not going to bother with that! Can't we just pound them into the ground?"

We got back into the car. I flipped in a CD—Nick Cave and the Bad Seeds, and our maroon battle tank lurched forward. Our agile, fast-moving campaign took on a new feeling: invulnerability.

We were each fueled by own our drugs and our own motivations. I was running moderately well on the Coca-Cola that I sipped, Kevin was happy and stoned on some pot he had smoked just before I picked him up, and Wayne was tweaking on crystal meth. I relaxed in the commodious, jovial atmosphere we created; nobody said a word that was not in jest, and nobody mentioned the contradiction of placing Grant Cogswell monorail-trade-marked signs just off Interstate 5 (it sort of felt like we were putting up Planned Parenthood billboards across from a fundamentalist church).

I cruised by a street corner and circled it twice. "What do you think, boys?" I mixed a little Peter Falk into my voice, for the hell of it. We were at an empty intersection near the University of Washington's medical center.

"Looks good to me."

I stopped the car, then said: *"Go go go go go!"*

Kevin and Wayne rushed out, hammers in hand. They opened the back end of the Volvo, took a yard sign, shut the door, rushed to the spot where I had pointed, and ran like frightened geese.

While they hammered, I jerked the car forward and sped away. At a side street, I hung a U-turn and stopped. I shut off the lights, and waited in the dark for fifteen seconds, counting them out. Then I flipped the lights on and retrieved Kevin and Wayne.

Back in the car, Kevin and Wayne compared notes.

"I think that went pretty well," Wayne said. "But I almost crushed my hand."

"My sign was falling apart," Kevin said. "I couldn't get a good grip on it."

The more signs we pounded in, the better we got. Wayne and Kevin moved with more efficiency, and I realized that I didn't need to drive away every time—at least, not when there weren't any other cars in sight. We stopped feeling the need to do a debriefing after each planting.

Kevin cracked jokes from the back seat. Wayne rubbed his shoulder; I had pulled away while his hand was still on the Volvo's back door, and the pain was spoiling his high.

"Oh, what about that spot at Sixty-fifth and Ravenna?" Kevin said. "That is a suh-*weeeet* spot. Thousands of people drive by there every day."

"Oh, yeah!" Wayne said. "That is some *prime* real estate."

"Oh, yeah, baby, prime real estate!" we said in unison.

After four hours, our energy ebbed, so we called it a night. We had planted 120 yard signs in all.

The placement of political yard signs became my private obsession. From the driver's seat, I became a nervous political auditor. My eyes searched the side of the road, looking for that second-long political advertising hit that let me assess not only my candidate but all of the city's candidates. I smirked at the other drivers; they were being subconsciously inundated with this ancient American marketing ploy. The fools! When they got to the polls on election day, they would not know how they came to vote for Grant Cogswell, but I would.

Every serious candidate in Seattle uses yard signs, though some candidates rely on them more than others. The only candidate who wasn't using any was Richard J. McIver, a fact that inspired hope in our overworked campaign. Maybe old Dick didn't care. Maybe he wasn't campaigning at all.

13

Seattle in the 1930s was home to a radical political party called the Washington Commonwealth Federation. Run by communists and socialists, the WCF was so powerful at one time that it almost overturned the state's entire economic order.

Here's an excerpt from Murray Morgan, the reliable chronicler of Seattle's lesser-known histories:

> In 1936 the [WCF] delegates stampeded the [state] Democratic convention. When the conservative opposition, who controlled the convention machinery, tried to use parliamentary tactics to neutralize the voting strength of the 'wild men from Seattle,' the assembled radicals, led by a former drama critic, a former history professor, and a former barber, simply marched onto the platform, took over the agenda, voted themselves power, and carried on . . . When the shouting died down and the Democrats read the minutes, they found the Party was on record as favoring the nationalization of all banks, public ownership of all utilities and natural resources, and production for use; but it was not on record as favoring the re-election of President Roosevelt.

Marion Zioncheck was a favorite son of the WCF, at least until it became clear that not even they could control him.

All of this occurred before 1941. Pearl Harbor changed everything.

In the city of Seattle there were six District Democratic organizations, comprising more than 1,000 Democratic precincts. Each of these six districts played an essential role in citywide elections—an amazing fact, considering that citywide elections are supposed to be nonpartisan. No city council candidate was legally required to declare party allegiance, but unless the candidate was independently wealthy and could therefore afford a battery of television ads to reach undecided voters, he stood no chance if he admitted to being anything other than a Democrat. Success in Seattle politics rested on the approval of these unknown and unelected custodians of the remnants of America's liberal values.

In mid-August Grant and I went to a meeting of the 43rd District Democrats, who met in the basement of a local church on the north end of Capitol Hill. This would be another test for us: Grant would be delivering his stump speech before a group of total strangers. "McIver might be there," Grant said. "I really hope he is."

The meeting had already started when Grant and I arrived. Grant took a metal chair facing the front, and I took a chair against the side wall, where I could survey the room. Richard McIver was easy to spot in this small pond of white people. With his avuncular face, peppery-snowy hair, and modest pot belly, the councilman looked perfectly complacent about accepting the re-election landslide that he must have expected. I shot him a hard look but he didn't notice.

This wasn't the official endorsement meeting. Candidates were invited to come, introduce themselves, and answer questions in preparation for the real endorsement meeting, which would take place in a few weeks. At least a dozen candidates were there. One after another got up to pay homage to the latest political cliché. *I believe in doing things the Seattle Way. I have faith in the future of this city. I want to move Seattle forward.* The local D's asked routine questions. It was a warm and pleasant day outside and it made no sense for any of us to be there.

Curt Firestone, a gray-bearded lefty from the 1960's, got up to speak. He was making yet another attempt for a council seat (the last time he lost, he had pumped his fists defiantly in the air, Fidel Castro-style, for reasons known only to him). Firestone was running for a different seat than Grant was, and he appeared serious about winning his race this time. At least he had edited the bombast out of his stump speech. His main platform seemed to be ensuring that Seattle's firefighters and police officers had better training equipment.

One Democrat sitting up front asked, "Who did you vote for for President in 2000?"

Firestone was ready for this. "I—did not—vote for George Bush," he said magisterially. "I have—supported—*many*— Democratic candidates in the past who have ideals that are in line with the true values of the Democratic Party. In the future, I will continue to support these Democrats."

The questioner persisted. "Did you vote for Ralph Nader?" His motives were now transparent. Nader the visionary in 2000 had become Nader the spoiler by 2001. No establishment Democrat could utter his name without spitting.

Firestone froze his smile, white teeth glittering through a dirty beard. "I did not vote for George Bush," he repeated. He wagged his index finger at the man. "I voted for the candidate in the presidential race who best represented the ideals of the Democratic Party."

I felt a loud, sarcastic bark coming on, but I suppressed it with a sigh. It sounded like a tire decompressing.

"But did you vote for Nader?" another man pressed.

"I—voted for the candidate in the presidential race who best represented the ideals of the Democratic Party," Firestone said.

I turned to the person next to me. "Sweet Jesus," I muttered. "Just admit it." The haggard, craggy man nodded politely.

It was McIver's turn. Grant remained expressionless. I held my breath. The man next to me said nothing.

McIver walked—swaggered, really—to the front and commented

on the neighborhood in which he found himself, mentioning a few small things he had done for it. Then he listed all the committees he sat on and all of the challenges those committees faced. Among these challenges was the debate over expanding the State Route 520 bridge over Lake Washington to accommodate more traffic.

"So, these are the kinds of important decisions we will have to make in the future," he concluded, without saying where he stood on any of those important decisions.

This was our opponent. Hardly the apex of evil, Richard McIver was a genial bureaucrat with few ideas, a lot of money, and lazy endorsements. In our minds, he represented the biggest problem in the American political system.

A young woman near the back of the room stood up. Leaning forward, with her hands on the back of the chair in front of her, she announced with heartfelt earnestness that she planned on living in Seattle for the rest of her life. I looked around, thinking people would start applauding, my hands outstretched so as not to fail to join in. When no one did, she continued.

"Isn't it sad," she purred, "that the current city council lacks the racial and ethnic diversity that it had five or six years ago?"

McIver agreed that that was, in fact, sad.

Someone else asked McIver about some irate African-Americans who were criticizing city hall and any black who was a part of it. No names were mentioned, but the question was clearly about Omari Tahir-Garrett. To the crowd's pleasure, McIver scoffed at these individuals. He also blamed the media for stirring up controversy by creating false black leaders. After he received the applause that was his due, he sat down.

I bit down on my tongue and restrained myself from elbowing the man sitting next to me. These meetings might be entertaining after all. I looked around the church basement and asked God to help me behave myself.

Grant followed McIver. His shoulders were pitched forward and his head was aimed at the cement floor, as if he were trying to run while being weighed down by a battering ram. When he found the imaginary X where all the other candidates had stood, he raised his head.

"Hi, my name's Grant Cogswell and I'm running for Seattle City Council position number eight, Mr. McIver's seat." He pointed at the incumbent, like the cocky young hitter calling his first home run.

Grant gave what would later become his boilerplate speech. He billed himself as the co-author of the first monorail initiative. He named McIver's largest blunder in office, trying to kill the monorail—and therefore, trying to kill effective public transit. He called for public transportation that would work. He threw in a few poetic flourishes about the city and the disappearing salmon.

And then he got angry.

Grant attacked the policies and attitudes that were threatening Seattle's environment, its neighborhoods, and its quality of life. "We can't expand the 520 bridge!" he said, referring to McIver's speech. "I grew up on and off the area where the I-90 was expanded, and look what happened to it!" He wasn't stumbling the way he did during the kickoff party, or meandering off topic as he did during the last volunteer party. He was concise and electric.

He was also taking a big chance. The other challengers weren't even naming their incumbent opponents, much less pointing at them. And Grant had gone further. He had questioned McIver's record. In other cities, this would have been routine, expected. In Seattle, it was outrageously confrontational. Three hands flew into the air as soon as Grant looked finished.

"You seem like a one-issue candidate," said the man who had quizzed Firestone about Nader.

Grant shot back: "I'm not a one-issue candidate, but I do think transportation is the most important issue, and you only gave me a few minutes to speak. There are a lot of issues facing this city. Affordable housing—my best friend had to move out of town because he couldn't afford to keep his business running here.

Independent police oversight—" Grant spoke in a rush, but his reply was shot through with personal touches, and his answers had enough of the right political buzzwords to prove that he understood buzzwords. By the time he was done, everyone was clapping.

He walked back to his seat and looked at me with an expression that said, *Let's go. Now.* I waved goodbye to the craggy-faced man who had been sitting next to me, and we left. Outside, Grant silenced me with a sharp gesture. "Don't say anything," he hissed, "until we're farther away." One hundred yards out, he turned and made pounding motions with his fists. "I kicked ass in there," he said. I pushed him from behind, jumped on his back. "Stop it," he said, waving me down.

Later that week we drove to the University District, the neighborhood surrounding the University of Washington. The next campaign stop was the King County Young Democrats, who were having an introductory meeting, another precursor to a real endorsement meeting. I was confident here. What young political junkie wouldn't be swept up by Grant's brash idealism? The KC Young Dems were meeting in the University Heights Center, a large old building that was suffused with a musty, historical smell. The meeting was sandwiched between a room for ballet and a room for kung fu.

There were about a dozen Young Democrats present, and twice as many candidates. The Young Dems were hustling about, setting up tables and refreshments, handing out name tags, and rubbing elbows with the candidates. Grant and I busied ourselves putting up campaign posters, then we tried to look engaged and engaging.

We stood in the center of the room armed with what we hoped were thousand-watt smiles. Nothing happened. Grant wandered away from me on the theory, I'm sure, that we'd be more effective working opposite sides of the room. I kept smiling, and tried to devise a plan, a way to corner a Young D without being too obvious or desperate. But they were moving too fast. I tried tugging one on the sleeve, but she was gone before I could reach her. I couldn't tell if she had seen me or not.

I didn't understand the purpose of all this bustle. There weren't *that* many people in the room.

From where I stood, I noticed Greg Nickels walk into the room. Nickels was a county councilmember who had been running for mayor since January; a lot of people thought he was going to win. He was a colorless public official with no intelligent proposals of his own, whose campaign consisted of nothing but clichés about the strength of Seattle's neighborhoods. Grant and I had only recently had a conversation about him in the Geo. What repelled me about Nickels was how, as a young man, he had dropped out of college to pursue a career in politics. Wasn't college the best place to test your political ideas, and wasn't politics merely the process by which the best ideas were fought over? Why would anyone vote for someone who so nakedly put ambition before education?

As I watched, four Young D's ran to him like groupies hoping for a backstage pass. The volume in the room doubled. Nickels beamed; he didn't even seem to mind that the casual sweater wrapped around his shoulders was getting slightly mussed.

Realization dawned, and I felt exposed in my naiveté. The Young Democrats were swarming only some of the political candidates—the well-moneyed incumbents and the veterans of the local Democratic machine. Nickels was a winner, someone who had more authority than anyone in the room and would soon have even more. Every one of those Young D's probably wanted to do him a favor, maybe several, to make sure they were remembered by their first names.

A Young D brushed my shoulder on his way to the Nickels mob, and as I fought down a rising nausea I lunged for his polo shirt. I let go just as quickly. His expression was disturbing in some unspeakable way: His eyes were shiny and glossy, but not open. So transparently—*political*. My hopes of finding kindred spirits in this place evaporated. I knew at some point I'd transfer that expression into some bizarre nightmares—of multi-lipped animals with reptilian brains, and of weird, strategically behavioral calculations that possessed no substantive meaning.

"Hellooooo!" Pat Griffith, a school board candidate, pounced on me, eager to impress, wearing glasses suitable for a parent/teacher conference. I hastily told her that I wasn't a Young Democrat, and she looked downcast. But then she relaxed, and we talked about the usual things candidates talked about, like who had the best yard signs and how to survive the stress of the campaign trail. We were both relieved to appear occupied.

I struck up a few more conversations with some other candidates, and even shook the flaccid hand of City Councilmember Richard Conlin, who was in the process of blowing every bit of his first $85,000 before the primary, an astounding sum for a city like Seattle. I was wedged somewhere between contempt and jealousy, though, when I saw Conlin pigeonhole a baby-faced Young D for a few words. *How come I can't do that? Why can't Grant?*

Only one candidate in the room didn't seem to care about any of it. He came in, sat down, adjusted his custom-made suitcoat around his shoulders, didn't put up campaign posters on the walls, and didn't look around. His indifference to the system was enviable and horrifying. He was Richard McIver.

It didn't make any sense. McIver was the least visible incumbent running for re-election, and his ties to the local Democrats were not particularly strong. I wondered why he seemed so unconcerned. I ticked off the possibilities in my head:

1) McIver's old and has made peace with himself. Doesn't care for ass-kissing.
2) He's disgusted by the electoral system and wants his council record to stand for itself.

*3) He's black and knows he's well-positioned to win
with liberal white voters. That woman at the 43rd District Dems was just the tip of the iceberg.
4) He knows Seattle incumbents never lose.
5) Sound Transit has already promised to make him a
well-paid lobbyist if he's voted out of office.
6) He knows something we don't.*

But then I realized what I had done. I had gotten lost in reverie
in the middle of a crowded room. I panicked. *I'm alone! Looking
pensive and solitary! Without anyone nearby!*

Grant came up to me.

"I gotta talk to you," he whispered. He looked like he wanted
to grab my arm. Had I forgotten something again? Remit
envelopes this time? Or scotch tape?

Grant told me that he had been inspecting the table near the
front of the room that had been set up for candidate literature
when he saw something that made him wince. Next to our
brochures, he said, someone had placed the text of a television
news report in which Grant had been quoted. The story was aired
the night of the 2000 election; a TV reporter had been cruising the
Washington State Democratic Party's election party, looking for
something unusual, and had come across Grant. Naturally, Grant
was happy to shoot his mouth off for the camera.

"We didn't leave the Democratic Party," he had said. "The
Democratic Party left us." The reporter also noted that Grant was
wearing a Ralph Nader button.

In other words, it was now public knowledge that Grant was
seeking the endorsement of a group of people he had openly
insulted the year before.

"Don't turn around," he said, voice still low. "I'm trying to
figure out what I'm going to say when I get up there." He sat down
to think and I walked over to look at the offending document. I
tried to be discreet. Sure enough. The story was right next to our

quarter-page flyers, a hastily printed computer document, with the offending quote highlighted in yellow. I wanted to pocket the document, to run into the bathroom and eat it, but Grant had specifically told me not to touch it. I couldn't think of anything better to do, so I joined him back at his seat near the middle of the room.

It made perfect sense for Grant to have adored Nader in 2000. He was a lone figure in politics, a man who dared to challenge a system that was only interested in raising money for itself. Not even the Democrats had thought that George W. Bush, the GOP's "uniter," would be as right-wing as he was now starting to appear. The stakes in 2000 just hadn't seemed that high.

"Hey," I said to Grant, forgetting his request to keep quiet, "Who's that guy sitting next to McIver, the guy with the craggy face?"

"That's Paul Elliott, his legislative aide. You sat next to him at the Forty-third Dems. Looks like he's managing the campaign, too."

Then it occurred to me. "He's—"

"—probably the guy who put that quote next to my stuff," Grant said.

Silence. I tilted my head toward the ceiling. It was pretty high. If it had collapsed at that moment I wouldn't have minded so much.

A young woman sat down on the other side of Grant. To my surprise, she recognized me. It was Selena Davis, a part-time aide of Judy Nicastro's, a freshman city councilmember whose narrowly successful campaign Grant had worked on. I had met Selena the year before, when she had considered moving into a room in my house. She had seemed poised and mature for someone in her early twenties, and she had told me at that time that she was interested in politics, but I hadn't realized that had meant joining these sycophants. I forgot our predicament and started to chatter away.

But she cut me off.

"I'm sorry," she said to Grant. "I didn't realize who you were. I'm not supposed to be seen with you." Then she got up and moved to a seat toward the back.

Grant's posture stiffened further. I grabbed my mouth with both hands.

The meeting came to order. The president of the Young Democrats of King County noted with pride how many candidates were present—the packed room was now about 60 percent candidates, 20 percent campaign managers, and 20 percent Young D's—so she had to regretfully inform us that candidate speeches would be strictly limited to two minutes.

The first person to go up was Dave Reichert, the King County Sheriff seeking reelection. Tall and iron haired, he looked like a deputized extra from *Gunsmoke*. He gave a forgettable song and dance about how it was good to be the people's sheriff. Then he entertained questions.

"Are you a Republican or are you a Democrat?" someone asked, rather archly.

Reichert used the same evasive condescension that Firestone had used at the Forty-third District Dems. "This is a nonpartisan race," he said, and added that he didn't think it was a good idea to be inserting politics into such a vital law enforcement post. Next question.

The Young Dems badgered him again about his party affiliation. And Reichert evaded them again. And the longer I sat through this clumsy attempt to root out the sheriff's political bent, the more I longed to start laughing at everyone in the room. I realized in that moment how deeply my career as an alternative-weekly reporter had affected my personality: I didn't know how to behave at public meetings. I had learned to snicker or talk out loud whenever I found something funny or irritating. In high school I had been well behaved to the point of obsequiousness, but as an adult I had no idea how to control myself.

"Are you a Democrat or are you a Republican?" someone repeated.

It was no secret that the sheriff held predominately conservative values. But who cared? Wasn't his job to enforce the law? Wouldn't the time be better spent asking about more relevant issues, such as "What do you feel are the Sheriff's Department's biggest priorities in the coming year?" or "How do you feel about racial profiling?" or even "Why haven't you caught the Green River Killer yet?" There were at least a dozen questions that would have been more productive than this farce.

More importantly, what were they were going to do to Grant when his turn came?

We were only eight minutes into the meeting and I was already about to implode. I squirmed. My face grew flush and hot and I started to make small mewing noises.

A bizarre sound threatened to push its way out. I knew exactly what it would sound like—an old man choking to death at the dinner table. To salvage a little self-respect, I forced my vocal chords to change the noise into a sentence. "Ask him if he voted for Gore or Bush," I bleated.

Four or five people heard me. Grant scowled at the chair in front of him. I bit down on my tongue as hard as I could. It hurt.

Grant's turn came. He moved to the front of the room. With only 120 seconds to establish his political worldview and describe his ideas for change, he plunged into it by criticizing McIver and light rail and promoting monorail. He tried to save his explanation about the Nader quote for last.

"Time!" someone called.

"—and I really wish someone would ask me about that little piece of paper that's up at the front table there." He tried to cover his frustration with a grin, but he could only manage a contorted scowl.

No one, however, asked about the little piece of paper that was on the front table. Everyone was looking at Grant and smiling, for a host of different reasons. As soon as his turn was over we fled. We found out later that he didn't get a single vote in the straw poll.

And then things got worse.

At the 11th District Democratic pre-endorsement picnic, Grant frantically trailed Paul Elliott, our opponent's campaign manager, as he showed the quote to that district's members. Between bites of hot dogs and corn on the cob, the Dems nodded disappointedly, like nineteenth-century Masons hearing about someone breaking one of their codes. Nobody asked Grant about his policy ideas, and Grant lost the endorsement.

At the 36th District Democratic meeting we didn't see it either coming or going. News of the quote had gotten there ahead of us, having spread like an airborne virus, and Grant lost the endorsement.

They were openly hostile in the predominately black Central District, home of the Thirty-seventh District Democrats. The revelation of Grant's Nader support was followed by yelling and shouting—"Ralph Nader is *not* welcome here!" one man screamed—and the situation was only mildly relieved by Stan Lippmann, the attorney/physicist candidate who opposed rubella vaccinations. Lippmann spent half his allotted time defending Grant and scoffing at the idea that Nader had ruined the 2000 election. But it didn't matter. Nobody asked Grant about any of the issues, including how his ideas might affect Seattle's minorities. Grant lost the endorsement.

At the Thirty-fourth District Democratic endorsement meeting, Grant's frustration began to show.

"This isn't working," he said. "We have got to do something before we lose another endorsement. I'll take this side of the room, and you work that side over there. We need to talk directly to the individual district members."

"What do I say?" I asked.

"I don't know, *lobby* people. Talk to them about me, monorail—I don't need to tell you what to say. You know all this stuff."

Scouting around, I spotted what appeared to be a friendly, elderly couple. "Excuse me," I said. "I'd like to tell you a little bit about my candidate, Grant Cogswell."

"Who?" the old man rasped.

"Grant Cogswell!" I shouted, noticing his hearing aide. It was behind the oxygen mask.

"Oh. Who's he running against?" the man asked.

"Richard McIver!"

"Is that the colored guy?!" he shouted. "No! We can't vote against the colored guy! There needs to be at least one of those!"

Stunned by this inverted bit of political correctness, I sat down and contemplated the ends of my shoes. Here was a side of Seattle I didn't see very often. Before I could stand up again, the meeting was called to order. Grant lost that endorsement, too.

Part of the problem was that each district endorsement meeting operated differently. Would Grant be allowed to speak, or would someone have to speak for him? How much time would be allowed for debate? Was there time for a rebuttal or were there going to be questions from district party members? Grant and I walked into each meeting with only a vague understanding of what had to be done, and by then it was too late.

There was no particular reason to suspect that anything worse than usual would happen at the 46th District, an organization located in the north-central part of Seattle. I knew nearly nothing about that area of town, except that it was less dense than Capitol Hill and more centrist in its politics. I assumed that it was also wealthier. Tara hopped in the car with us and we headed out.

Once there, in a cafeteria-type room in a generic meeting hall, we learned that the candidates were not allowed to speak for themselves. At least one member had to give a speech for the candidate, with another member seconding the endorsement speech with a shorter speech. It felt like we had stepped into a low-rent country club.

Cleve Stockmeyer, a maverick attorney and veteran monorail activist, volunteered to speak for Grant. He made a ringing speech, arguing that Grant was a candidate with a vision. "Isn't it time we had somebody who pushed for big ideas for a change?" he asked. Stockmeyer pulled the crowd gently toward us.

But McIver had state senator Ken Jacobsen, who was experienced in the hardball politics of the Olympia legislature. Jacobsen didn't mince words. He went right for Grant's throat.

So what, Jacobsen said, if McIver wasn't a big-idea man? He fixed potholes, and that counted for something. Pointing at Grant, Jacobsen said. "If Gore hadn't been in Washington and Oregon trying to get the votes of those who voted for Nader, he would've been in Florida winning votes there."

He added: "Make no mistake—these people put George Bush in the White House, and now it's time for payback!"

The applause was thunderous.

Grant didn't say a word after we lost the endorsement. "Let's just drive in silence," he told me. We did. When I dropped him off at his apartment, instead of marching off with purpose, he leaned on his girlfriend and dragged his feet.

"Why the hell are we going through all this, anyway?" I asked Grant the next morning at Victrola. "This is totally pointless. We're investing all this time appealing to a group of people who are so overwhelmed with pettiness that they can't even ask you questions about real issues. This is a *city council race*, for fuck sakes!"

"Because this is how things are done," Grant said tightly, adjusting his seat for better back support. There was a more specific reason. It was August and nobody else was even remotely interested in listening to a city council candidate speak. The Democrats were the only show in town.

We tried to create an independent speaking tour for Grant. We didn't have much success until Grant received permission from the owner of a popular outdoor theater to talk to his patrons ten or fifteen minutes before *The Wizard of Oz* began. There would be several hundred people in attendance, more than all of the district Democratic meetings combined.

I didn't drive Grant that night; I was too busy crunching some voter statistics we had just received. So Grant and Tara borrowed my car. Tara drove while Grant tried to think about what he would say to all of the families that he would be standing in front of.

They got to the theater with plenty of time before sundown,

only to discover that the theater had moved the year before, and neither of them had any idea where it was now located.

Hal, who was still helping our campaign, called Grant's cell phone, gave Grant the correct address, and urged him to hurry. The movie was going to start in five minutes, with or without him.

Grant, thinking that the theater was just around the corner, abandoned Tara and the Geo and broke into a run, but he was wrong. He screamed into his cell phone for directions, and Hal yelled back, until neither could understand the other. Grant was drenched in sweat, but he kept running.

"Christ!" Grant said. "You know, just forget it. Forget it! I'm not going to be able to give a good speech even if I got there now! It just isn't going to happen!" He hung up on Hal.

Grant looked up to see Tara approaching him in the Geo, and he cursed and stomped. When he reached my car, he got in, took over the steering wheel, swore, revved the engine and then gunned it. He vacillated. Maybe, he thought, he could get to the theater before the movie started. He gave up just as quickly.

Grant got out of the car and swore some more. Not knowing what else to do, he took his anger out on my car. He planted his foot right into the car's fading red metal, throwing his whole body into it. He kicked it five or six times in all.

The frame of my Geo gave with an abrupt popping noise. Tara yelled and Grant stopped, suddenly conscious of what he was doing.

Grant thought the car would elastically retain its shape, the way a crushed plastic two-liter bottle of Coke pops back when it's filled with enough air. The Geo's rear cheek, however, never undimpled. Like the dust from the old Kingdome that I had never washed off, Grant's dent became an indelible mark on my car. It was one of the lowest moments of the campaign.

The district Democratic endorsement meetings were over, and only the King County Democratic Party endorsement meeting remained.

Grant was led into a small room, alone, where he was directed to sit at a long table. Seated around him were some of the county's highest-ranking politicos. The man running the meeting was seated at Grant's left. This man, who didn't seem to have a name, refused to look at Grant.

"We have documentation that you have been quoted as saying you want to hold the Democratic Party's 'feet to the fire,'" the man said. He did not phrase this as a question, nor did he provide the documentation; Grant, however, was expected to respond.

Grant paused, baffled. No such quote existed. "I don't recall ever saying anything like that," he replied. "I did say I voted for Ralph Nader, yes." But he pointed out that he had been a member of the Democratic Party for thirteen years before Nader ran for president in 2000.

He received some grilling about his Green Party affiliations. One person, a woman, asked him a question about monorail, but it seemed to be out of sympathy rather than genuine interest.

When the meeting adjourned, Grant remembered his manners well enough to force the meeting chair to shake his hand, even though the man still wouldn't look him in the eye. Then he strode out, smirking.

"Let's get the hell out of here," he told me. "Gladly," I said. I threw the injured car into first and drove us home.

14

The Pearl Harbor Naval Base in Hawaii was attacked at 7:55
in the morning on December 7, 1941. Japanese dive-bombers
and torpedo planes killed or wounded nearly 5,000 soldiers and
civilians and wiped out much of America's naval fleet in a few
short hours.

Fear thundered all down the West Coast. Seattle, the "Gateway
to the Orient," is closer to Tokyo than any other city in continental America. The city's strongest men—its loggers, its dock
workers, its fishermen—hid in their houses every night with the
lights turned off.

Hoover's G-men immediately rounded up 150 Japanese-
Americans in Seattle on the flimsiest of evidence. But more was to
come. America's super-patriots immediately denounced anyone of
Asian descent. They argued, "How can we be sure?" President
Roosevelt, whom many liberals now lionize, ordered that thou-
sands of Japanese-Americans be rousted from their homes on Skid
Road and elsewhere and shipped off to camps in California and
Idaho. A handful of Seattle's softer-spoken leaders tried to put in
a few good words for their citizen neighbors, but to no avail.
Everyone was trapped by the vastness and narrowness of their
own terrors.

And where was Marion Zioncheck, zealous activist and fearless
radical? Where was he to make appeals for reason, to assert the
law in its most just form? Why didn't he use his stature in Congress to protest? Zioncheck had already wiped his hands of the
whole mess. He had left America alone, to deal with its problems
without him.

But that's getting ahead of the story.

The clock radio went off. At the top of the hour, 8 A.M. Pacific time, NPR's Bob Edwards read the headlines. There were two. "The twin towers of the World Trade Center have been hit by jet planes, and have collapsed. In Washington, D.C., the Pentagon . . ."

Disoriented and only partially dressed, I stumbled downstairs to the living room to find SnowWolf watching television. The images on the screen were violent: Two planes, a holocaust of fire and smoke, and two of the tallest buildings in the world were destroyed. Before they fell, one could make out the silhouettes of people leaping from them. They jumped without grace, hope, or meaning. From another angle a plume of smoke enshrouded lower Manhattan.

It would take time to understand who was responsible, but details soon emerged. A tiny band of fanatical contrarians on the margins of the Third World had decided to declare war on the whole show. Not only did they hate globalism, capitalism, and democracy, they despised the very concept of Western society, with its cities, its vices—everything. Their response was to try to bring down the entire structure, steel beams and all, in one abrupt, suicidal ambush.

A smaller news story crawling across the bottom of the TV screen made me wince with reflexive embarrassment. Seattle Mayor Paul Schell had announced the closing of the Space Needle. With this self-important gesture he singularly failed to acknowledge the obvious: The World Trade Center attack reduced our city and its pretentious icon to a remote province, as relevant as a Michigan fur trading post to the eighteenth-century French. And what moron would want to go to the top of *any* tall structure today, anyway?

Doug and Emily came by, lingered for a little while to stare at the television, and quietly left. SnowWolf went to bed without a word.

I called Grant and got his voice mail. I called his cell phone; it was turned off. There was no point in throwing rocks at his window, or it felt that way at any rate. I started doing household chores. I swept and mopped the entire common area, and when I had covered the thousand square feet of floor space, I started over. I dusted, put some books on the shelves, straightened out furniture, paced, and thought about cleaning up the basement and mowing the lawn. *(If you can't keep your own house in order,* I thought, *what hope do you have?).* Instead I ran upstairs and sent out a campaign email to our spam list, a message that I had failed to send the night before. I went back downstairs and sat on the couch again and watched the news, which was now on a nauseating repeat mode.

I reached Grant sometime around 11 A.M. He had no idea what was happening. He didn't own a TV. I drove over to his apartment. He eyed me skeptically and said he wanted to get a few things done before I showed him the news.

"Grant, the Twin Towers are *gone,"* I said. "Manhattan is completely covered in smoke!"

"You said that," Grant said. "And we'll go watch the news in a minute. But right now we need to pick up some materials from a few volunteers." Tara looked at me sympathetically but didn't say anything. I saw that two months of campaigning had made Grant come to believe that I no longer had a reliable sense of proportion. Or perhaps Grant had become so focused that he wasn't going to let anything distract him, not even a terrorist attack on American soil.

We dropped off some materials at a volunteer's house and picked up some other materials at another volunteer's house.

When we returned to my house I saw that I hadn't turned off the news. Grant saw the images and sunk to the floor, pounding the spotless hardwood with the palm of his hand. I nodded to myself, swept the floor again and talked to myself. I said things like, "Well, this is it, isn't it? This really is *it."*

I drove Grant home. It was agreed, without either of us saying so, that the campaign was on hold. I wandered out to Volunteer Park, where a crowd was spontaneously gathering with candles and blankets, but I felt self-conscious and left. Later in the evening, some of my housemates gathered on the first floor and agreed to get drunk together. Emily and Doug went out to do errands and came back with their arms loaded with alcohol. Doug seemed pleased with the new community spirit that infected the house, no matter its source, and SnowWolf turned to Emily before he left for work and asked why she was so upset over something that had occurred thousands of miles away. I later recalled in gauzy detail how I had wandered barefoot across the street to a neighbor's house and interrupted her in the middle of a date. I had slurred, stammered, and babbled about getting her help in an upcoming campaign fund-raiser—an unusual intrusion, as I barely knew her. Then I had gone home and blacked out.

The next day Grant and I met at Victrola. We tried to talk about the campaign but the conversation quickly looped back to the terrorist attack. Then heavy silence.

My mind kept returning to the time Grant and I had watched Andrei Tarkovsky's movie *The Sacrifice* in an art-house theater. The characters agonize over the news that World War III has started. As they wait for the nuclear bombs to fall, the camera lingers on people pacing around darkened rooms. But that's not really why I remembered the movie. In a seat in front of us, a man with thick facial hair had been eating popcorn, attacking the crinkled bag with savage indifference to the rest of the audience. No one but Grant had the courage to tell him to stop; he reproached the man with such energy that the man put his bag on the floor and did not touch it again. I sat outside Victrola hoping Grant would say something to puncture the silence, explode in anger, give expression to my hamstrung emotions.

Evan Sult, an artist and musician, wandered by. Evan—tall and lanky, whose eyes were red and raw—said, "I joined the alternative community for a *reason*." His voice quivered. "It was a deliberate choice that *I* made." Despite the shorthand, we understood what he meant. We had all chosen to live as far outside of mainstream culture as we could. We had all been critics of American policy, foreign and domestic, and had all tried in our own ways to change those policies, or at the very least to educate ourselves on why those policies were bad. But the attacks were making everyone rethink everything. Was this more than just an attack by terrorists? Was mainstream America to blame for having been so willfully ignorant? Were we to blame for not having shown more reverence the last time we heard the national anthem?

Evan disappeared into the coffeehouse and I said to Grant, "There's some damage control you probably need to do."

"What's that?"

"I sent out an email to our list this morning about the campaign pub crawl that we had planned this week."

"That probably wasn't a very good idea."

"Well, it's worse than just that. It was really flippant. Wa-a-a-y flippant. I don't know what I was thinking. I've been getting flamed all morning."

"So what do you want me to do?"

"I'll have to send you a copy of what I sent out, and some of the flames, and you can write something sensitive and calming or something."

Grant agreed.

"I feel really shitty about this," I said. I couldn't decide if it was soothing or disconcerting to see Grant so calm.

"Nobody's thinking about pub crawls right now. Should we cancel them?"

"I don't know. Let's see what tomorrow looks like."

While the appropriateness of campaign pub crawls was debatable, taking a short break to drink with friends was not. We met at the Rendezvous, a dive bar in the Belltown neighborhood. It had low ceilings, nicotine clouds that started at your waist, red velour walls, a beehive-haired barmaid named Dodi, and a permissive attitude toward the local winos. The Rendezvous was the kind of place one might have found on Seattle's old Skid Road. It was scheduled to be closed, scrubbed down, refurbished, and reopened as a clean, friendly environment for the urban hipster set. Just a few weeks earlier this development had struck me as a tragedy of the highest order.

Some of our closest friends were there. There was Matt Fox, a veteran of grassroots politics who had led the charge against the Seattle Commons, a mid-1990s plan that envisioned a Central Park for Seattle. It would have been a wonderful idea had it not involved removing hundreds of small businesspeople from stores that had been in their families for generations. Matt was dating Lisa Herbold, who was also there. A legislative aide to councilmember Nick Licata, the city's only consistently progressive city councilmember, she did the policy research that put her boss on the losing side—often by an 8-1 vote—of almost every battle that took place in city hall. Herbold sported a nose piercing, rolled her own cigarettes and was raising a teenage daughter by herself.

Across from Herbold sat Evan, who had once been the drummer for Harvey Danger, a band that peaked in the late '90s with the single "Flagpole Sitta." I had never thought of Evan as a rock star, primarily because he was always talking about his other obsessions—graphic design, writing, and comic books. Evan was dating Paula Gilovich, who sat next to him. She was a social worker, a writer, a small-press publisher, and a novelty sex-shop clerk who was obsessed by Ronald Reagan's influence on America.

Lisa was pointing her finger, interrupting someone with her usual brassy style. "It's not just that! It's not just that America has a double standard foreign policy or that almost no one in America has health care. Why do people keep moving here? If everyone hates us, why do people keep moving here? This *is* a great, rich country. That's why."

What I found so comforting about my friends was that I was never able to adequately define them. Not a single one of them knew how to fake a disinterested expression in a dance club. None of them had attempted to make a pile of dough off the New Economy. What separated them from the riffraff was that they were actually *doing* something, politically and artistically, and they supported the efforts of others who were trying to do things, too. They had all made deliberate, personal decisions about how they wanted to live their lives, and they had put money at the bottom of their priorities.

Grant was engaged in earnest discussion with Evan about the counterculture and its role in society. Evan looked ready to give up; Grant was telling him not to. "I have to look at everything and ask myself, 'What am I doing? Am I doing enough?' It doesn't make sense at first, but the individual becomes more important than ever now." Grant was reaching for his activist-poet self, the anarchist/populist/optimist who truly believed that things would work out in the end, if only we all got involved, gave money—tapped into *it.*

It had been a long time since I had played around with drugs, but as I watched Grant pontificate, it was as if I had been mixing pills all night. He looked bigger, and fuller, as if he were the only person in the room, but at the same time distant and unreachable and none of what he was saying made any sense.

Fear overwhelmed me. What if we lost? What would I do then?

I left the Rendezvous around one o'clock. My head was throbbing from drinking alcohol for the fourth night in a row. I stumbled upstairs, threw my door open, and dropped onto my bed, thinking only about brushing my teeth and falling asleep. Or maybe just going to bed with my cigarette polluted clothes on. But then I remembered that I had some campaign emails to send, so I hauled myself up and headed for my office.

When I checked my email, I saw that Grant had finally written the damage-control message I had asked him to.

"If anybody believes that it is frivolous to try and get a bunch of our supporters out to a bar, I would say exactly the opposite," it read. "After all the tears and anguish and mind-numbing horror of this week, camaraderie, warmth, fellowship and yes, release, are what we all need. More crucial than anything right now is that we come together one-on-one and talk, and reinstate our feelings of community, provide an atmosphere of clear thinking and peaceful intent."

I read it with a prick of jealousy. Every time I attempted something eloquent or heartfelt, it came out sounding frivolous or the opposite, honest to the point of insincerity. Grant made it seem natural and easy. I arranged our spam list and hit "send."

Right at that moment I heard a distinct clicking sound from behind the wall that separated my room from Doug's. It sounded familiar in a way I did not want to contemplate. A score of old memories came flooding back—of Memphis, Bill Clinton jokes, and NRA hats.

I walked out of my room and knocked on Doug's door. He was sitting on the floor against his bed, facing his piranha tank. The fish jumped.

"You bought a gun," I said.

Doug lifted a white cloth that was in his lap. "Just today," he said. "How did you know?"

"Can I see it?" I asked.

Reluctantly, Doug handed the gun to me. It was a 9 mm Glock, the same kind of semiautomatic that I had once shot at a gun range. It was black, cool to the touch, and heavier than I had remembered. Doug held the ammunition clip in his hand.

I had forgotten about Doug. He had been in my peripheral vision, like a car zooming into my blind spot. He hadn't shown much of a reaction on the morning of September 11. As I recall, he had stood there, not saying anything, not moving, his face expressionless, his empty hands resting at his sides. Later he had gotten drunk with the rest of the housemates, enjoying himself as if he had discovered for the first time what it was like to be the life of the party.

The day after, while the rest of us nursed hangovers, Doug had retreated to his room and turned on his TV set, but not to watch more news coverage. He watched the bloodiest movies in his DVD collection—*Pulp Fiction* and *Reservoir Dogs* topped the list. From my office I could hear round after round of ammunition being fired from his speakers. And now this.

Guns are strange consumer objects. Nobody ever thinks about making them any color but black, silver or army green. You could never get an aqua-colored Glock the way you could get an aqua-colored computer. In the global marketplace, corporations didn't need to work very hard to create a demand for them.

I handed it back to Doug, barrel facing away from both of us.

"Well, just keep it out of the common living areas," I said.

"No problem." He set it back on his cloth, which I now saw was one of his bedsheets.

I wanted to ask Doug why he had bought the gun, but I was afraid of the answer. So I said, "So, uh—what are you doing this weekend? This would be a great weekend to go fishing with your brother, wouldn't it?" Back when I had first met him, Doug had spent his weekends fishing out in the country. He had seemed happy, then.

"No, I haven't seen him in a while," he said.

"I mean, not that I know anything about fishing—" I said.

"—I'm trying to save up the money and buy that hundred-gallon tank for my piranhas. It's gonna be awesome!"

I rarely saw Doug in the days that followed. He was putting in full days at his weekday job, and disappearing on Saturdays and Sundays, for his part-time job. When he got home from either job, he'd go immediately to his room. From time to time, I caught glimpses of him on the porch, smoking cigarettes and dumping his empty beer bottles in the recycling bin, but he would return to his room without delay.

But I heard him. At night, in his room, with the door closed. For twenty minutes he would load and unload the cartridge from his Glock. *Click click. Click click.* Then silence. Then *click click—click click* again. The wall that separated us had never seemed so thin.

15

Marion Zioncheck loved big band and swing music. Populist,
urgent, devil-may-care, they were suited to his lifestyle. By 1936
Zioncheck was widely known as the "playboy" congressman. It
was big news when he was spotted dancing all night long in a New
York club. His favorite song that summer was Irving Berlin's "Let
Yourself Go," perhaps because he was about to.

"Let's go over everything," Grant said.

It was Sunday, two days before the primary election. We were
sitting around a table in a volunteer's apartment, for our weekly
steering committee meeting. I normally led the Sunday meetings,
but Grant was in charge today. His controlling style had
returned.

"Do we have Re-bar lined up?" he asked, consulting his notes.

"We're all set," I said. "I still have to tell the media where we're
going to be, though."

"Do we have people set up to hang our big banner on the
Aurora bridge during the morning and afternoon rush hour?"

"Oh. Yeah. We got Chris. He said he'd be able to do that."

"Chris? Who's that?" Grant said.

"You've met him," I said. "He emailed me out of the blue a few
weeks ago. *Chris.* You met him at the Belltown pub crawl. He even
emailed me his résumé, though I was afraid to open it because he
sent it to my email as an attachment, and you know how I don't
open attachments from unknown people—"

Grant cut me off with a look. "He's real gung ho," I finished.

The candidate consulted his list again. The rest of us waited.

"Have we got any volunteers committed to taking a day off work on election day?"

Hal Colombo was in charge of this task. "Well, I couldn't get anyone to agree to do that," he said.

Grant made a face. Hal saw this and hastened to add, "I mean, that's asking a lot, you know—but we do have a number of people planning on coming out."

"How many?" Grant said.

"I don't know. Ten, maybe a dozen. I'm still waiting for people to call me back. People are still depressed about the terrorist attack. They're recovering."

Grant made another distinctly sour face. He made a mark on his paper.

"I want four volunteers working in teams of two running into the bus tunnel at University and Third," he said. "One team will be heading south, the other north, so they'll hit the buses on both sides of the tunnel. They'll run in, hand out as many flyers as possible, then they'll get on the first bus that shows up. They get off at the next stop, pass out literature there, get *out* of the bus tunnel, then cross the street and get back in to the bus tunnel on the other side. Back in the tunnel, they'll do the same thing, catching the first bus and going back to where they first got in. Then they switch sides and start all over again."

"I don't understand," I said. "They get in the tunnel where and then get out where? And they're passing out flyers the entire time? Why can't they just stay where they are? Why do they have to run around like that?"

"Pay attention, will you?" Grant said. "We need to reach people who already ride Seattle mass transit. So the volunteers get on the bus at University and Third, then get off at the very next stop. Then they switch sides of the street and go back into the tunnel. They're getting on and riding the bus, then getting off again and riding the bus, but they're always returning to the same bus tunnel station."

"But why can't they just—"

"And the reason they can't just stand in one spot is that you're not supposed to pass out campaign literature in the tunnels, that's why. It's illegal. But if they move quickly, they can hit a lot of people at once and not get caught."

I shook my head. But it didn't matter. I wasn't in charge of the volunteers.

The primary election would be our first real test in the race. Grant had to place second, beating the three other challengers to Richard McIver, and he had to do it by a wide enough margin to seem like a credible threat to McIver in the November general election, seven weeks away. He could get good numbers on his own, proving that his support was strong. Or McIver could draw poor numbers, proving that his own support was weak. I bragged that we were going to keep McIver under 50 percent of the primary vote, but none of us really knew what was going to happen.

There was solace in minutiae. There were printing companies and mailing companies to handle. There was a last-minute effort to raise more money. Grant had managed to raise almost $20,000, a profound sum given his distaste for fund-raising, but not a lot when the goal is to mail literature to every registered voter in the city. We sent a limited mailing to voters around Capitol Hill, which we assumed constituted Grant's base.

On the eve of the election, I retreated to my office, where the only sound to interrupt my thoughts was Doug fiddling with his Glock. George Howland from the *Seattle Weekly* called and asked me where we were going to be on election night, and after I told him he wished me luck. The rest of the time I kept busy organizing the scraps of paper that had piled up on my desk. I could have used a beer, but I was too poor to buy any, and I didn't have the guts to ask Doug for one.

I woke up late on September 18—a luxurious ten o'clock. I stretched, brushed my teeth, showered, and cautiously inspected the second floor to make sure Doug wasn't around. Downstairs, SnowWolf was playing a video game on his Sony PlayStation, hunched so close to the television screen that it was hard to believe that he could see anything more than pixellated fuzz. I sat on the couch and watched. He was kickboxing a leopard-like creature with the help of a humanoid that could, on command, turn into a giant, lightning-quick mole.

"What are you playing, SnowWolf?" I asked, after some time had elapsed. SnowWolf was his gamer name, the name he preferred to be called. His real name was Charles.

"*Bloody Roar 3,*" SnowWolf said.

My cell phone rang, and caller ID told me it was Grant. I let him leave a message. No doubt he would provide a curt directive that I could follow without direct contact.

I turned back to SnowWolf. "Hey, man, I'm real sorry about that voicemail I left on your machine last week," I said. "That was really out of line." On the message I had screamed and swore at him for proposing to get a DSL line without proper house (read: my) permission.

"It's OK," he said. "I figured you've been under a lot of stress lately."

Terrorist attacks, personal attacks—I had never seen SnowWolf get upset about anything. Just leave him to his graveyard shift and his video games and he was fine. The strangest part of it was that everyone generally agreed that he was the friendliest, most unselfish person who had ever lived in the house.

I wandered into the dining room to gaze out into the back yard. The lawn hadn't been mowed in more than two months—I saw a clump of grass attack a squirrel. Our brand-new electric mower sat unused in a storage space behind a door in the kitchen. I went back to my room to toy with my CD collection and stare at the ceiling.

Around 11:30 A.M., I drove downtown to an ugly slab of concrete known as the Westlake Mall. The area was clogged with activity, the lunchtime business crowd mingling with the daytime shoppers. On the perimeter stood the candidates and their volunteers. Despite the crowd, the Grant Cogswell metro blue T-shirts and posters stood out. I had to admit, Grant had chosen an excellent color.

I pulled up alongside the mall on Pine Street. Hal Colombo greeted me at the car. He opened the back door and started taking yard signs from the back seat.

"Where's Grant?" I said.

"You mean your wife?" he said. "I think he's down on the other side of the mall."

"How'd that bus tunnel thing go? Did you guys hand out flyers down there?"

"Oh, you know, we didn't do that," he said.

Hal, it seemed, couldn't get the volunteers to cooperate, and since he didn't like public buses anyway, he didn't push them very hard. This sent Grant into a fury. He gathered a crew together on his own and tried to draw the plan on the back of an envelope. But his diagrams made no sense whatsoever. The volunteers solved this problem by pretending to understand before wandering off.

We staked out the northwest corner of the mall, a small battalion of Grant Cogswell supporters, a dozen or so in all. Grant's campaign had produced more supporters than any other campaign. I waved my sign and hooted.

I tried to do a little campaign math in my head. Of the 400,000 Seattle registered voters we could probably expect about 70 percent or fewer of them to actually vote. Of those voters, about 60 percent had already voted by absentee ballot. Of the remaining voters, many had already voted at the polls. There were hundreds, arguably thousands of people passing by, but many of them were suburban commuters who couldn't vote in our race. There was a chance we would be on the noon or perhaps the evening television news, but there was also an equally good chance our signs and volunteers would be ignored or edited out in favor of the top mayoral candidates.

But who knew? Maybe nine of our supporters who had forgotten to vote today would now vote, after seeing our signs. Or maybe seven completely ignorant people who normally wouldn't have voted today would be guilted into doing so because they had seen the political rally at the Westlake Mall, and they would choose to vote for Grant and his mass-transit ideas simply because they saw his name and his logo on my sign.

On the other hand, we might have accidentally reminded sixteen pro-McIver people to vote. Or maybe two of the people passing through Westlake Mall were members of the Seattle Poetry Slam, a group that Grant had bashed some time ago in the *Stranger* for being boring and uncreative, and we had inspired them to vote against Grant because they hated him so much.

I let out a tremendous scream. The thing I was learning about political campaigns was that one should never try thinking about or questioning them. Some people shouted along and congratulated me for my enthusiasm.

Later that evening, I drove to a hardware store for some miscellaneous supplies, then to my girlfriend's house to borrow her laptop. Then I drove to Re-bar, a dance club wedged between Capitol Hill and downtown.

Re-bar was once predominantly gay but it had become a favorite hangout for straight hipsters, too. I had been there a few times before, the first time with Grant, who had taken me with him to a Modest Mouse show. It was our primary-night election spot because it was close to downtown, which meant that if Grant was doing really well in the polls, the media would have an easy time tracking us down. It was also the only place we could get for free.

As I approached the entrance, I saw Chris, our gung ho volunteer who had agreed to hang Grant's eight-foot banner over a bridge on Aurora Avenue for three hours earlier that day. I greeted him vigorously.

Chris handed me the banner.

"I wasn't able to put the banner over the bridge," he said.

"What? Why not?"

"I can't talk about it," he said glumly. "I'm sorry." He walked away.

The bar was dark inside. I asked the bartender where I could set up. She had no idea what I was talking about, so she went to look for Steve the owner, who was asleep in the back room. Soon he was shuffling up to the bar to greet me.

Steve's thin hair was matted down and his left cheek was flushed red from the pressure of the couch he had slept on. He peered at me wearily through thin metal-framed glasses.

"You guys are going to be done by nine or so, right?" he asked. He had a slow, raspy voice, though this might have been caused by his recent awakening.

"No," I said, "We're probably going to be here until midnight or so. This is an *election*. The results won't start coming *in* until nine."

Steve was slow in digesting this information. "I don't normally host this kind of stuff in my bar," he said defensively. "I'm doing this because I like Grant." We could use his office to set up the laptop, but he told me that no more than two people at a time could be inside the office. Steve also told me that I couldn't spend long periods of time on the Internet because the bar needed the phone line to run credit cards. He then sloughed off toward the bar.

Our supporters trickled in. I recruited my girlfriend, one of the first, to turn one of the blank poster sheets into an election results poster, with a space for raw results and percentages that could be updated periodically with index cards and a little tape, like an amateur golf scoreboard. Steve had a television, but the reception was so bad that I turned it off.

We hung our banner behind the stage. Someone had arranged for a Pixies cover band to play while we waited for the results, and they showed up early to set up equipment. We placed the election scoreboard prominently at the end of the bar while one of Steve's employees started collecting a nominal cover charge. In Steve's office we connected to the Internet and found the county's election Web site, and I put a volunteer in charge of monitoring it.

The party was coming together so well that I felt comfortable enough to buy myself a beer. Shortly after I did, a volunteer grabbed my shoulder. "I think you're wanted up at the front of the bar," he said. When I protested, he persisted. "Just go up front. There's a problem."

Near the entrance, Steve was pleading with a man who had just arrived. The man was throwing his hands in the air, shouting expletives, attracting the attention of everyone in the room. "Please. We can resolve this if you just calm down. Now, Daniel, maybe you guys can all talk about this so we can reach some sort of compromise—"

I ventured a hello. The stranger swiveled around. His eyebrows were black and stood out from his forehead like coils of razor wire. He was taut with anger and his eyes burned.

I stared back as hard as I could. I was not going to lose this battle, I decided, whatever it was about.

As it turned out, Steve had booked the gentleman who stood before me to play after nine o'clock. The gentleman—Daniel—was supposed to debut his DJs that night for a regular series of heavy metal Tuesdays, and he was a little perturbed to learn that we had no intention of leaving the bar until midnight.

Daniel shoved a piece of paper into my hand. I didn't read it. I didn't want to lose the stare-down. I could guess what it was, though.

"I'm sorry, but so what?" I said. "We've got flyers announcing our event, too. They were probably posted in the same places you posted *yours*. Do you want to see our flyers? Kevin, go show this man our flyers." I had no idea if we had flyers on hand or not, or even if Kevin was standing next to me, but it seemed like the right thing to say.

"I was just profiled in the *Stranger*!" Daniel said. "People *know* I'm going to be playing tonight! It's my debut! If they come to see my debut, and I'm not up there, they're not going to come back!"

"Well, we're in the *Stranger* calendar, too! What am *I* supposed to do?"

"You can get out of here, is what you can do!"

I sputtered for a moment. "Listen, *this* is an election. I'm sorry, but we've got more at stake than you do with your DJ night. *You* can always come back and play another time, and if you're any good people will come see you, I'm sure. Do you know what's at stake with this election? This doesn't happen every Tuesday."

"Guys, puh-*lease*," Steve said, rubbing his face with his hands.

The argument began in earnest. We had the advantage in that we had gotten there first, but Daniel benefited from what appeared to be a naturally explosive disposition. Steve stood between us, begging us both to be reasonable, but neither of us was interested in compromise. Grant couldn't afford to have heavy metal playing at his election party, and Daniel was similarly cornered (there were a few older people in our crowd wearing preppy clothing, which very well might kill a heavy-metal mood). We both urged Steve to make a summary judgment, only to pull back at the last moment for fear that the judgment would not be in our favor.

Daniel stormed outside. Steve followed him, and I followed Steve. Daniel got on his cell phone and ignored both of us. Steve looked at me, told me to work it out with Daniel, and retreated into the club. One of our campaign advisers came out to recommend that I find another venue for our party. I looked around helplessly. Someone told me my girlfriend wanted me. I walked back inside and consulted with her. She told me she had interviewed Daniel a few weeks before, and his behavior had terrified her.

I searched the room desperately. Where was Steve? Where was Grant? I walked back outside.

"I can't deal with this bullshit," Daniel was saying. He was on his cell phone. "Fucking amateurs! And they got a fucking Pixies cover band playing! I can barely believe this shit!"

I saw Grant at the front door and gave a shout. The candidate stepped onto the sidewalk with the air of the invincible. He was poised. His back was straight and his shoulders were sturdy. His jaw was thrust forward like a boom on a sailboat. He looked positively—electable.

Grant told us to resolve our differences. "I am *not* going to get involved in this," he said. And that was it. Turning, he went back inside the club.

Daniel and I were both caught off balance. We circled each other and tried to decide what to do next. Daniel went first, trying to sound reasonable. "Look," he said. "Grant seems like a pretty good guy. I would have voted for him if I'd had time to vote today, but I'm scheduled tonight, and I can't miss my debut."

I was losing my will to fight.

"Would it help if we paid you to leave?" I asked.

"How much?"

"Hundred bucks. A hundred-fifty."

"Can't do it. This is my debut!"

I held onto my empty beer bottle. The simpler option seemed to be right in my grasp—how hard would I have to bash this asshole to get him to change his mind?

"Two hundred," I said. "*Three* hundred dollars to get out of here and leave us alone."

"Three hundred bucks?"

"That's my final offer." I would have to figure out later how to count that as a campaign expense. Did the elections commission filing papers include a space for bribes?

"OK," he said. "Three hundred dollars. I can do that."

We barely had three hundred dollars left in our checking account. But I had said it. "Wait here. I'll check with Grant."

Grant was chatting with our ACLU-appointed attorney (who was trying to win our case in time for the general election) and a man in his mid-thirties. He grabbed me. "Hey, I want you to meet this guy," he said. His tone was positively breezy. "He gave us the maximum contribution. He said he was mad at the way the Democrats treated us at their endorsement meetings."

I jumped on the man and gave him a bear hug. Fortunately, everyone laughed.

I pulled Grant aside and explained the situation.

"No fucking way are we giving that guy three hundred dollars," he said.

"So what do you want me to do?"

"I don't know. You handle this. Get Steve to get rid of him. *Stall* him."

So I stalled, filibustering with declarations and apologies. I retracted my bribe, then filled the air with useless talk until I needed water. Daniel fumed, but I could tell that I was wearing him down.

Finally, Steve pulled Daniel aside and told him he wasn't going to get to play tonight. Steve then pulled me aside to let me know that I had won. Daniel, who by this point had changed from whatever he had been wearing into a black kilt, sulked in the corner with one of his similarly attired friends.

I started running. The election! "Hey, good to see you. Please get out of the way," I said. I pushed my way through the crowd. Who were some of these people? It was surprising that I didn't recognize everyone. Maybe we really were gaining momentum.

Steve's office was a narrow storage room, with boxes and papers everywhere. No wonder he would only allow two people in there at a time; two felt like a crowd. A volunteer was there, fiddling with the laptop. "Let me see," I said. We had to hug each other to switch positions.

The King County Elections Commission web site was packed with data. Seattle City Council position number eight was near the bottom. Richard McIver was hovering at 50 percent. Grant was in second place at around 24 percent. The three other candidates split the rest.

I started writing numbers on the index cards. When we posted them a murmur of congratulations went up around the bar. We were going to survive the primary, and the incumbent was not demonstrating extraordinary support.

We watched the numbers change as the night went on. McIver's poll numbers started dropping—first to 48 percent, then to 45—and ours started to rise. We stuttered to 26, then up again to 27 percent. The other candidates' numbers didn't move.

Sometime before 11:30, Grant decided to give his primary-night speech. The band cleared the stage and the crowd quieted. Grant stood in front of his giant campaign banner.

"I want to thank everyone, especially now, during these terrible times. People have been telling me all week about how they want to give up, that politics doesn't mean anything anymore. I want to say exactly the opposite. I can't say enough how important it's actually become—"

Grant was eloquent and heartfelt; nonetheless, his speech filled me with anxiety. I looked around for an exit. Then I realized that it might look bad if the campaign manager walked out on the candidate during his speech. I chewed on my tongue instead.

"—so please enjoy yourselves tonight. And if you could remember to make a contribution, we have plenty of remit envelopes near the front. We also have a volunteer sign-up sheet. These last seven weeks are going to be the hardest."

A DJ—our DJ—took over. I turned toward the bar and concentrated on what I would be drinking next. Steve pulled me aside again, this time to give me a campaign contribution of two hundred dollars. It was turning out to be a pretty good night.

There was a commotion near the stage. The music had stopped, too. Grant was grabbing the microphone again.

"Hey, hey," he said, by way of getting everyone's attention. "Ladies and gentlemen, I wanted to apologize for the song that was just played. That was not at all appropriate given the current political climate. It was a mistake and it shouldn't have been played."

"What was the song?" I said. "I didn't even hear it."

" 'Killing an Arab,' " someone next to me said. By The Cure, apparently. "It was the DJ's opening song."

"God," I heard someone else say. "I wouldn't have even thought of that."

16

The year in which Marion Zioncheck was first sworn in to Congress was one of one of the most tumultuous, transformative moments in American history. The newly elected Roosevelt and the Democrat-controlled Congress began passing sweeping laws and creating ambitious programs to help lift America out of the Great Depression—programs like the Civilian Conservation Corps, the Public Works Administration, the Tennessee Valley Authority, the National Recovery Administration, and the Agricultural Adjustment Act. Social Security and Aid to Families with Dependent Children (the original 'welfare' bill), were still to come. Roosevelt's influence wouldn't be slowed until he tried to pack the Supreme Court in 1937.

Zioncheck thought FDR wasn't doing nearly enough. Millions were out of work, and the rich were fiercely resisting change. People were starving, and the only institution big enough to help was the government. At some point, he believed, things were going to come to a head.

Eleven weeks down, seven to go. Traffic moved along Twenty-third Avenue as if nothing was the matter. I knew because I kept a nervous watch from the front porch.

I had another hour before Grant woke up and started his day. My hands shook, and I felt skeletal, insubstantial. I got up and began walking to Fifteenth Avenue. A few times along the way I broke into a run.

On Fifteenth, I bought both daily papers, a plain bagel and a banana at the health food store, followed by a cup of black coffee at

Victrola. I turned a metal chair toward Grant's apartment building across the street. As I skimmed the papers I avoided the international and national news. There was very little about the Seattle city council campaigns, although there was a large photo on the metro page of Grant's blue-shirted volunteers at Westlake Mall. But for the most part the news was all about terrorism and Mariners baseball. Despite my efforts, one article caught my eye:

> . . . "People are panicked," said Alan Goldman, owner of Central Gun Exchange in downtown Seattle. "They watched what happened at the World Trade Center, and every pronouncement out of the government's mouth since then has been: 'War.' "
>
> Since the attacks, Goldman's sales have jumped about 30 percent—with one out of every six customers a first-time buyer. "They're buying a little bit of everything," from semiautomatic pistols to assault rifles, Goldman said . . .
>
> . . . . It's not unusual for the department to experience increased applications following high-profile crimes and during times of unrest, when people fear for their safety. That happened after the World Trade Organization protests in November 1999, Nordberg said . . . The current spike [however] appears more extreme.

I had once lived in a Memphis apartment building where two-thirds of the residents owned handguns. It was unsettling at first, but then I got tired of worrying about it. It was disturbing in an entirely different way to think about all the Seattle residents picking out their first firearms over an incident that had occurred 2,400 miles away. Who were these people—skittish soccer moms with new Berettas locked in the armoire? Or were they all like

Doug? Was there a small army of defiant misfits hiding with Glocks and .45s under the city's polite veneer?

I threw the papers down and ran home.

Back in my room, there were two messages on my voicemail. The first was a jubilant message from one of our ACLU-sponsored attorneys. The judge had ruled in our favor: Grant had won the right to criticize Richard McIver in the general election ballot pamphlet statement. The second message was from Grant. "The lawyers just called," he said. "We won the lawsuit and I'm being bombarded with media calls. This is really great, but we need to move fast. *Now.* We need to get a press release out, and let's see if we can have a press conference or photo op for our victory, and I want to be on KIRO radio first thing tomorrow morning, and—"

And so it begins again, I thought. Then I was diving, head first and with arms extended, for my candidate.

That evening, we huddled in a corner of Olympia Pizza & Spaghetti House. We had to avoid Victrola because too many people were interrupting us, coming up to Grant to congratulate him for surviving the primary. Plus we were broke. Grant was using campaign money to buy dinner, a perfectly legal tactic, since we were discussing campaign business, and Olympia Pizza was one of the only places that would take our campaign checks.

Grant slammed his notebook on the table and told me how he and Wayne, by then our volunteer coordinator, had managed to secure a second car for the campaign. They had been at Victrola, complaining about how they needed another automobile, when a young woman, a total stranger, approached them. She lived on Capitol Hill and never used her car—did they want to borrow it? Right there, on the spot, she gave Wayne the keys to her Honda.

"I couldn't believe it," Grant said. "I stood up and went like this." Arms wide, he mouthed a hallelujah in the pizzeria, just as he had done at the coffeehouse. Even at his most joyful, Grant didn't like to yell inside public places.

The story gave me a brief rush. We had won our lawsuit, gotten a second campaign car for a committed volunteer coordinator, and had made it to the big show, the November ballot. And Grant was in high spirits. It would be tough, he said, but we could win. McIver had not received an overwhelming majority. There was discontent—we just had to exploit it. We both had our notebooks out. Grant said, "Make sure you write this down. This is important," but he didn't need to say it.

Number One: Money. "We raised $20,000 before the primary," he said. "That was when we were just one of five candidates. Things get faster now. We need to raise—" his head was cocked to the side, the math churning in his head—"Forty thousand more. No. Fifty thousand. We can raise seventy or eighty thousand by the time this thing is over."

Eighty thousand dollars. It didn't even seem like real money, partly because I had never had that much myself.

"What about fund-raisers?" I asked.

"We need to have several," Grant said.

"I'll call Anne again—"

"Don't bother. I'll call her at this point."

"Jonathan Raban!" I said abruptly. "What if we got Jonathan Raban to read at one of our fund-raisers? Like a highbrow literary reading?"

"Now *that's* a good idea!"

"I know someone who can reach him for us. We could probably charge a lot of money."

"Great. Great."

Number Two: Message. "This is what I want," Grant said, his arms outstretched to take in the entire pizzeria, the whole of Seattle. "I've got it all figured out. I want to make new campaign signs. They have to be square. And they will only have three words on them." With a sweeping gesture, he motioned how these words would run, from top to bottom:

SAVE
THIS
PLACE

This sign, in our signature metro blue and white, would not include Grant's name, except for the obligatory—and tiny—"Paid for by Grant Cogswell for Seattle City Council" line that had to go on every single document, sign, and T-shirt that we printed.

There was something tremendously tantalizing about the idea. Such a sentiment encompassed the WTO protests, the terrorist attacks, and every federal, state, and local problem imaginable. On the other hand, I had no idea what he was talking about. *Save this place?* What did that mean? Surely he meant the same issues—transit, salmon, affordable housing—as before? Though I wanted to believe otherwise, no single person, no single campaign, could save everything. To even try was to invite madness. And why change our campaign strategy now? What was wrong with the monorail logo, which was excellent candidate branding? My stomach tightened. Were the terrorist attacks derailing Grant's sanity?

True to style, Grant did not ask me for my opinion. I was free to argue with him, or not. I wanted to argue but hesitated. Declarations like these by Grant were either utterly serious or only serious at that moment, as if he were momentarily in the grip of a fever. I had heard Grant make dozens of such eccentric vows in the past, all uttered with formidable gravity, only to see him move on without mentioning them or even remembering them again. I didn't yet have the ear to distinguish between the two.

"It sounds interesting," I said, measuring my words. "Let's discuss it at the next advisory committee meeting—"

"Fine. Put it on the agenda." He moved on.

Number Three: Volunteers. "We need to bring Wayne into these meetings," Grant said. "I want volunteers everywhere, all the time. I want to make sure that we've got people outside grocery stores passing out literature every weekend, in as many neighborhoods as we can get them to. I want people outside farmer's markets for however much longer those are still open. I want to keep sending volunteers to mayoral candidate forums. And I want more volunteers with us pretty much wherever we go."

"We'll have to sit down with Wayne," I agreed. How reassuring it was to be able to put an assignment on my list, and then cross it off a moment later.

The last point on the agenda was going to take the longest. That was *Number Four: Pamphlet Statement*. With the success of our free-speech lawsuit, we could now use the candidate statement to criticize our opponent. However, the submission deadline for a general-election pamphlet statement was only two days away; we had to write and edit our statement right away. Grant was convinced that, short of finding the money to run a barrage of television ads, the pamphlet statement was the best chance we had to reach voters.

We took out blank pieces of paper and wrote down ideas. The crux of a good pamphlet statement, I was learning, was not only the careful use of language, but also the strategic use of spacing, italics, and boldface. We had to obsess over every typographical trick. The Seattle Ethics and Elections Commission insisted on only a few things—no graphics other than the candidate's picture, a 400-word limit, and a strict use of size and font (Helvetica 10-point).

Grant's pamphlet statement for the primary election (before we won the lawsuit) opened like this:

Sound Transit has $2 billion.

You decide.

Should they build: a slow, expensive train, running on neighborhood streets, that will never be extended to Northgate?

OR

a quiet, cheap, safe and fast Monorail we can
afford to build now and easily expand to serve
the region?

Sound Transit is hopelessly over budget, but still
insists on spending billions on a system that will
get less than one out of every thousand cars out
of traffic. The funds to extend light rail to
Northgate are now postponed indefinitely:
"There is no Phase Two," staffer Paul Matsuoka
admitted recently . . .

. . . Seattle needs someone who will push for
effective public transit.

I have been an activist for the Monorail because
the issue of transit affects every corner of our
lives and the health of our city . . .

We had taken a risk, consuming 178 out of our assigned 400
words to establish Grant's major idea. That was a tactical decision.
With so many others competing against McIver, we had decided to
make Grant stand out by playing up his issue and playing down
his candidacy.

Now, with just two people left in the race, Grant would have
to emerge as a full-size candidate, a leader people could trust.
This was more than a tactical decision: It was an emotional one.
Ideas were supposed to come first, not personalities, but until
the election was over, we would have to accept that this wasn't
really true.

"We have to push the point immediately," I said. "We need to
think of this as an inverted pyramid, like a newspaper article.
The most important stuff goes first, then down the line." Since
we were the challengers, and since we had won our fight against

the city to criticize Richard McIver, we quickly knocked out an introduction:

> The incumbent, City Council Transportation
> Chair and Sound Transit board member Richard
> McIver, has presided over our traffic mess for
> the last five years while offering no solutions for
> this crisis.

We savored that paragraph for a moment. It felt good to name McIver. With very little back and forth we added:

> Our city desperately needs effective mass transit.
> Instead, regional forces want to widen SR 520
> and I-90 for cars, which will jam our city streets
> and fuel sprawl, making Seattle a less pleasant,
> less affordable place to raise our families.

Then we reminded voters that there was someone who could and should be held accountable for this crisis:

> Mr. McIver's Sound Transit light rail plans are
> $2 billion over budget, and their scaled-back
> alignment will not reach the U-District, North-
> gate, or SeaTac as promised and will not carry
> suburban riders within our lifetime.

And then we had to throw in Grant's standard arguments for why we needed mass transit instead of wider highways for automobiles:

> Good transit protects the environment, and pro-
> motes social justice, allowing working people
> and the poor, disabled, and elderly easy access to
> employment, housing, education, and culture.

"Of course," I said, "Nobody really wants to give up their automobile. Everybody loves mass transit. They just love it for other people." Grant acted as if I hadn't said this.

One hundred thirty-two words later, we had gotten to Grant's qualifications ("I co-authored the Monorail Initiative (I-41), creating the Elevated Transportation Company . . ."). It wasn't perfect, but it wasn't bad, either.

"It needs something to catch people's attention right away," Grant said. At the top of the evolving statement, he wrote, in a careful script, the letters thickened to indicate boldface:

Transportation is Seattle's #1 problem.

I noted how crazy people who wrote letters to reporters put everything in capitals, boldface, and underlined. Grant didn't find this comment funny. So I added, "So the general thrust is a throw-the-bum-out idea."

We looked past each other for a minute, lost in thought. I said, abruptly, "We gotta start thinking like those activist groups do when they send scare-the-bejeezus-out-of-you fund-raising letters. Somewhere in there we need to stress the real danger of letting our city go without a real transportation plan. We should use that line you mentioned once, the one about Seattle not becoming L.A.? Wasn't it, 'Do you want Seattle to become L.A.?' "

"No. I said, 'If we don't do something soon, Seattle will become like L.A., only with rain and trees.' " Grant said.

"Whatever, but that's too long. If we go with my way, we'll save a bunch of words. One, two—it's seven words versus sixteen. And we should rely on rhetoric here, not a declarative. Make people respond, 'Hell no, we're not L.A.! We're Seattle. There's no way we're going to allow more highways so we can become another L.A.' " Southern California was an easy target; I had heard many Seattleites talk about how they had "escaped" from it. L.A. evoked an instant, hellish image: Fifty-lane highways, smog, congestion, flashy people brainwashed by the ever present sun and the most recent blockbuster. We put that sentence in what was now the third paragraph.

We were 190 words in. We had given Grant's transit spiel, now what?

There were three ways we could go: We could attack McIver some more, we could declare additional positions for Grant, or we could present more information about Grant and his qualifications. Attacking McIver made sense, but the problem was that the incumbent was a lifeless target. No strong, deliberate attack on him, other than on his transportation record, was going to resonate with anyone.

So we decided to weave together the last two ideas, to promote Grant as we promoted his positions.

> **Affordable housing:** Skyrocketing housing prices and high property taxes are making it difficult for lifelong Seattleites to stay here. All the more reason the city needs to spend money wisely and work with the private sector, the federal government, and Community Development Corporations (CDCs) on creative solutions to house Seattleites at a price we can afford. For this reason, I worked to elect Judy Nicastro and Nick Licata, and also managed the county initiative campaign **against public funding of the stadiums.**

Populism. Fiscal responsibility with a class-conscious sensitivity. Then:

> As a journalist, I've covered issues of fair trade; I also worked on I-63 to protect salmon, and helped create Seattle's first on-the-street program to bring medical supplies, food and clothing to Seattle's **homeless youth.**

The "journalist" part was a bit of a stretch. Grant had written very few things for the *Stranger* that counted as journalism. But we couldn't call him a music and arts critic. Besides, that was four words against us, where "journalist" was just one.

> We must **preserve our public housing**. We
> need **independent police review** in order to be
> fair to cops and citizens.

"The police guild hates the idea of independent police review," I said. "With a fucking passion."

"I don't care about the police guild," Grant said. Fair enough, but it still felt like fence-straddling.

> If elected, I will demand social and fiscal
> responsibility in our city government. Seattle
> needs representatives who have a vision of what
> this city can and must be. I'm not trying to start
> a political career. I ask for your vote because I
> want to protect our diminishing quality of life,
> and to save this place we love.

I thought the line about Grant not wanting to be a career politician was going to sound disingenuous. And I was beginning to wonder if it was true. Grant liked the line and insisted that it was true, so it stayed in.

The last line was a standard reminder, in all caps:

GRANT COGSWELL FOR CITY COUNCIL

When we were done, Grant was convinced that we had the best possible ballot pamphlet statement we could have written. It felt all right to me, but it was demoralizing to think that people were choosing their candidates based on four hundred words. Why couldn't we talk more directly about the city's most difficult issues, like all the mentally ill homeless people, or the full extent of our public housing problems, or even the insidious consequences of gentrification?

I felt a wave of apathy. I couldn't care less if a bunch of middle- and upper-class Seattleites got stuck in traffic or killed off their native species of fish. Didn't I dream, in journalism school, of being a correspondent in the toughest parts of Latin America— Guatemala, Columbia, wherever the action was? Who could be obsessed about anything anymore? Didn't thousands of people just die in New York in a single day?

Grant broke my reverie.

"What's wrong?"

"What?"

"You're giving me that look like you want to say something," Grant said. "Is everything OK?"

"No," I said. "Wait—yes. It's nothing. It's—it's just hard to keep doing this day after day, without a break."

"Tell me about it," Grant said. "I'm not sleeping, my back hurts, and I'm getting as fat as a whale. I'm telling you, this shit is hard. When we're done with this, we're going to Mexico. We're going to do it the way Nick Licata did after he won in ninety-seven."

"Yeah," I said, without enthusiasm. That didn't really sound like a great idea anymore. "How are you keeping it together?"

"I'm not," he replied. "But I have to. If I don't keep going, I'm going to go mad."

Looking down at the table, I saw that Grant was holding his pen like a weapon. Politics was the one thing keeping him sane.

17

*For his first three years in office, Marion Zioncheck played by the
rules and was respected by his legislative colleagues for it. He
gained a coveted seat on the House Appropriations Committee, as
well as the House Naval Appropriations Subcommittee. After
handily winning reelection in 1934, he was assigned by House
Democratic leaders to fill the position of party objector. The
objector's job was to read and become familiar with every piece of
legislation coming before the House and to object to any proposal
that didn't conform to the party's platform. This was tedious
work, but it was pivotal, and for a political climber it was an
opportunity to rise within party ranks.*

*Transcripts from the Congressional Record of 1935 intimate
how seriously Zioncheck approached his job. There were quite a
few moments when the "radical" Zioncheck respectfully sub-
mitted to moderate senior colleagues, or interrupted a fellow radical who was making a point about social injustice, simply because
the point wasn't germane to the discussion at hand.*

*But Zioncheck was growing increasingly restless. He was a self-
styled dreamer and doer, not a bloodless bureaucrat and policy
wonk. Back in his apartment, with Hulet Wells looking on, the
congressman paced and gnashed his teeth.*

The next morning, Doug and Emily caught me as I was running
out of the house. "This is Merlin!" Doug gushed. "He's going to
live here. He's our new roommate." Emily was jubilant, too.

"That's great!" I said, taking in the young man who stood
behind them. Merlin, who told me that he was a Cornish College

theater student, was lean and buoyant. I guess I had skipped the house meeting when he had been invited to live with us. Or maybe Doug hadn't gotten around to telling me about it. "Welcome!" I added. "Sorry to say hi and run, but I really gotta get going."

I picked up the candidate and we drove across Capitol Hill to a sidewalk outside Union Station, where a crowd of protesters had gathered. Inside the building, the Sound Transit board—which included Richard McIver—was moments away from officially approving a fourteen-mile route for light rail.

The print reporters and television crews took no notice of our arrival, and it quickly became apparent that they weren't interested in quoting Grant. Nevertheless, Grant shouldered his way through the crowd and struck up a few conversations with the activists that he knew, while I hung back to listen to the recitation of facts and statistics that had been marshalled against Sound Transit's light rail plan. It was nearly two billion dollars over budget and it was going to divide the minority community of Rainier Valley in half. If that weren't enough, Sound Transit had to cut seven miles out of the route voters had approved several years before; it would not go all the way to the Seattle-Tacoma International Airport, as the agency had once promised. Commuters were expected to take a bus for the last mile.

But the protesters had no clout. The Sound Transit plan was approved twelve to four, with McIver voting with the majority.

"What happens now?" I asked, strapping on my seat belt. Sound Transit was not going to wait for our insurgent campaign to stop them. They were not going to wait for Grant to don his polar bear suit.

Grant looked past the windshield, jaw tight. "We can still stop it," he said. He did not say how. Grant's rhetoric about stopping Sound Transit wasn't going to change. And the campaign went on as if nothing had happened. It didn't seem to matter. From what I could tell, nobody was paying any attention.

We kept campaigning. And driving.

The post-primary world seemed to be mostly about wooing the smaller special interest groups. Organizations, many of which we had never heard of, barraged us with questionnaires and forum invitations, claiming to be able to influence anywhere from one hundred to two thousand voters. They included the King County Nurses Association, the anti–highway bridge expansion people, the SeaTac International Airport anti-noise activists, the Washington Parent-Teachers Association, the Friends of the Seattle-King County Library, the Friends of the Burke-Gilman Trail, various social service groups whose names never stuck in my head, the Black Women's Caucus, the anti–light rail people, and the King County Women's Political Caucus. We frequently lost these questionnaires, only to find them the day before their filing deadline.

The loudest activists in the local political scene were those involved in animal issues. Their forums were the best attended, their knowledge of the issues was the most commanding, and their emails were the most humorless. In a city boasting one of the highest pet ownership rates in the nation, this shouldn't have been as surprising as it was. People in Seattle may not be talented at socializing with humans, but they loved their animals.

At a meeting with Wayne and me at Victrola, Grant handed me an envelope. "Take care of this, will you?" he said.

I opened the envelope and pored over its contents. It was a statement from an organization calling itself "Seattle Pro-leash." Their statement was titled, "The Dog Problem What is to be done. 14 Point Program." The points included banning dogs from apartments, banning citizens from owning more than one dog, a five-hundred-dollar fine if a dog was discovered to be unlicensed, and a requirement that property-owning citizens must pass a written and performance test before being allowed to own a dog.

There was a check enclosed. It was signed by a woman named Ellen Taft. She had given Grant the maximum allowable donation of six hundred dollars.

"Oh my God," I said.

• • •

In the early 1990s, Ellen Taft was a Capitol Hill resident, fortyish and married to a successful computer software programmer. She considered herself a socialist and a bohemian, even though she would later support city ordinances that cracked down on the homeless. Taft wasn't politically active, but she was politically aware, and she believed in the power of the ordinary citizen to effect change in government.

One summer afternoon, Taft took her daughter to Volunteer Park, which was not far from her house. They went to the children's area, where Taft let her daughter splash around in the wading pool. Taft saw a man come up to the concrete edge of the pool with three large dogs at his side. To Taft's horror, the man took the dogs off their leashes; the dogs immediately lunged for her child near the center of the pool. As the dogs charged, Taft leaped, and reached her daughter first, but by no less than a jaw's length. She swept up the girl in her arms, away from the animals. Taft screamed at the dogs and their owner, but all four slunk away without apologizing. What's more, none of the other parents around the pool joined in her outrage. One man whispered to her, "God, don't you just hate dogs?" but that was all.

Some months later, Taft was jogging in the same park when she saw a different man unleash his dog. As she watched, another man tried to tell the first man to put the dog back on the leash, but instead the dog owner got so angry that she thought a fistfight would break out. Taft fled, doubly panicking as she remembered that dogs tended to chase after runners. Taft had been bitten by dogs before and had a scar to prove it.

Everywhere Taft went after those incidents she saw danger in Seattle's public spaces. She saw a man at a bus stop roughhousing with an unleashed pit bull; Taft worried for any child who might get in the way. She went to a local beach and saw dog excrement in the sand—wasn't that some sort of health hazard? Why wasn't anybody picking it up?

She did some research and came across a number of academic articles about zoonoses, diseases shared by humans and animals. Rabies was an obvious, nasty one, but there were others, like toxicariasis, which is caused by the roundworm toxacara, which could leave 15,000 eggs in a single gram of puppy poop, and could cause all kinds of horrific problems if ingested by a toddler. Leptospira was another feces-dwelling threat—a spiral-shaped, contagious microorganism, that could cause bleeding, jaundice, and severe respiratory problems.

More research, this time on city ordinances: Only a fraction of the people in the city licensed their dogs, and almost nobody obeyed the city's leash laws, which were never enforced.

Taft no longer felt safe outside, for herself or for her daughter. Since no one else was doing anything, she knew the responsibility fell to her.

She attended parks department hearings, and began speaking at them during the public comment period. She listed the problems that she wanted addressed immediately, like prohibiting dogs and other pets from playground areas and children's wading pools and enforcing the city's leash law. With her outspoken style, Taft found herself embroiled in an ugly fight. Dog lovers were beginning to organize, and they were willing to go to great lengths to attack their enemies. Her name and phone number became public knowledge, and she became a frequent target for threatening and prank phone calls, hate letters, and false magazine subscriptions. She found loose dog poop in her front yard almost every day. Some people suggested that she move out of town. The experience was embittering.

It took seven years for Taft to lose patience with the system and with the people who heckled her. When she got up to speak in 1998, she asked—again—why there were no signs in the city parks prohibiting dogs from children's playgrounds. But, before letting the question fall into the bureaucratic vacuum, Taft pulled out her checkbook. "How much does it cost?" she asked. "I'll pay for it myself." To her satisfaction, this tactic worked; the department was embarrassed and the signs were installed.

It was a victory, but there were still the problems of feces and unleashed dogs. And a battle was brewing between dog lovers and everyone else. The *Seattle Press,* a community newspaper, wrote an exposé on the rising tensions in the city parks, describing illegal gatherings known as "puppy clubs" or "pooch packs." Dozens of dog owners were meeting at secret locations, forming loose social networks, and letting their dogs roam free. the *Press* noted that dog owners were routinely breaking city code, "with a latté in one hand and an [unused] leash in the other." Many of these people openly bragged that they knew what the law said but didn't give a damn.

City officials proposed a compromise: the off-leash area. A section of a park would be cordoned off with a fence, and people could let their dogs run around in it without a leash. The rest of the areas in the parks would remain mandatory leash areas, under penalty of a fine. It sounded great to a lot of people, but Taft was appalled. The city already had good laws governing dogs in parks—if those were just enforced, without compromise, everything would be fine.

Taft filed suit against the city to shut down the off-leash area in Volunteer Park—*her* park. She hired an arborist to study the health effects of dog urine on trees, and she hired private detectives to take pictures of people cavorting outside the off-leash area with their unleashed pets. She had aerial photos taken. In all, she paid $30,000 in legal and other fees. In October of 2000, a judge in the King County Superior Court ordered the off-leash area be taken down. The court order was only a temporary injunction, but it was enough. The city conceded, and victory was Taft's.

Aware of how her activities had made her unpopular with her neighbors, Taft found one last use for her private detective. She got him to install a surveillance camera on the front of her house. Taft made it well-known throughout the area that if any dogs were allowed to relieve themselves on her lawn, she would know exactly who was responsible. Then she withdrew from public life.

Grant Cogswell was the only city council candidate to whom Ellen Taft sent a campaign contribution check that election season. She gave him the money because she agreed with his ideas on mass transit.

"Listen," Grant said. "I don't have time to deal with this. Will you call the woman who sent us this check and thank her for me?"

I groaned, but agreed. There was only one thing comforting about the letter—it wasn't filled with the boldfaced, capitalized letters of the demonstrably insane.

The next morning, I sat in my living room, with the TV muted and the phone at my side. I dialed Ellen Taft, praying that I would get an answering machine. I could leave a perfunctory message— *Hi thanks for your contribution please feel free to call the campaign if you need anything from me, click*—that sort of thing.

A man answered. Why, yes, she was home. Hold on.

I lost my nerve when she picked up. "Hi, this is, um," I said, "I'm Grant Cogswell's campaign manager. I'm calling about your contribution—Uh-hm, thank you."

"I want fifteen minutes with him," she said.

"Uh. OK. Well," I said. "Yes. I think that can be arranged. Let's see now—" I pretended to be flipping through Grant's campaign schedule, which I didn't have.

Taft asked, "Do you have any city councilmembers supporting your campaign?"

"Well, Nick Licata is on our side, quietly, I guess, and—"

"None of them are good for anything," she interrupted, "except for Heidi." That would be Heidi Wills, whose first move in office was to pick a losing fight over the prohibition of circus animals within Seattle city limits.

"Well," I said. "We can put you down for 10:30 A.M. this coming Thursday, but I may have to call you back."

I called Grant to tell him what had happened. His reaction was, "Oh, wonderful."

"Don't worry about it," I said. "I'll let it go for fifteen minutes and no more, and then call you on your cell phone with an urgent message. You can break away from her gracefully."

Grant said, "Did you see that email exchange I had with Joe Haptas?"

"No."

"I sent it before I left the house. He's from NARN." The acronym was meaningless to me, but I found the email waiting for me when I went upstairs and turned on my computer; NARN meant National Animal Rights Network.

The animal rights group had pressed Grant on whether he would re-introduce a vote on a circus animal ban. Grant had answered succinctly: He was not interested in being the leader on such an issue. A flurry of emails followed, and Grant finally replied: "Whoa. Please reread my response more carefully. I believe you asked me to take the lead on it. I said no . . . I WILL support it IF SOMEONE ELSE INTRODUCES IT, THEY HAVE THE VOTES, AND IF I DON'T HAVE TO TRADE MY PRIORITIES FOR IT." Pleased with this all-capped answer, the NARN spokesman counted this as a victory for circus animals, and endorsed Grant, which helped us pick up a couple new volunteers.

I immediately forwarded copies of the entire exchange and the subsequent endorsement to the media. *See how blunt my candidate is? That's one rare honest politician.* George Howland of the *Weekly* was the only one kind enough to email me back. "Hey Phil . . . I don't know what I wrote that makes you think that I think you guys are not running an honorable campaign. I think you guys have run the best challenge to an incumbent this year. I think you have the best chance of pulling off an upset, but I still think it would be an upset. Good luck!"

I felt an exhilarated surge. George Howland of the *Weekly* was a really terrific guy.

I headed to the bathroom; it was noon and I still hadn't found time to shower. I found myself standing in front of Doug, who was changing the water in his baby piranha tank. My hands were balled up in fists.

"Sorry," he said. "Do you want to use the bathroom?"

"If that's OK with you," I said.

"Sure, go ahead. I just finished."

"Thanks," I said. "Aren't you done with that? Changing the water in the tank, I mean?" I was beginning to wonder how much this was affecting our water bills.

"Not yet. They'll be old enough pretty soon."

"Oh."

"Uh . . . ?"

"Yes?" I said.

"Did you have to tell everyone in the house about—" he trailed off. He didn't want to finish his sentence.

"About what?" I did want him to finish his sentence.

"—about my toy?"

"Your *gun*?"

"Well, yeah."

"Doug, everyone has a right to know that there's a gun in the house."

"Yeah, but," he hesitated, suddenly inarticulate. "It's no big deal."

"I had to tell everyone. Sorry."

In the shower and on the drive over to Victrola, one thought occupied my mind. He called his 9-mm semiautomatic a *toy*. And I could still hear him tinkering with this "toy" whenever he was home.

"Are you OK?" Grant asked when I reached the coffeehouse.

"No," I said. "I'm not. West Seattle, right? I'm relying on you to get us there."

"Take the West Seattle Bridge and I'll direct you from there to the Admiral Benbow. God, what is the *matter* with your car?"

I was beginning to smell it too—a pungent confection of human sweat, used coffee cups, carboard signs, and leaking oil. It didn't bother me that much. "Sorry," I said mechanically, "I don't have the time to clean it out."

We were heading to an event put on by Charlie Chong, a one-time ally of Grant's. Several years before, Chong had been a fire-brand populist who got elected to city council by opposing giant spending projects like the Mariners and Seahawks sports stadiums. Once in office, he made city hall more accessible to its citizens, responding swiftly to constituent complaints and insisting that official meetings were always made public. But Chong let his ego overtake his idealism, and he gave up his council seat to make a quixotic bid for the mayor's office in 1997. He was defeated in a landslide, and his mainstream appeal evaporated. He stayed active mostly by hosting monthly political dinners with his remaining loyalists, some of the only genuine conservatives in Seattle. We were hoping Chong's endorsement would appeal to this disaffected bunch; his support might be worth several hundred votes.

"McIver's not going to be here, is he?" I said. We were seeing the incumbent two or three times a week now, at various forums.

"No. Charlie's endorsed me, and this event's only for me. The Admiral Benbow—this is it," Grant said. I parked the car.

The bar had the interior design of a pirate ship about to break in half. A wooden floor, steering wheels and brass fixtures in strange locations, and odd, shiplike curves jutting out of the walls. A handful of salty old customers lined the tired bar. Charlie Chong was waiting for us at the edge of the Benbow's banquet room.

I looked around the dim room. Everyone was over forty and had faces creased with distrust. Grant seemed confident, though; he had dusted off an old "I'm with Charlie" button to prove his credentials. Rather than mentioning social justice, he planned on focusing on how much Sound Transit's light rail was costing taxpayers.

Dinner first. I sat next to Midge Batt, a neighborhood activist with a crisp sense of outrage. She told me that she and many of her colleagues were willing to listen to Grant because they despised

Richard McIver. The year before, McIver had had the gall to laugh as he cast a vote against her group's agenda for a subsidized parking lot. I faked a look of horror as best as I could and told Midge that Grant treated every citizen's views with the respect they deserved.

Chong got up to speak, and soon Grant took the floor and delivered a slightly edited stump speech in the bar's stale air. His posture was straight and his voice was polished and pitch perfect. Grant asked if there were any questions and I began to daydream about crawling back into bed.

A heavyset old man wearing an abnormally thick coat for the late summer weather raised his hand. As he stood up, he convulsed with disgust.

"There is one thing you said that makes me not want to vote for you already," the man said, by way of introduction, "and that is that you say that you are an environmentalist!" Using shouting techniques usually heard on cable talk shows, he launched into an extended tirade about liberals, especially environmentalists. Grant made a few diplomatic but firm interjections—"No, it doesn't" and "That's not what I said"—but he was swept away by the citizen's blitzkrieg attack.

The man stomped his foot, turned on his heel and stormed out of the room. As he swept past Chong, who was guarding the door, he pretended to spit.

"C'mon, Helen!" the old man said. "I'll be waiting in the car!"

Then he was gone.

Few could hear Grant over their own confused murmurs, but he tried to regain control with a nervous chuckle. "Well," he said, "It looks like our civil discourse has broken down." His hand was trembling; I could see tiny eddies in the glass of water he was holding.

No one spoke for a moment, but then a man near the front tried to defuse the tension. "He was out of line," he said, "But you've gotta understand that he's got some legitimate complaints."

"Yeah," piped in another. " 'Environmentalist' is a real yellow-flag word around here. Saying that is taking a real risk. I mean, you may as well be a Muslim on your way to a mosque in this day and age than be an environmentalist." This was said with utter seriousness.

Just as the room started to calm down and as other, more politely stated questions were being, the old man with the coat returned, barreling past Chong until he was in the middle of the room.

"Helen, will you come on!" he bellowed.

All eyes swiveled away now toward Helen, a diminutive woman sitting next to her husband's empty chair.

Helen didn't move. "But I have a question," she protested weakly.

The man exploded again. "I'm not going to sit here anymore and listen to this asshole!" he said. "I'm not going to put up with this bullshit anymore. I'll be outside!" And once again he stormed out. Grant called on Helen, who asked a fairly technical question about Sound Transit's light-rail plan, and Grant answered with a fairly technical answer. Helen then gathered her purse and left, stopping only to say a few words to Charlie Chong on her way out.

"Do you realize," one man asked, "that you're not going to get everything you want out of city hall? Charlie didn't, when he was there."

"I know that," Grant said, relieved that the question wasn't about environmentalism, "but that's why politicians compromise. I'm willing to trade to get the things I want." He hadn't told me he was going to say this. I wondered what, exactly, Grant was thinking about compromising. What had happened to "Save This Place"?

Later, everyone apologized for the man, explaining that he had recently had stomach surgery. Almost everyone I spoke with afterward said they appreciated Grant's honesty and added that they would vote for him, but no one promised to do anything more for us.

And so the campaign trundled on. We were picking up votes here and there, but each step forward was a battle that left scars. And the election, still five weeks away, seemed slippery and unreal, like a fish that's just out of reach of a hungry bear's paw.

INTERLUDE: The Tragedy of Marion Anthony Zioncheck

When they write about him at all, Seattle historians place the onset of Marion Zioncheck's downfall on New Year's Day in 1936, when he was arrested for the first time. I'd argue that his end actually began some months earlier, when he fought his last major political battle. Abruptly spurning the cautious pragmatism that had gained him respect in Congress, Zioncheck banded together with twenty-three other insurgent House legislators to form a radical voting bloc. This group produced its own sixteen-point economic plan for America that called for vast new amounts of money for education and drastically higher taxes on wealthier Americans. Zioncheck and his colleagues tried pushing parts of their plan to the House floor, but it proved too extreme for the FDR Democrats, and it was crushed just before the end of the 1935 legislative session, by a vote of 310–38.

As 1935 drew to a close, Hulet Wells saw Zioncheck pacing the apartment, grinding his teeth and making cryptic midnight phone calls to his mother in Seattle. Then things got strange.

In the early morning hours of New Year's Day, Zioncheck was drunk and looking for some friends in a hotel. Not finding them, he woke up everyone in the building by throwing the operator's switchboard open and wishing all the guests a Happy New Year. He spent a few hours in jail and was fined for drunk and disorderly conduct and for disturbing the peace.

Zioncheck started seeking out trouble. The Associated Press reported that he was caught driving a brand new roadster at seventy miles an hour. Police only caught him when he had to slow down for a truck. Taken back to the station, he blew cigar smoke in the booking officer's face. Zioncheck refused to show up for his court date, so the judge ordered him physically dragged to court if necessary (it was). Zioncheck was under the impression that as a U.S. Congressman he was immune from prosecution.

Zioncheck also grew belligerent on the House floor, breaking countless unspoken rules about how congressmen should conduct themselves among their peers. He called members of the Supreme Court "old fossils" and proposed a resolution to cut Postmaster General Farley's salary down to a dollar a year. He argued bitterly that congressmen should be above the law, and that they deserved better parking privileges. Moreover, he grew derisive of standard parliamentary procedure, and his undiplomatic comments toward one colleague nearly caused a fistfight. Tom Blanton, a physically impressive anticommunist from Texas, jumped out of his chair and exchanged heated words with Zioncheck. Other politicians and House staffers had to hold the two men apart to keep them from killing each other.

Around this time a D.C. secretary named Rubye Nix called Zioncheck on the telephone. She thought his antics were funny and wanted to meet him. After they had dated only a few times, Zioncheck proposed to her. She agreed. "She asked me down and so I went down and looked her over," Zioncheck told reporters, a score of whom were by now following his every move with a jocular sort of awe. "She was OK." Whatever had gotten into Zioncheck, the media was clearly enjoying it. He was good copy. His fellow legislators in the House gave him and his new bride a standing ovation. Rubye promised people that she would tame his wilder instincts, but she was just a kid from Texarkana and had no idea what she was in for.

On their honeymoon Zioncheck got speeding tickets in Virginia and North Carolina. In Puerto Rico, he crashed a borrowed car, and avoided prosecution by asserting his status as a congressman. He got drunk with a local fisherman whose services he had hired;

he broke through an iron gate with a second automobile, provoking the gate's owner to wave a pistol in the air and challenge him to a duel; he tried to return his inebriated new fisherman friend to the wrong house; he threw coconut shells out of his hotel window; and he telephoned the U.S. Naval radio station to send the Marines to come protect him.

"He went next to the Virgin Islands," Murray Morgan wrote, "where he was noticed lapping soup from his plate at a swank hotel and biting the neck of the chauffeur assigned to pilot his car." Hulet Wells (who by this time had left Zioncheck to work elsewhere in the government) refused to believe the part about the chauffeur, believing that the press was now taking certain liberties with his boss's growing legend, but he was helpless to make Zioncheck behave.

As his antics continued, the press attention grew. From January to July of 1936 his activities made their way from the back to the middle of the newspaper, and finally to the front page. The *New York Times* alone wrote dozens of articles about him. He was also covered by *Time, Newsweek, Collier's*, the wire services, and of course by his hometown papers. Some, like William Randolph Hearst's papers, treated him with contempt, others, like the *Times*, seemed to want him to be even more daring and original. "In his recent efforts there is a forced note," said an unsigned article that remarked on the "playboy Congressman's" adventures in New York City, where he drank and danced all night in the clubs before jumping into a Rockefeller Center fountain. "The first fine frenzy which thrilled a continent has spent itself."

Wells was as confounded as everyone else by Zioncheck's behavior. Struggling to find a rationale for it, he sought explanation in the young fields of psychology and psychiatry: "His lapses were caused by the onset of mental aberration, though it had not yet reached what the psychiatrists call the 'manic-depressive' stage. Until the climax he lived a kind of Jekyll-and-Hyde existence. Most of the time he was an earnest, hard working legislator, devoted to his ideal of improving the economic system and promoting the welfare of those who suffered from unemployment and needless poverty. Then quite suddenly there would come an amazing change in his personality."

People didn't start to worry about Zioncheck and his wife until the couple returned to Washington, D.C. from their honeymoon. Zioncheck got into a fight with his landlady, who was trying to evict him. The papers ran a photo of a violent, enraged man physically dragging a woman through the door of his apartment. Zioncheck, the landlady claimed, broke her hip. Reporters were also there when Rubye walked out on Zioncheck; naturally, she had no idea what to think.

Around this time Wells tried to step in; he arranged to have a doctor talk, casually, to Zioncheck. "The doctor's opinion was instant and positive," Wells later wrote, " 'His mind has given way,' [the doctor] said. 'There is no doubt about it, but there is nothing we can do just yet.' "

"It was now only a question of time," Wells continued, "until his sanity was questioned. This happened on the first of June, after his wife had left him. He had driven his roadster over sidewalks and through traffic lights to leave a present at the White House for President Roosevelt. The present consisted of empty beer bottles and a box of ping pong balls. He was taken to Gallinger Hospital for mental observation." Reporters got their fill of that story, too: pictures of Zioncheck in a straitjacket, claiming that he was being kidnapped; an article about how he briefly escaped doctors to give the media one more screwball interview; a heartfelt promise from Rubye that she would stand by him.

After a few days of observation, Zioncheck was declared insane. He was transferred to a sanitarium in Maryland, but he escaped by climbing a seven-and-a-half-foot wire fence and outrunning asylum staff. He made his way back to Washington, D.C. a penniless fugitive. He went straight to his office, where he locked himself in and drew his shades down. The House sergeant at arms, a friend of Zioncheck's, kept police at bay and worked out a deal in which Zioncheck could return unmolested to Seattle. Rubye came home with him.

He claimed that he was a victim of persecution, that he had been "shanghaied" into the sanitarium, but people back in Seattle, normally so forgiving of their eccentric politicians, didn't know what to think. Many blamed his enemies for exaggerating his escapades, but many more were ready to throw him out of office, embarrassed that the only attention their city got was through the antics of a clowning congressman. More than a dozen people filed for his House seat in August of 1936, and the Washington Commonwealth Federation, once his staunchest supporter, withdrew its endorsement. The congressman reacted erratically to this news: He first said he was going to withdraw from politics but then changed his mind and filed to run for reelection.

On August 8, Zioncheck went downtown with his wife and his brother-in-law to his office in the Arctic Building. He went upstairs to "get some papers." After a few minutes, Rubye grew worried, and got her brother William Nadeau to go upstairs to find out what he was doing. The office was on the fifth floor, and Nadeau found Zioncheck's office door locked. He had to get a janitor to open it for him. He found Zioncheck at his desk, scribbling frantically on a loose piece of office stationary. He told Zioncheck to hurry up, that they were waiting for him.

A few moments later, Zioncheck was making a wild dash toward an open window. Nadeau tried to catch him but couldn't. Zioncheck jumped through, plunging to the ground below, his body turning like a stick. He landed head first in front of his wife, who was sitting in their car, and died instantly.

The paper that Zioncheck had been writing was his suicide note. It was unfinished and bordered on the incoherent. "My only hope in life," he had written, "was to improve the condition of an

unfair economic system that held no promise to those that all the
wealth of a decent chance to survive let alone live."

The mostly forgotten legend of Marion Zioncheck is the uncomfortable, darker side of the American dream. He was the Mr. Smith
who went to Washington and failed, the young European immi-
grant and early twentieth-century Everyman who couldn't grasp
(or refused to believe) Horatio Alger's credo that one lived in
America simply to make an enormous pile of money for oneself.
He was seized with the foolish idea that altruism could be combined with ambition to change society for the better. His sincerity,
his utopianism, and his narcissistic frustrations ran too deep to
contemplate. And when he was finally destroyed, it was through
an act of violent self-negation, an embarrassing implosion that left
his enemies still standing. It's a powerful, discouraging lesson for
anyone who believes that the individual can still make a difference
in the world.

Grant Cogswell discovered Zioncheck as most people in Seattle
do, through the tantalizing, brief profile of him in Murray
Morgan's garrulous *Skid Road*. Grant was captivated by what he
saw as Zioncheck's romantic, divine madness, and he did a little
more digging. He discovered that Morgan had skimped on a
number of details, especially relating to Zioncheck's suicide note.
Morgan had edited it to make grammatical and logical sense;
Grant preferred it exactly as it had been written, straddling the
realms of idealism and lunacy.

The allure of Zioncheck consumed Grant, who set out to immor-
talize him. When he was finished, he had written a poem that ran
404 lines in all, an epic address to an unknown martyr:

Every day some nobody
becomes somebody else's Christ.
You are mine now, Congressman:
I have looked for you long afternoons

at the doorways of supermarkets
and in the cold bleach-scented halls
of the Seventh Circuit Court of Appeals
and some years back, on far-flung nights

in front of motel cable TV,
in Texarkana, before I knew
your wife was living someplace there.
We fight in hallways, in kitchens, in bed,

draw blood on beaches that spent all night
washing out the detritus of play:

Grant, who in 2001 was a few years shy of Zioncheck's age when he
died, used historical facts, regional landscape imagery, and personal
stories to influence his poem. Grant's Zioncheck was a man who, in
life, understood the world all too well; in death he is a ghost who
still cries out for social and economic reform. Grant delivered the
Zioncheck poem at a local bar on what would have been the congressman's 100th birthday (Grant believes he was born in
December of 1900, though some say 1901). He gave out black T-
shirts to his friends; on the front was a reprint of Zioncheck's suicide note; and on the back was the date and location of the reading.
    Grant roared:

Marion Zioncheck for President of Death!
is my new campaign: your plea
wins just one vote in this house, my own
I take you myself like a first love
your nails thick in moss and mud;
Marion Zioncheck for President of Death!

It was quite an extravaganza. A blond high school cheerleader
warmed up the crowd, and two rock bands followed his reading.

Grant never made it a secret that he wanted to resurrect Zioncheck, so that a new generation of activists could have a spiritual father. The incredible, awful thing is that, barely halfway through our campaign, I became convinced that somehow we had done just that.

18

Victrola was nearly empty. Grant and I were in a far corner of the café. An alternative rock band I couldn't identify was playing on a stereo in the background. I was making a half-hearted attempt to cheer up my candidate.

"So what did Ellen Taft want? For you to launch a crusade against dog owners? To send beagles to the King County Jail? Did you tell her about the time you owned a pug and you attacked my car with its poop in a plastic bag? That scared the hell out of me, by the way, but it *was* funny."

I had apologized, too. Because I had lost track of time and not phoned Grant until his meeting with Ellen Taft had run thirty-five minutes, instead of fifteen.

"I have to learn to control my temper," Grant said in a low voice. "Tara threatened to leave me if I didn't."

The day before, he had been in such a rage over the campaign that he had almost thrown a chair across the room. He didn't, but only because Tara was nearby and her expression stopped him. Instead, he had walked into the closet and thrashed at something she couldn't see. It turned out to be an old laptop computer; Grant destroyed it.

Tara had added up the emotional toll that the campaign was taking on Grant, on her, and on their relationship, and she was horrified. The sleepless nights over fund-raising. The transformation of his personality from sensitive to maniacal. The constant anger—she couldn't forget how Grant had dented my car. And now this, another explosion. She had said, "Enough," and had started gathering some of her things together, telling Grant that she had gone through crap like this before, with other men, and didn't want to go through it again. She wanted her old boyfriend back, the one who wrote poetry and spent time with her and who wasn't killing himself trying to take on the whole world at once.

I knew this was a moment when I was supposed to be supportive, and I tried to feign sympathy. It wasn't easy. Sixteen hours a day without a break had used me up. Grant was on his own now. I just didn't have the guts to say so to his face.

"So," I said, "What are you going to do?"

"I've got to control my temper," he said. "That's it. I've got to learn to relax if I'm going to keep doing politics."

"I came up with an idea for that guerrilla art I was telling you about," I said, scrounging for a change of subject.

"Oh yeah?"

I had befriended an employee from the *Seattle Weekly,* a friend of my girlfriend's. Together we had conceived, under the influence of alcohol, a funny but harmless prank on George Howland, the *Weekly's* likable news editor. This employee would take about twenty-five or thirty Grant Cogswell posters and plaster George Howland's office with them. Howland, who had repeatedly said that we were incapable of winning in November, would have to admit that we would stop at nothing to beat our incumbent opponent.

"Funny," Grant said. I wasn't sure if he had really heard me.

Grant asked me what I was doing with the rest of my day. I reminded him of our plan. We had a list of names and addresses of Seattle voters who favored monorail, and with the right kind of campaign literature, we could create a targeted campaign mailing that would rival the best-funded candidates in the city. "The only thing missing from the plan," I said, getting some of my old energy back, "are some volunteers to do our data entry work for us, but I think I have the answer—high school students."

"Hmmmn."

"The Northwest School requires its seniors to work on a

political campaign of their choice. I got ten students drawn to you, Grant Cogswell, the young, hip candidate. I'm meeting them tonight."

"Great, great," he said. "Young, hip."

I left Grant to pick up Evan, our musician friend who had been so inspired by Grant's words after 9/11 that he had volunteered for the campaign. We drove to a historical archive in suburban Bellevue, where we sifted around in some old files until we found a photo of the monorail on the day of its 1962 unveiling. We scanned this into Evan's laptop. Later, Evan manipulated the image, erecting a scaffolding behind the monorail and placing Grant's name on it. When the image was touched up and given a uniform sepia tone, it looked like a genuine piece of photographic history. Anybody driving down Fifth Avenue thirty-nine years ago would have seen both the monorail and a neon sign for Grant Cogswell, glowing like an electronic billboard for a posh hotel.

The students were the next part of the equation. Wayne, our volunteer coordinator, and Hal Colombo, our ex-volunteer coordinator, agreed to help me organize them. "Meet me at my house," I told Hal. "Seven-thirty." I devoted the rest of the daylight hours to working on press releases, sending email, and doing some anti-McIver research.

It was going to be a long night. After stopping at the grocery store for chips and soda for the students, I tried to rest on the porch. The horizon before me stretched into the other side of the world and the sun stumbled like a man failing a sobriety test. The cars along Twenty-third Avenue turned their lights on, one by one. Hal disrupted the moody silence by showing up early and cracking jokes about how he couldn't believe that he had been entrusted to work with private school girls. I offered him a beer, but he cheerfully declined. I helped myself to one anyway.

Our youngest volunteers arrived half an hour late; the student leading the caravan had gotten lost. Piling out of their cars, they talked to themselves in the blithe way that teenagers talk. I invited them inside. I probably should have put my beer away at that point, to set a better example, but I didn't. In fact I got another one. I was getting a little tired of worrying whether absolutely everything I did reflected poorly on Grant.

I ran the meeting like a focus group at first, quizzing the students on everything they knew about the campaign. The bulk of their opinions had been formed by the *Stranger,* which meant that to them Grant was a hipster folk hero, the very essence of romantic idealism. They drank all the caffeinated beverages and polished off two bags of chips. I didn't want to be cruel, giving them only data entry work, so I assigned them a mixture of data entry and yard sign construction. I also got some of them to pass out flyers outside grocery stores.

Doug and someone else, I couldn't tell who, were in the kitchen cooking dinner. I thought I could hear Doug talking, but I was too caught up in the meeting to listen or even care. An hour and a half later, the students left, as loud and as carefree as they had been when they had first entered, maybe even louder.

It was dark outside, though the air was warm. I threw my empty beer bottles in the recycling bin outside. They landed at a bad angle on a high mountain of glass and fell with a clatter on the porch. The recycling container was so full of Doug's empty bottles that there was no room for mine.

After saying goodnight to Hal I locked up the house for the night. There were about eight things to do on my list before I fell asleep. But when I reached the top of the stairs, I stopped. There was a note taped to my bedroom door. It was from Doug. Each letter looked like a knife slash.

> Phil.
>   I believe you should put your management
> duties to work. I.E. The garbage Emily has
> behind her room. The garbage under the sink,

kitchen. Lawn duties: Put someone on the list,
me, I don't care. The living room: What are we
going to do with the extra couch? Basement is
disaster please fix I will help. Bathroom upstairs
tub needs Draino., I believe—should fix it.
Emily's cable needs work maybe. You could
help, Also we should get all the housemate's shit
out of our neighbor Joan's garage. She keeps getting on my case thinking I manage the house.
YOU should manage the house

Thanks
Doug

The self-appointed populist had given me an ultimatum. I must
have set him off by taking over the living room so casually.

He was standing in the stairwell, watching me. I saw that mad
grin that preceded his ridiculous laugh. Was he drunk already? He
had to be. And he obviously thought he had me.

Fuck him.

I ran into my room. Doug, surprised, yelled after me. I slammed
my bedroom door and ran into my sunroom/office. Doug didn't
give chase, but he didn't have to. Instead, he ran through his room
and into his sunroom. Throwing wide his sunroom window, he
looked out and over into mine. He wouldn't stop yelling. I told
him to wait a fucking minute.

Doug's disembodied head appeared from the other side of the
sunroom. He looked dangerously close to falling. Now that was a
nice image. My problems would disappear. I'd be back in control
of the house and wouldn't feel obliged to attend the funeral.

But he didn't fall, and he wouldn't stop yelling.

"Just a minute!" I screamed.

I looked at Doug's list and counted. Eight items. I opened up a
document in my word processor and started typing. I bulleted

eight points, one for each complaint. I shouted back at him demanding patience. When I was done I printed out a copy:

Doug,

I'm too busy to get into a long-winded discussion with you about house management stuff. The note is helpful because I have a list of things to address. I will address everything, point-by-point.

• *The garbage under the kitchen and sink will make a fine chore if you want to clean it out and put your name on the chore list (I don't think I've seen it up yet).*
• *I told you some time ago that I was not going to mow the lawn again this season due to my allergies. You said at that time that you would mow it . . .*

And so on. Writing and editing press releases and letters to the editor had definitely sharpened my memo writing skills.

The old printer grumbled, then shot out two copies.

The phone rang. It was Wayne. "Is this a good time?"

"I want to talk to you!" Doug again.

I realized that my list of the high school kids was downstairs, and that I would need that list to talk to Wayne. I asked him to hold on.

I threw the door open and ran downstairs, hurling the memo at Doug's head as I passed him. I talked to Wayne, firing off a staccato list of instructions. By the time I was back in my room we had hung up on each other.

Doug rushed in after me.

I dashed into my sunroom and sat down at my chair. Doug burst through the French doors and stood, seething. He had me cornered. It had never occurred to me to lock the door to my room. I had never needed to.

Doug hadn't read my note. He did so now. Then he crumpled it up in his fist.

"No!" he said.

"What?"

"What is this, this *bullshit?*" Doug threw the paper to the ground. It joined several other crumpled up pieces of paper that were already on the floor. "Do you expect me to just read this thing and be happy and go away?" He let the question hang in the air. We both fumed. I wondered if Doug had been rehearsing in his mind how he wanted this conversation to go.

"You get this huge rent discount, and what do you do for it? You stick up a chore list on the refrigerator, you put a cleaning rotation list on the bathroom wall every once in a while, and you look after the bills, but that's it!"

"First of all—"

"C'mon! This house could be so much better than it is, but you're not doing anything. The yard, the basement—no one's going to do any work around here if you don't take charge. So take charge! This house is a place we all could be proud of, but it's going to shit!"

My hands twitched uncontrollably.

"Do you know what this campaign means for me?" I said. "I'm trying to get a job here! I don't know if you realized this or not, but I'm unemployed!"

Doug talked over me, "—When you first got this position, I thought you were doing a great job. So tell me, what happened? Can you just answer me that? What happened?"

"If you don't like it here, why don't you move out?" I said.

"No," he said, ready this time. "Why don't *you* move out?"

"I don't have to!"

"Neither do I!"

Stalemate. Doug was angry and drunk, and I was angry and trapped. Hovering above me as he was, I was also exceptionally nervous. My housemate had never seemed this big before.

"We both know that you can't do your job here if you're on the campaign. I can do a better job than you can. So let me."

"Fine, Doug. Fine! You want to be the house manager this month, go ahead."

"Really?" Doug said.

"Yes. Yes! OK! I'll tell the landlady that you're doing all the work and that you're getting the rent discount this month."

"OK," he said suspiciously. "Thanks."

"Now will you leave me alone?" I said.

The phone rang. Grant. "Hey, we need to meet. Did you forget?"

"Shit. Fuck! I'm on my way."

Grant got to Victrola before I did. "What's wrong?" he said as I sat down. "You look terrible."

"My housemate's lost it. He's a raging alcoholic with a gun who wants my job as house manager."

"Jesus," Grant, the recovering alcoholic, said.

"He's nuts. He's obsessive and he's bought a gun to protect himself from God knows what after 9/11 and we just got into an argument."

"Your hands are shaking."

I told Grant everything. This took a full ten minutes, since Grant knew practically nothing about my domestic problems. He listened, but then he wanted to talk about the campaign, because there were things to do. We separated an hour later, and I went home. The first floor of my house was dark, just as I had left it. Seth, the new roommate (*When did he move in? And who did he replace?* I couldn't remember), had left his things in the foyer. I thought I recalled Emily telling me that he would take care of them soon.

Doug was waiting for me at the top of the stairs. He had probably heard me come in. His expression was pained.

"Phil, can't we talk about this some more?" he said.

I went into my room, and this time I locked the door behind me.

Doug wasn't finished, though. He went into his sunroom, threw open his window again, and tried to plead with me. Don't hate me, he begged.

The stress, the exhaustion, and, finally, Doug's whiny tone, pushed me over. I couldn't stand it any longer.

"You want to be friends now?" I hollered. "You think that's the way it works? You've been challenging me and questioning me and talking about me behind my back for weeks—hell, *months*—and now that you've gotten your way, you want to be *friends*? Who the hell are you? You think you can do a better job than me? Go ahead. Do it. *Prove* it."

It all came out. "So go ahead. Call the landlady. Call her. Get an agenda of all the shit you want to get fixed. Write yourself out a list. Envision yourself a mover and a shaker in your own teeny tiny little world. Then listen to her bitch and moan about money, and try to deal with her. She'll blow you off. If you really think that she's going to let anybody turn this house into a place that we can actually be proud of, then—you're a bigger, more delusional alcoholic than I thought you were!"

Doug turned his head until it faced the ground below. Slowly, he withdrew inside.

Alone for the first time that day, I climbed into bed and stared at the ceiling. I thought of the refrains of popular songs and fragments of lines and scenes from *Dr. Strangelove*. In five weeks, this will all be over.

Click click.

Did I imagine it, or was Doug playing with his Glock?

Click click.

There it was again.

I imagined Doug, too drunk to stand, sitting on the bed with his Glock, contemplating the wall that separated me from him. I could see him staring down the barrel of the gun, down its smooth black metal, at me on the other side. Doug didn't read, so he was probably thinking of movies, not literature. Was he thinking of Tarantino or

Scorsese? Personally, I'd have said this was a Larry David script that had somehow turned into an episode by David Lynch.

And what was that music he had just turned on, all soft and gooey?

Leonard Cohen?

I knew almost nothing about Leonard Cohen. I only owned one of his CDs and I never listened to it. The only male vocalist I liked who could be described as "ethereal" was the late Jeff Buckley. The rest of them, including Cohen, seemed like pansies.

Click click.

I had to admit, though, that I wouldn't have picked Cohen to be the singer-songwriter (from *Canada*, right?) you'd listen to before you loaded up a Glock and shot someone cold. Cohen was girlie suicide music.

Holy shit—was Doug going to kill himself?

Unless—

Unless that CD had the song from the *Natural Born Killers* soundtrack, where Cohen sounds hard and grim, like his vocal cords have absorbed too much cigarette smoke and the only thing on his mind is murder.

I called my girlfriend. "Can I come over?" I said.

When Grant asked me if I was all right, I told him I could keep going. I shouldn't have. As I retold the story of Doug to friends that week, I found myself increasingly uncertain of whether or not he had really played with his gun that night.

Instead, I pressed ahead with my guerrilla campaign prank. I dropped by the Capitol Hill apartment of S——, my anonymous connection to the *Seattle Weekly*. I had thirty Grant Cogswell signs with me. S—— and I exchanged a few good-humored remarks and I left, feeling giddy. Our act of guerrilla politics would go down exactly as I had described it to Grant. S—— would enter the *Weekly* offices late at night and cover the offices of George Howland with poster board. We would all—Grant, Howland, me, and

S—— get a chuckle in the middle of the most stressful times I had ever lived through.

That night I could not sleep. I threw punches at the mirror. This was going to be great! Howland was such a good guy, how could he not find it funny?

But then it would be over, and the campaign, with its sheer drudgery and its unending anxiety, chaos, and monotony, would still be there.

Well, carpe diem, then. I'd turn this stunt into a spectacle.

Sneaking up on my computer I roused it from its sleep. I tapped out the following message:

> The Grant Cogswell Campaign poked a little fun at *Seattle Weekly* News Editor George Howland last night when it managed to plaster his entire office with 25 Grant Cogswell poster signs . . .
>
> . . . The Grant Cogswell Campaign employed the tactic because the *Weekly* fails to understand the sheer and absolute inevitability of the Grant Cogswell Campaign. While the *Weekly* endorsed Cogswell for the primary, it described a vote for Grant Cogswell as being a "protest vote" . . .
>
> . . . The Grant Cogswell Campaign hopes that Mr. Howland can take a good, clean joke— while at the same time betting that the prank will serve as a hearty warning to other local journalists who might dismiss Grant Cogswell for Position 8 on the Seattle City Council.

By the time I was done I realized that I had written a press release. I added a few more paragraphs and cut and pasted the entire text into an email. I could barely suppress my laughter. In fact I was holding it back only because I did not want to wake Doug and get shot. I found the folder on my computer containing all of the media email addresses. I inserted them into the 'bcc' line of the email. Then I hit the 'send' button. It was so easy. My laughter could be suppressed no more, so I smothered my face with a pillow and cackled until I was gasping for air.

"What are you laughing at?" my girlfriend asked. She had come over because I had begged her to.

"This is gonna be great!" I said.

The next morning, I woke up early to check my email. There weren't many messages, a few from Wayne and one from Thomas Shapley, an opinions page editor at the *Seattle Post-Intelligencer*. I didn't know Shapley personally, but Grant and I had good feelings about him. He had already written a pro-monorail column. He must be an ally.

His email was vague. "Warning? I don't like warnings. Please specify so that I may adequately prepare to address such a threat."

I responded lightly. "Can't do that. Then you can prepare for it." Send.

Shapley's response was immediate: "Thank you for verifying the fact that you have made a threat. As to preparation, it would seem that those who make threats would do well to prepare for any legal and political results that may come from having made those threats, or having carried them out. And thank you, too, for giving new definition to the kind of campaign you are running and the quality and character of your candidate."

I looked at the date on the email Shapley had sent. October 11, 2001, exactly one month after September 11. Anthrax was in the news and people were buying guns and nobody was in a very humorous mood, especially when reading a press release that invites a jokey comparison to terrorism.

Soon I was clutching my stomach and bowels and writhing like a dying fish on the floor.

I got in my car and drove to the *P-I*. I asked for Shapley. He was in a meeting. I told the receptionist I'd wait. I sat there for twenty minutes, trying to maintain some semblance of composure.

Shapley came out, a bearded man with a stiff bearing and a contemptuous demeanor. I apologized in every way I could, then let
him rebuke me until he was out of adjectives. He did not invite me
back into his office.

I drove to the *Weekly*. When I announced myself the receptionist gasped in disbelief. She paged Howland, but he wouldn't
see me. Yes, the receptionist said, he's very upset. Moreover, the
employee who had helped me could get fired.

Queasy, I returned home and tried calling Howland three times.
He wouldn't pick up his phone, I sent an eight- or nine-paragraph
apology to him. Then I sat and waited. Howland finally emailed
me back. He thanked me, assuring me that the joke wouldn't be
mentioned in the *Weekly*, and that was it.

But that wasn't it. S—— could get fired and our entire campaign hung in the balance. If we lost the *Weekly* endorsement for
the general election because of my juvenile stunt, we had no
chance of winning the election. Grant and I both knew this. When
Grant heard how bad the situation was, he was almost past words.
"I trusted you," he said through clenched teeth. He hung up on me
and called some of the veteran politicos on our advisory committee
for the kind of advice I normally provided. Neither one of us got
any sleep that night.

The next day, the phone rang. I picked it up. "This is Alisa
Cromer," the voice said, in a way that meant I was supposed to
know who that was. I didn't, but I pretended to, and in a moment
I realized that I was talking to the publisher of the *Weekly*.

"Thanks for sending that email to George," Cromer said
brusquely. "He appreciated that."

"Oh, you're welcome," I said, grateful to be able to confess to
someone. "You know, what I did was really, really stupid, and—
well, it was really stupid, and I'm sorry."

Cromer turned breezily curious. "Now when you and S——
broke into the office—"

"Wait a minute," I said. She was trying to trap me. "*I* was never in the office, and I'm sorry but I can't tell you who helped me." I rambled a bit at this point, but I basically repeated what I had said in the press release: No laws were broken, the whole thing was just a dumb joke, etc.

Cromer fell silent. A cold, calculated silence. "I don't want to get the police involved in this," she said.

"I can assure you," I said, "that it was someone who had *legal access* to George's office, but I can't tell you who it was." I repeated, "And no laws were broken!"

Another pause. "How would it *look*," she asked, "if we had to interrogate all the Muslim-American janitors in the building?"

Then she said something about anthrax. Still holding the phone, I fell back on the floor and started rocking back and forth. Wasn't this one of the most liberal publications in America? What was happening?

Still, I wouldn't give away S——'s name. Cromer and I hung up on each other.

19

Reality parted before me as if made of water. Or maybe I had crashed through it, indifferent to density. Objects lost their distinctness, their inherent noun-ness. Swimming before and below me, they slipped outside of my field of vision, gray blobs on a shifting gray palette.

I fell, blowing backward into the past

January 1998

The man bellowed in the middle of the restaurant· "You are my hero!"

He had grubby brown hair and a rough, untrimmed beard. His glasses were tiny granny spectacles, and he was wearing the kind of clothes that I later learned he always wore: a collared, somewhat billowy shirt of a muted color, enormous baggy pants for an enormous baggy body, and tremendous blue clogs over white tube socks. His name would soon be splashed all over the Memphis media, but I would know him as Big Thom.

We were in a run-down taqueria. The owners, who spoke no English, were friendly to us, perhaps because most Southern whites considered the restaurant too daring a place to patronize, or perhaps because the owners were naturally friendly. A lot of people in the South were. A coworker of mine had spotted me and had called me over and introduced me to Big Thom.

Big Thom had a big laugh that employed both his massive belly and his sarcastic lower lip. His praise referred to an article I had written that lampooned the D.A. for proving after six months of intense undercover investigation that topless dancers were sitting on patrons' laps when they weren't supposed to. With a few hundred dollars one Friday afternoon I proved that the D.A. and his police investigators were a little naïve about the city's underground sex economy. Since Big Thom apparently worshiped me, I liked him immediately.

Big Thom was an activist. I couldn't tell what exactly he was active about, because he spent most of his free time browsing the Internet. But Big Thom said he was an activist, so I believed him. He read the *Nation* and kept the latest Michael Moore book next to his toilet. He was in his late twenties, hung out with radicals and vegetarians who lived in co-ops, and ran a weekly poetry slam. He drove a beat-up Volvo and was obsessed with hating yuppies and loving Public Enemy and Wu-Tang Clan. As jaded and worn down as I was, I found him refreshingly acerbic.

"I'll be there when the revolution begins," Big Thom boasted, smothering his steak with hollandaise sauce. "And you're going to encourage it. We don't have any guns, but we can get some at one of the pawn shops in the 'hood."

At the time I had a wretched case of insomnia. At night I became a prowler in my own apartment and during the day I turned into a motorized zombie flitting through red lights under the illusion that they were merely symbols in a colorful dream. As I paced the darkness of my apartment every 4:00 A.M. I kept clear of two overflowing boxes of police reports and trial transcripts that spilled out of my desk and onto the floor. In a year-long fit of madness I tried to save a man's life from the electric chair, hoping that success would earn me a robust, celebrity-style fame. The case had dead-ended for me the month before, hinging as it did on two witnesses with conflicting, vague testimony, one of whom had fled (at best guess) to Minnesota. The other had been shielded from me by her mother in a broken-down shotgun shack on the south side of town. My editor refused to publish my findings without better evidence, and he wouldn't let me waste more time pursuing the case, so I had given up.

Time passed. We saw each other at another restaurant in December of '97. I waved listlessly and joined him. He told me news that I myself had reported the week before, that the KKK was planning a rally in Memphis.

Someone, Big Thom told me, was going to have to stand up to the Klan.

I said that I knew that, and in that moment we both knew what the other was thinking. Big Thom and I had spoken often of wanting to do something that would break through the shallow thinking of the average, deluded American, to prove that dull-witted acceptance of the status quo was wrong, that change was possible. Now, for the first time in a year, I was able to forget about the man on death row that I could not help. The KKK was coming to Memphis, Tennessee, on Martin Luther King's birthday, and they had to be confronted. Here was something I *could* do.

We met later that night over beers, and had soon settled on a course of action. I wrote an editorial with a provocative headline: "Calling All White People." I said that black people should stay home, but that all available Caucasians should come out to oppose the Klan, which was, after all, the white man's problem. I included Big Thom's name and phone number and encouraged people to join his new group, which he had named Memphis Against Racism, or MAR.

Things moved fast after the editorial was published. Big Thom got forty phone calls a day and TV reporters, who now had a face to attach to anti-Klan stories, jumped in; one news station ran teasers of the upcoming anti-Klan rally, gleefully wondering if violence would break out. The media called Big Thom a "local businessman," and police officials considered him the sole authority on the anti-Klan rally. After some negotiations, the city allowed both groups, Klan and anti-Klan, to rally on the south side of the courthouse.

The KKK arrived. Perhaps fifty in all, they donned their sheets on the courthouse lawn before moving to their assigned station on the southeast court steps. Big Thom's group, about the same size as the Klan's, convened at a coffeehouse on Beale Street before marching to the southwest court steps. Big Thom had a bullhorn, others carried signs and wore green armbands, self-styled emblems of peacekeeping. Big Thom's group was almost completely white. A sea of independent African-Americans showed up, too, hundreds of them, a few carrying video cameras—motivated, it seemed, not by ancient grudges but by a possible Kodak moment.

The street filled with a thousand, possibly two thousand people, but police had cordoned off an area only large enough for Big Thom's crowd estimate of five hundred. Claustrophobia and irritation mounted as the elbows, shoulders, and thighs of whites and blacks became entangled, and police on horseback and in riot gear added to the general sense of unease. Moreover, no one was happy about being prevented from even seeing the very thing they had come to see—the KKK. Memphis police had strategically parked city buses to block them from everyone's view.

Big Thom, standing on the courthouse steps with his bullhorn, saw everything. Klan members, he noticed, had all the freedom they wanted to move around on their side of the courthouse, while the anti-Klan protesters, his people, did not. He was torn over who to fight, the Klan or the police, and soon succumbed to a classic liberal problem, the desire to take on everything at once. From his perch above the crowd, he chanted, "Jesus was a man of color!" Then, "Are you [police] here to provoke or protect us?" and "Fuck the police!" Big Thom was on fire.

With a press pass around my neck, I was milling about on the Klan side of the courthouse when the police decided to disperse the crowd. I saw the tear gas canisters arc upwards, floating lazily, like frisbees caught on a cushion of air. I did not see them land, but when they did, a white thick fog enveloped everything. I plunged into the chaos to try to help some college interns I had left there, but only ended up getting knocked to the ground by the noxious fog.

The police escorted the Klan safely out of the area and attacked the anti-Klan crowd with tear gas and pepper spray. Most people fled, but a few lingered, sitting on the street and curbs forcing officers to spray them individually. Big Thom was hit on the ear with a tear gas canister, and his glasses were knocked off his face. He accused a cop of being a Klansman in police uniform, and then he fled, too. Half an hour and a dozen broken downtown office windows later, order was restored.

A lot of the blame for the incident was heaped on Big Thom. The police department accused him of misleading them with his crowd estimates and his promises to organize a peaceful protest, and the daily newspaper scorned him for being so incendiary with his megaphone. Everyone stopped calling him a "local businessman." Now he was a "freelance graphics and Web-page designer" and a "former waiter." They dragged up embarrassing moments from his past, like the time he got mad and destroyed a computer monitor at an Applebee's where he once worked. My role in promoting him wasn't mentioned; the paper had an unspoken policy not to mention its rivals.

"It's your fault," one of my editors said. "*You* created him."

"He meant well," I said, which was true.

It took another year and many more months of insomnia to recognize how burnt out I really was. When I did, I left town. I moved west, believing that thousands of miles of traveling might give me a fresh start. I ended up in Seattle, in the tear gas clouds of the WTO protests, and with Grant Cogswell.

Questions broke the surface of my watery consciousness. Why was I drowning in self-doubt, narcissism's doomed little brother? I had devoted hours and hours to researching the death row case, to the point where I was convinced that the guy could be innocent. Why had I then given up on the story? I wasn't even sure if the man was still alive; I *was* sure that I didn't want to know.

A shout, a flash of metal, and the sound of brakes screeching pulled me back in the present. I was driving on a road that had narrowed. I had to veer into an open lane before we were killed.

"What are you doing?!" Grant yelled. "Use your blinker! Watch where you're going!"

"I'm sorry! I didn't see that guy!"

Grant had had enough. "If people see me in this car with you, and you're driving like *this,* they're not going to vote for me!"

And if idealism could freefall so easily into madness, was solipsism just the ledge from which one leaped?

20

My mind had wandered again. Kevin was asking me a question.

"Why do you put up with Grant, anyway?" he said.

We were looking down from a footbridge spanning a nameless segment of freeway that connected West Seattle to the rest of the city. It was late, about 11:30 P.M., and Kevin and I were supposed to find places to plant more illegal yard signs. The street gleamed with a film of oil and rain. An occasional car flitted by; drivers kept a wary eye on us as they passed below.

"Uh, Phil?" Kevin said.

"There's a spot over there," I said, ignoring his original question. "By the statues of the guys rolling on logs. That's a pretty good stretch of grass, don't you think?" The statues were supposed to be whimsical reminders of the water sport lumberjacks played, but to me they looked portentous and strange. Who wanted to watch a game where grown men fell off the only thing that kept them on their feet?

"Sweet," he said, with typical nonchalance. "How do we get over there?"

"Same way we came in. There's two fences to climb, but I don't see any other way. Do you?"

He didn't, so we walked back toward the side of the footbridge where I had parked the Geo. In addition to the fence, the area was protected by thorny bushes and shrubs.

The seasons had changed. Gray clouds had moved in, encasing the city in an ash-colored dome, isolating Seattle from the rest of the world and signaling the onset of a long, miserable season. The only thing worse than the clouds was the morning fog, which rolled in from the water, turning everyone into ghosts, amplifying the alienation that I already felt from this cool, unreadable place. I would have noticed the shifting weather earlier, but fear of Doug had forced me to move my office into the basement.

Kevin had asked me about Grant because, not too long ago, Kevin had bummed a ride in the car with us after a press conference. Grant had dropped his rigidly managed public façade and lost his temper, yelling at me about the things I had done and the things I hadn't done. Grant was not being insulting, exactly, just demanding in the way I had (somehow) grown accustomed. Kevin said he found this appalling.

"Watch yourself," I said.

The fence wasn't very well made. Its lower half vibrated like a rubber band, and its upper tip, the part we needed to heave ourselves over, was uneven and serrated. Kevin was twenty-one and fairly athletic, and he made it over cleanly. I was twenty-eight and only looked athletic in a scrawny, long-distance runner sort of way. I made it to the top just fine, thanks to a nice initial jump, but on my descent the right sleeve of my leather jacket snagged on the fence's pointed metal tips. I turned my head just in time to see the edge of the sleeve tear in half. I landed in the thorny bushes below the fence, not the softer vegetation I had aimed for.

"Oh-ho, man!" Kevin laughed as I swore. "Dude, that sucks."

I dusted myself off and tried to sound philosophical. "At least it isn't raining," I said. "So. Now that I've woke up half the neighborhood over there, let's go."

We walked down the hill, hefting the signs I had tossed over the fence. Kevin was as calm as ever. I thought he was going to whistle next.

I said, "What we need is a long row of signs, maybe twenty or thirty feet apart, so everybody who drives west along this road can see them. Let's put in a few and see how they look."

We set our stuff down and started pounding in the signs.

"Your question about Grant," I said. "I just don't know. I—" I was too embarrassed to finish. My mind was filled with meaningless mottoes. Sometimes in life you are going to fall. Sometimes you have to eat a ton of lumpy, parasite-ridden dog shit. Pursuing a higher ideal can mean sacrificing your pride. It was a shame that my memory always failed me; perhaps I could have stolen something out of *Bartlett's Book of Quotations.*

Besides which, I needed Grant, and I wanted to believe that Grant still needed me.

"You know that guy got fired from the *Weekly* because of what I did?" I said.

"I've got a friend who works there. He told me all about it. You really pissed off George Howland, didn't you?"

"*Fired.* And now we could lose the election because of me."

I took another yard sign and held it out for Kevin. This time, he hammered while I held. We finished and moved on to another sign, switching roles without comment.

"What I really need is a few days off. But there's no time. There's just a few weeks left." Afterward, I vowed, I would throw out my cell phone, hide my car keys, and swear off politics forever. Like the main character in Murakami's *Wind-Up Bird Chronicle,* I would find a well to hide in for a few days.

When the signs were hammered in, Kevin and I went back over the footbridge and tried to pound in a few more signs on the east-bound side of the freeway, but the shoulder was too narrow, and there wasn't enough dirt to anchor the sticks. Climbing back over the fence, I lost my balance again and fell into a pile of thorny bushes. Kevin helped me up. We drove around for more than an hour before concluding that there weren't many good spots in West Seattle for yard signs. We called it a night.

When I got home, there was a message from Grant, who needed some financial materials from my office in the basement, and it couldn't wait until the morning. The city Ethics and Elections Commission wanted to inspect our records. "I really need this," he said. It was 1:30 A.M.

He met me at his front door. "Tara's asleep," he said. "Otherwise I'd let you in. How you doin'? You look awful."

"I *am* awful," I said. "Look at this!" I held up my sleeve. "I tore it on a fence over in West Seattle putting up more goddamn yard signs."

Grant was wearing a dirty T-shirt and boxers and his hair was disheveled. He looked miserable.

"That's one really useful footbridge, the way they block it off like that, with fences and thorns. Shit! It cost me forty bucks to get this same sleeve fixed just last month!"

"Shhh! Keep your voice down, will you? My neighbors are asleep. Listen, I'm sorry. Is there any way we can pay for it to get fixed?" By we, I think he meant the campaign.

"Just forget it," I said. "We need all the money we have for our last mailings. See you tomorrow—ten o' clock at Victrola."

"Thanks for getting this," Grant whispered after me.

The next day, Grant, Wayne, and I met at Victrola. The agenda was the same as usual.

More money was coming in every day, but not nearly enough, so Grant was going to fall short of his eighty-thousand-dollar goal by about thirty thousand dollars. Our "secret weapon" mailing—the monorail postcard—was only aimed at fifteen thousand voters, several thousand fewer than our list seemed to promise. Our more generic mailings to absentee and poll voters had to be scaled back. After some debate, we decided on a somewhat complicated breakdown of these mailings to three-out-of-four and (the so-called perfect) four-out-of-four voters; we'd focus most of our attention on the neighborhoods surrounding Capitol Hill, where Grant's chances were presumed strongest.

We skipped any talk about skin color; Grant was white and McIver was black and nobody was talking about it and there was nothing we could do about it. Grant was armed with arguments and facts that cast doubt on McIver's record with minorities, but

McIver seemed to have rallied around him the city's most prominent African-Americans—the same African-Americans whose support for him had been tepid to nonexistent. I had tried to find someone in the black community who could give a penetrating argument in Grant's favor, but no one was willing to do it.

How wide was the racial divide? One of our supporters had even found a black small-business owner who supported McIver, even though McIver had voted to have the man's mom-and-pop store demolished to make way for Sound Transit's light rail line.

Instead, we talked about media. The *Stranger* had done more for Grant than for any other paper; Josh had been printing Grant's name and mailing address in nearly every issue since the primary election, directing his readers to support Grant. The paper's latest cover contained the headline: "Folk Hero: Why You Should Vote for Grant Cogswell." The story opened with a description of Grant reading his Marion Zioncheck poem in a local bar. The rest of the article was, as the headline suggested, a wholesale endorsement of Grant. Next to the cover story, an intern had written a sidebar about the dumb campaign manager who might have ruined the folk hero's chances for victory by insulting the news editor of the *Seattle Weekly* with a nonsensical prank.

The only other newsperson who was interested in our campaign was Jean Godden, the *Seattle Times* gossip columnist. Not only had she written about my prank, she had written a follow-up when my accomplice at the *Weekly* lost his job. The editorial boards of both dailies had endorsed McIver. As for the *Weekly*, they refused to mention the prank in print, but they had recently thrown in a few snide comments about Grant. The editorial board had not yet decided if it would rescind its pre-primary endorsement.

Grant's frustration over the prank was palpable. He was losing sleep and was overwhelmed by migraines, stomachaches, and back pains. But he couldn't bring himself to say anything more to me about it. I had accepted blame for the incident and had offered to resign, an odd offer from a volunteer, and no one had any doubt that I was a complete wreck.

"What's the big deal, anyway?" Grant said, flashes of his old loyalty returning. "Some people just can't take a joke!"

Neither Wayne nor I said anything. Grant added, "We can still win this thing!"

With just a few weeks left and with money running low, Grant wanted a stronger emphasis placed on our volunteers. He wanted more energy invested in getting them to stand outside grocery stores and on street corners. Wayne would be calling on me for assistance whenever he needed it. Grant asked Wayne if he could be relied on to get everything done; Wayne promised that he could. Then Grant and I stood up to go.

"Is that it?" Wayne asked. "Is this the end of our meeting?" He was still getting used to the terse way Grant and I ran meetings. I told him we were done, and we all left the café, parting on the sidewalk for our respective apartments.

Wayne called me later to ask for help. He had been getting scores of names and addresses of people throughout the city who wanted to put Grant Cogswell yard signs on their front lawns. Would I mind driving some signs out to these people? Sure, I said, I'll get that list from you and head out. Grant called me shortly after that to tell me that a few dozen Democratic precinct captains were willing to distribute our flyers for us. They would drop them off with other favored candidates' materials on people's porches and front doors: Would I please drive around and drop off piles of our brochures to these people? Sure, I said. I'll swing by and get *that* list from you, as well as another box of brochures.

Back in the driver's seat, alone, I swung north on Interstate 5, away from downtown and Capitol Hill. To my right and left sloped unremarkable little hills, solitary homes, exit ramps, and office buildings. South Park, Georgetown, Leschi, Lake City, Magnolia—I wasn't terribly familiar with any of the neighborhoods on my lists. I had visited them in the past, but with Grant; I had had no use for maps with Grant in the car. He would point and I would drive. Now I definitely needed one, and I had no idea where it was.

Driving by myself through the city for the first time in months made me feel more like a lost tourist than a campaign manager. With little information and little desire to seek more, I had always filled in the unknown spaces of the city with sloppy, unflattering brushstrokes. Now I paid closer attention. I went past the hideous Northgate shopping mall to sleepy residential blocks in the far north side of town, pleasant neighborhoods with gravel driveways and no sidewalks. I drove around Alki, the West Seattle area where Seattle's original founders had landed by boat; today it was all glittering waterfront views of downtown and burnished people in tight shorts and roller blades. I drove through Upper Queen Anne, a hilltop with expensive private homes made more private by the absence of windows facing the street. I sped through the low-rent blight of Aurora Avenue and Lake City Way—wide streets disfigured by car dealerships, the kind of neighborhood that every city must accept. And I was slowed to a crawl somewhere around the University Village shopping center, whose suburban mall enormity was suffocating the smaller independent shops near the University of Washington half a mile away.

At an intersection somewhere on the south edge of Green Lake I came to a stop. This was an untarnished neighborhood shaped around a placid body of water. Across the road, a handful of joggers were getting in a late afternoon run. Their immaculate shoes, their focused strides, their slightly moistened sweatshirts, their panting dogs, the glistening water; everything was arranged as it had been yesterday and the day before, as picturesque as a postcard, as carefully designed as a J. Crew catalogue. The only contradictory aesthetic element was the dingy sky, but that could be solved with some clever marketing. Call it another name, like "slate" or "light metallic," and the romantic lifestyle could be packaged for global export.

The more I explored Seattle, the more I thought of Jonathan

Raban and how wrong he was. Raban had posited in *Hunting Mr. Heartbreak* that Seattle was a malleable place, a soft city that could be shaped to one's own liking, as easily as one arranges a pillow behind one's head. It had appeared that way to me, too, when I had first arrived. But the fleeting glories of grunge and the New Economy had slipped unnoticed into the fog, and now Seattle seemed to me more like an elusive construction of a novelist, like the village in Gabriel Garcia Marquez's *One Hundred Years of Solitude* that disappears in the final pages, an ethereal figment of the imagination. Or the exotic places in Italo Calvino's *Invisible Cities* that the narrator implies may or may not have ever existed. Seattle was hazy, slippery, and unknowable; no wonder so many people here were such devout agnostics.

We had arranged an event at which Jonathan Raban was going to read, and it was the one thing I had been excited about in weeks. This was to be our third major fund-raising effort. Our first fund-raiser had drawn precisely three people and raised $150. The second had been canceled because a volunteer in charge of scheduling the bands had hired a band called the Honky Meters, and Grant had not wanted to campaign against the city council's only black official using a band that had a racial slur in its title. This last fund-raiser, Grant insisted, had to be different; we had to draw a big crowd and raise some real cash, period.

The usual preparations for a fund-raiser were made—a DJ, drinks, and the same campaign propaganda I'd lugged around in my Geo for nearly four months. We held the event at an art gallery in the concrete desert that separates Capitol Hill from downtown. Yard signs were plunged into the ground outside the site, which was at an art gallery in a squat little building. I arrived early to help get the room ready. Someone else opened the doors, and by the time we had set up the DJ's equipment, Raban was sitting in a chair across from me.

His face was mostly as I had expected, from the author photos on his paperbacks. A solid, long head; a penetrating, intelligent gaze; a prominent, regal nose and chin. But his real face had more lines. They weren't bad lines, necessarily, but they were dignified and—*arched*. He seemed to be a man who wanted to be intrigued.

"Mr. Raban," I said, or gushed. He looked up from his seat with an expectant smile. I heaped praise on him for everything I liked about one of his other books, *Passage to Juneau,* which was a lot.

He thanked me warmly and smiled, but then let the smile die on his lips, and added nothing more.

I opened my mouth and closed it several times, as if I was trying to chew something that had already gone down my throat. Shuffling my feet, I backed away, and then moved to the front of the room to watch the entrance for potential contributors.

Josh Foit came in and I pounced. "Thanks for that write-up in the *Stranger!*" The tone was sarcastic, a familiar and welcome relief from the fawning appreciation I had just used.

Josh looked baffled. "It was pretty fair," he said.

"It wasn't the article," I said, backing off. "It was the picture of me you used. You got it from the old staff photo wall. I'm drunk in all of those pictures. I looked like a clueless chucklehead."

He gave me a sympathetic look. Then he shrugged and, in the tradition of political journalists everywhere, entered the fundraiser without paying.

The evening began, and soon Grant was introducing himself, speaking for a few minutes about the campaign, how close we were to winning and how we really needed everyone's help in the final days before the election. He then gave Raban a brief introduction. Raban stood up and didn't talk about our campaign, other than to comment on how good it was to spend an evening discussing charming things like municipal politics at a time when everyone's attention had been diverted to the caves of Afghanistan. Then he read from *Passage to Juneau,* the part when he leaves Seattle on a small cruising ketch. It was one of my favorite moments in the book. From my folding metal chair, I saw

everything Raban saw from the deck of his boat as he sailed out
of Puget Sound:

> The lie of the surrounding land gave no inkling of
> the sea's profundity. Suburban hills, low and
> rolling, sloped gently to the water's edge. The
> woods had been cut down to make way for looping
> crescents of identical $500,000 homes, pastel-
> painted ranch-style bungalows, built of cinderblock
> and Sheetrock, clad in color-coordinated vinyl.
> Through binoculars, I could see their barbecue grills
> and picture windows; striped sun-loungers on
> decks; buzz-cut lawns terminating in a meager strip
> of rocky beach . . . impeccable lives were being con-
> ducted right on the lip of the abyss.

The abyss. I allowed myself a huge, contented smile. Maybe I
didn't need to go to the bottom of that well; maybe I could make
do with a stack of books from the public library.

The reading ended, and I was back in the reception area, dutifully trying to grab last-minute contributions.

In front of me, the gallery owner was hanging out with his girlfriend. A stylish couple, they always made me slightly nervous; I
knew nothing about the art scene and nearly nothing about contemporary art, and assumed that they, in turn, didn't know or care
too much for politics. But when they got my attention they immediately started praising Grant and my decision to run his campaign. "What really impressed me was how sincere Grant was,"
the gallery owner said, sounding amazed. "When he talked, his
passion for local politics was—truly inspiring."

"That's why I joined the campaign," I said, giving my stock
answer. "Grant can really motivate people, and he's got a lot of
integrity, too." The gallery owner told me we could keep some of

Grant's yard signs outside the entrance, I thanked them, and they left, entrusting me as they went with the responsibility of locking the place up.

I went over to Grant, who was sitting on a bench in the now-empty gallery. "Wasn't that great?" I asked.

"Great?" he repeated. He held up a pitifully small stack of remit envelopes. "We only made seven-hundred-fifty dollars tonight," he said.

We had invested three hundred fifty dollars in the fund-raiser, only about fifteen people had come, and none of them had been new faces hoping to learn more about our insurgent campaign. Our momentum had crested and fallen like a wave smashing on the rocks.

Grant walked away. I had no idea how he got home, since I didn't drive him.

21

Grant closed the car door. "Where are we going this time?" I asked.

"North Seattle, to our last community forum. Just get on the highway and I'll direct you from there."

The accelerator needed a hard stomp to get into traffic, but for once Grant ignored my driving. He had a sheaf of papers in one hand and his cell phone in the other. A slender black cord ran from his phone into his ear.

"What are you doing?" I asked.

"Last-minute contributions," he said, and hushed me with his hand. "Hey Tom, this is Grant Cogswell, I just wanted to thank you for your last check and touch base with you again. We're in the final two weeks of the campaign and we're really close to making enough money to pay for this last mail-out. I know you've given before but we'd really like your help just one last time." He gave his number, thanked the voicemail system again, and hung up.

"Hey!" I said. "That was pretty good."

"This is nothing. I'm just going over the list of people who already gave. These people already agree with me. I have no shame now. It was the cold calls in the beginning that were awful."

Traffic on I-5 was surprisingly light. "Well, we're going to need the money," I said. "We gotta get past that mistake you made."

"It wasn't a big deal. Why bring that up again?"

Grant had forgotten to record a seven-hundred-dollar check he'd written to Homer, our printer, in the campaign checkbook. Out of sheer luck it didn't pose a problem for weeks.

"Then," I said, disguising satisfaction with resignation, "suddenly everybody needed to get paid. Wayne wouldn't have been upset if his check had bounced, but the mailing company certainly would have. They don't trust political candidates—they would have refused to mail out our campaign literature to the absentee voters. We wouldn't have reached twenty thousand voters, our targeted, precious three-out-of-fours and four-out-of-fours.

"And that," I said, "never bothered you?"

Grant was silent for a while, then he said, "But this isn't a problem now, is it?"

"No. Thank the Lord."

"Then let's forget about it. The way I see things, a mistake is made, we handle it, then we move on. As soon as it's gone," he made a vanishing gesture, "it's gone and I don't worry about it anymore." A reasonable, exasperating position.

I drove and Grant made phone calls. Between hang-ups and voicemail messages, he threw me quick asides about the stress, about McIver—our usual conversation. I replied with short, sour one-liners. It was more ritualistic than real, a final effort to maintain a certain rhythm and harmony inside the Geo.

I parked the car outside a boxy community center. Grant got out of the car after I confirmed that he looked great.

Inside, Grant headed for the stage and I found a place near the back of the room. I spotted Paul Elliott, Richard McIver's campaign manager and legislative aide. Just one glance at him and I knew he wasn't putting in a hundred hours of work each week the way we were—fifty-five, tops. Elliott saw me and gave me a small hello. I nodded back. With the Ralph Nader incident well behind us, we were slowly warming to each other. I no longer thought of him as a troll with a dirty knife.

Grant and McIver shared the stage. The format was different from nearly every forum we had attended; here the two candidates were allowed to exchange comments and rebuttals. *This* forum actually resembled a democratic debate. Grant and McIver's speeches were essentially the same as their usual speeches, but now they took turns, speaking in smaller time frames.

It struck me that the two men were positively enjoying them-selves—and each other. Their responses weren't sharp verbal blows but a patter of polished rhetoric, each candidate aimed to outdo the other.

"The writing is on the wall for Sound Transit's light rail," Grant said, his arm sweeping the air before him, a gesture executed with such vaudevillian exaggeration that it caused McIver to nod appre-ciatively and clap his hands together. Four months of campaigning against each other had turned them into a well-rehearsed act; I half expected them to want to take their show on the road after the November election.

Well, it's finally happened, I thought. *Racial harmony has at long last been achieved.*

Elliott pushed a piece of paper at me. He and some of the other campaign managers were taking bets for a pool, and he wanted to know if I wanted in. Dashing off my answers, I predicted with a glum perversity that all the incumbent candidates would lose, as well as a few other far-fetched scenarios that had provided Grant and me with our early campaign energy. I handed him five dollars and said goodbye. "See you on the other side," I said. The election was about three weeks away.

Back on the road, Grant got a phone call. One of our well-con-nected volunteers wanted us to know that the *Seattle Weekly* hadn't withdrawn its endorsement of Grant. "Oh, thank God." Grant shouted. I was so relieved I lost control of the car, narrowly avoiding a Ford Escort.

With that problem out of the way, I gave in to my other fear:

"I'm telling you, Doug might try to kill me," I said, scanning the pavement for big potholes. There were quite a few of them. Grant didn't respond so I continued. "Did I tell you about the time I passed him on the stairwell? He was walking with his right hand behind his back. I swear he had his gun tucked in the back of his pants."

"Listen," Grant said. "You have *got* to deal with this. You're not focused."

"I must be hallucinating," I said. "I can't even say with total certainty that he was really playing with his gun that night I fled the house. I *think* he did. And how do you propose I handle this? I can't talk to the guy. He's irrational. A *Glock,* for God's sake."

"I don't know, what about the landlord? Can't he do something? I want to help you but I can't. This campaign has taken everything out of me. And every time you even talk about this you bring me down. I do a bad job speaking in public any time I hear you go on about this stuff. You *need* to take care of this."

He was right. I had to try to be more upbeat. "Have you listened to that new Modest Mouse album yet?" I said. Their latest release, *Everywhere and His Nasty Parlour Tricks,* had been in the front display of a record store we had passed on our way to somewhere else. I had bought two copies, one for me and one for Grant, to help smooth things over between us.

"Not yet," he said.

"It isn't very good," I said.

Doug's behavior had again changed: Now he had authority. I watched, ambivalently, as he moved around the common areas of the house in the evenings with the force of a small tornado. He called the landlady about the mold problem in the bathroom. He bought Liquid-Plumr and unclogged the bathroom sink and shower drain. He checked in with Emily about the bathroom stench. He got rid of our ratty old couch when Seth, our newest housemate, donated his newer couch to the first floor. He spent an hour examining the basement storage area to see what kind of mess he was really facing. He made sure all the new bills were posted for everyone to see; in fact he was so excited by his new position that he posted one bill twice.

Then, just as abruptly, he lost interest. He was already working two jobs, his regular job and the weekend job at the pet store, and the lack of free time was giving his face a hounded look. I watched with equal ambivalence as he sunk into another lapsed state of anxiety and depression. The grass still needed mowing—it was approaching knee level in some places. The basement remained a mess. And he was having no luck getting Merlin to wash his own dishes. Soon enough, he was retreating immediately into his room at the end of the workday.

And he kept playing with his gun. *Click click—click click.* It was even more disturbing now; I imagined Doug sitting in his room, downing beer and dwelling on his failure as our house manager.

I had to act. At the very least, I had to warn the others about Doug's recent erratic behavior.

Seth was first. I knew very little about him. I knew, for example, that he wanted to find the time to register to vote, but he never did. He was not pleased with my news about Doug, especially since he had just moved in. Seth suggested I reason with Doug, get him either to give up his gun or agree to keep it locked up. I approved of this idea in principle, and then went to go hide in my room.

Merlin Whitehawk, the twenty-two-year-old theater student, was next. I knew very little about him, other than the fact that he had registered as an absentee voter at my urgings.

I caught him on the first floor, at the dining room table, studying Shakespeare.

"Merlin," I said, "Doug's bought a gun, he's unstable, and not too long ago we got into an argument, and now I'm afraid he may try to kill me."

Merlin tightened his jaw, perhaps to indicate that he didn't want to be disturbed the night before an exam. His reaction made me want to admonish him for not washing his dishes, but that felt trivial, so I left him alone and again fled to my room.

I dreaded my encounter with SnowWolf almost as much as I dreaded confronting Doug, for different reasons.

What baffled and disturbed me most about SnowWolf was his voting record. Statistically (psephologically) speaking, SnowWolf was a four-out-of-four, a perfect voter, the only one in the house (I had, to my shame, missed a primary election the year before). As a result of this, he was the only resident inundated daily with mailings from all the political candidates, from the school board challengers to the mayoral front-runner.

In other words, SnowWolf, the dedicated introvert, lived outside society. His double, Charles, was a responsible citizen. I would have felt much better about this if I had known who he usually voted for, and why.

When I caught up with him, he was sitting on the living room floor in front of the television, again playing *Bloody Roar 3* on his PlayStation; he appeared to have advanced a few levels, although I couldn't tell for sure. It was still morning, about 9:30, though of course this was kind of late for him to be awake. "Charles, I need to talk to you," I said, my voice tight. I couldn't bring myself to call him "SnowWolf" at such a time.

I tried to sound as rational as possible. "You know that I'm under a lot of stress with this campaign, but you should also know what's been going on here lately," I said.

He didn't say anything. "Doug and I got into an argument the other night, and it wasn't a very *good* argument," I said.

Unlike the terse summaries I had given Merlin and Seth, I gave a patient, detailed account of my campaign, Doug's campaign, Doug's Glock, and his behavior since September 11, and the night I fled the house in terror. Doug may have a problem, I concluded, and we needed to be nice to him, especially if he was armed.

"OK," Charles/SnowWolf said amiably. He returned to his game and I returned to my room.

Emily, I knew, would be sympathetic. She was a social worker, and we shared the same political sensibilities.

I intercepted her returning to the house one early weekday afternoon for a late lunch. To get her attention, I spun my car into the neighbor's driveway and nearly took her out, right fender just missing left hip. She seemed even more taken aback when I advanced on her with a crazed look in my eyes.

"We've got a problem," I said, and told my story.

To my relief, Emily was just as scared as I was. She also provided me with some new details: "He was downstairs in the living room a few days ago playing with his gun! I saw him and I got really nervous. I said, 'Doug, please don't play with that thing in the living room. You're making me really nervous.' And he was laughing! He was messing with the chamber and he played with it for a really long time. I got him to leave the living room, but he was still laughing on his way up the stairs."

Emily was from the South; people with guns had never really scared her before. "But the way he was playing with that gun—it was really, really frightening."

"He called that gun his 'toy,'" I said. It felt good, having a social worker agree with me.

"You're right," she said. "I think he's been exhibiting some really strange behavior lately."

"He's completely unpredictable," I said, happily. "I think he's lost his mind."

We agreed that we'd each call the landlady and ask her to intervene. If she wouldn't, and if the danger grew too great, we would find friends to put us up somewhere else, away from the house and Doug.

The next day, I called the landlady from my cell phone outside Victrola and told her everything that had happened. As I talked and paced, I was unhappily aware of the implications of the conversation. I felt like a member of the *Peanuts* gang turning to the never seen principal to settle my schoolyard dispute. The landlady's laryngitis only enhanced this sensation.

Then I said, "The gun wasn't the first sign that Doug's been having problems. I think it was the fish."

"Fish? What fish?" she interrupted hoarsely. "No one in that house is supposed to have fish. If I recall correctly, and I think I do, there's a specific item in the lease that says you're not supposed to have fish."

I stopped pacing. Shit. I had let it slip that Doug had fish.

"Doug told me you had given him permission to have fish," I said. "You did know that he has a fifty-gallon tank in his room, didn't you?"

I heard the landlady take a sharp breath. For a moment she seemed to forget her laryngitis. "A fifty-gallon tank? How big is that? My gosh, that sounds awfully big. No, I don't think you told me."

"I know *I* didn't tell you," I said. "He assured me he had already told you."

A long, uncomfortable pause. "I think he called and asked me if he could have some fish, but he made it sound like it was a tiny goldfish tank."

"Goldfish? *Nooo*. They're not goldfish." Gossip got the better of me. I had already betrayed Doug, or so it felt, so protecting him now was moot. "He has two *piranhas* in his room." I added, "And a lot of little baby piranhas. He's breeding them for profit."

I watched a minor traffic jam erupt on Fifteenth Avenue—a fast-moving SUV, a jaywalker, glares, indignant shouts and waves, and then a miffed sort of calm—while I waited for the landlady to digest what I had told her.

"Oh, dear. Oh, dear," she said. "That could get me in a lot of trouble. Do you understand why I have a rule against pets in the house?"

She said she had to check with her attorney about what she should do, and she hung up. And I was left standing on the sidewalk wondering how a conversation about a paranoid alcoholic with a gun had turned into a complaint about an avid hobbyist who kept too many fish in the house.

The landlady called me back half an hour later, when I was on the road running errands. I plugged my hands-free earphone into the phone and accepted the call.

She instructed me to tell Doug to get rid of his fish. "The lease clearly states that he can't keep pets," she said.

"What about the gun?" I asked.

She wasn't sure what to tell me. Her lawyer informed her that she couldn't infringe on his Second Amendment rights. I had every right to tell Doug to keep the gun out of the common areas of the house, "I already did that," I said.

She repeated her concern about the fish. "Those aquariums are too big," she said. "What if we get another earthquake? What if they break?"

I sighed. "I'll tell him to get rid of the fish," I said, "but he's not going to be happy."

I found Doug cleaning up in the kitchen. He'd made some Vietnamese porkballs, and for once he appeared to be in good spirits. The very fact that he was out of his room and eating dinner was a good sign.

I scrutinized his clothing; I didn't see the bulge of a gun, but his T-shirt was large and loose and from my position I couldn't see his backside.

"Hey, Doug, we need to talk," I stammered.

"Sure. About what?"

"I—had a conversation with the landlady the other day. We talked a little because—because she wanted to know why I wasn't doing my job as house manager. I—she wanted to know what was going on, and I started telling her about all the changes in the house, and about my campaign, and about the new housemates, and at—some point in the conversation I mentioned your fish. And she said, 'What fish?'"

I let this hang in the air.

Doug looked at me, not understanding. "Well, so?"

"You're not supposed to have fish in the house. It's in the lease. No pets, no fish, no nothing. You may have told her about getting a fish tank, but not about a fifty-gallon tank, and now she's worried what would happen to the floor if the tank broke for some reason. I'm sorry, but she told me to tell you: Not only can you not buy a hundred-gallon tank, but you're going to have to give up the fifty-gallon tank. And the piranhas, too. All of them."

Doug almost dropped the frying pan he was washing. "You can't be serious," he said.

"Of course I am. I'm sorry I let it slip that you had fish. I didn't mean to tell her, it just came out." Discomfited by the silence, I added hastily, lying, "I didn't tell her they were piranhas, though."

"But I don't understand. She told me I could have them."

"That's not how she remembers it. I think she thought you wanted to keep a small goldfish bowl, but not a fifty-gallon tank."

Doug set his frying pan down. He drooped. He looked small and harmless again. "I have to get another beer," he said. "Do you want one?"

"Uh, sure," I shrugged. We walked upstairs together.

On the second floor, Doug swiveled. He was angry. "I can't get rid of my fish. I've *always* had fish."

"I understand, but—"

"No, you don't understand," he said. "She told me I could have them. I called her out of the blue and said, 'I was wondering if I could keep a few fish in my room.' And she said, 'Well, I don't see why not.' And that's when I went to the pet store."

"Can't you sell them early? Can you still make a profit off the babies?" I asked.

"It's not that," he said, searching for the words. He looked down at his empty hands.

"You were right," he said. "I'm sorry. Most of this house stuff isn't your fault. It's *her*. I called her up and asked her about all the things I've been getting on you about, and she wouldn't help. *She* didn't want to pay for the garbage behind the house by Emily's back door. *She* didn't want to take responsibility for *anything*. She said, 'Cleaning up around the house is you guys' job.' You can have the job of house manager. I don't want it. I can't work with her. She's impossible. She could make this a great house to live in, but she doesn't care. She just wants to collect the rent."

Doug went into his room and grabbed two cold Coronas out of his fridge. When his back was turned, I looked frantically around his room. I didn't see his gun anywhere. When he turned around to hand me a bottle, I took it and thanked him, then I brought up the issue I really cared about.

"You've been worried about *that?*" he said. He took a swig and gestured dismissively. "Don't worry. I locked that up. It's locked up."

"It is?" This was news. "The night we argued, I didn't know whether you were going to kill me or kill yourself—I was worried about you," I said.

Doug looked at me differently, a recognition of some sort lighting up his face, but he didn't say anything. I had run out of things to say myself.

I turned to leave. Before I made it out of his room, he said, "You know, you're all right. We have our differences, I mean, but you're all right. And you can keep your job as house manager. I don't want it."

I didn't know what to say. "Good night, Doug," I said.

22

The final week.

The landlady called me on my cell phone. I excused myself from Grant and Wayne and stepped out of Victrola so I could hear her. I probably shouldn't have given her my number; cell phones were costing the campaign nearly $1,000 a month. But Grant didn't seem to care, especially since he himself made personal calls on his cell phone, and it wasn't as if the elections commission checked things all that closely.

She had talked to Doug. He had agreed to sell his piranhas by February, although the breeding pair might take a little longer. Her concern, she stressed, was that the giant fish tanks would burst, spilling water everywhere, destroying her hardwood floors. In short, everything we had already discussed.

My real concern was how Doug was taking this. I hadn't seen him in days. I interrupted her to ask.

"Very well, I think," she said. "He seemed pretty calm and rational about everything."

"What about the gun?" I asked impatiently.

"He's said he's locked it up. He's assured me he's locked it up. Have you seen any evidence of it lately?"

"No," I conceded. "I haven't heard it or seen it. Not in the past few days, at least—since he and I talked."

"Well, if he's acting up with the gun in the common area, you have to call the police, and get a report written out. It's the only way I can do anything if there's a problem. My concern is that something's going to happen, and I won't be able to do anything about it."

I agreed to keep her informed, thanked her for talking to Doug, hung up, and went back inside the coffeehouse, where Grant and Wayne were finishing.

Grant showed me a sketch he had made on his calendar, for November 6, Election Day. He had drawn a nuclear mushroom cloud. He made a rumbling, exploding sound under his breath. November 6. For months it had been a date that seemed years away. Could it be so close?

Wayne handed me a few addresses. He was too busy to get stacks of literature to some volunteers. Would I mind doing it? Of course not, I said.

"We can still win this!" Grant said to us. And to himself.

We all walked out together. I had missed most of the debriefing, but I already knew everything that could possibly have been said. We had hosted two parties since the Jonathan Raban fund-raiser. The first involved sign painting, in which long pieces of thick, brown paper were used to make giant posters that could be hung on bridges across the city on election day. Grant would have been happier with this party if he had not thrown out his back showing the rest of us how to paint the signs. The second party, our final volunteer party, had been sparsely attended and frustratingly anti-climactic. The only new attendee was someone from the Washington Conservation Voters, a new environmental group that did not endorse us, we were privately told by some members, because the group thought we would lose. Wayne, Grant and I all suspected that this stranger was a spy for the McIver camp, as she had left with only vague promises to volunteer for us.

As expected, McIver had won endorsements from the *Seattle Times* and the *Post-Intelligencer*. We had won the *Stranger* and had kept the *Weekly*. The media attention disappeared after that; the city council races were just not considered important that year. Grant had even admitted to being a bisexual in order to get more coverage. He hated talking about his sexual orientation; it was nobody's business, he believed, and most people assumed he was straight. But the sexual orientation issue was a chance for more press, so he came out. He was written up in one of the smaller gay publications and then everyone forgot about it.

The last campaign mailing, to a modest number of poll voters, was a scant few hours from going out. Grant's yard signs were all over town, on lawns, on public median strips, and other illegal spaces. The Grant Cogswell blue-beknighted volunteers were working on street corners and the entrances of grocery stores all over town. At least, this part of our overall strategy was working.

Grant was tense. I was already defeated. Wayne was tired but exhilarated; politics had given him a new lease on life. He had vowed to stop doing meth.

Even with all the last-minute chaos, I arranged to have the high school students from the Northwest School interview Grant as part of their class assignment. We had the interview at my house, when Doug wasn't home. I didn't sit through the entire interview, which took place at the dining room table. Instead I retreated into the kitchen and began cleaning up. I could hear the students pressing Grant to show them his tattoo. A delighted cheer could be heard coming from the dining area.

Grant and the students left. Merlin came home. As he ran up the stairs, I called after him. "I did your dishes for you. I don't want to do them again. Do you understand me?"

Before we knew it, it was election eve.

The evening began badly. Doug was playing his butt rock so loud that Emily could hear the music in her basement suite—this was one of those moments that Doug bragged about, when the people in Bellevue, across Lake Washington, got a taste of his "real music." Emily ran upstairs, pounded on his door, and yelled at him to turn it down.

Doug came to the door, drunk. He yelled back at her, over the music. "I don't have to turn it down! I can play my music as loud as I want! It's not quiet hours yet!" Emily retreated. Doug played the rest of the song and then, in a fit of apparent remorse, turned his music down.

Later that night, I went to the video store on Fifteenth Avenue to rent *Fists of Fury*, the Bruce Lee flick. I wanted the movie I watched to feel appropriate, somehow, to recent events, and Lee fit quite nicely into the local lore. An émigré like so many other Seattleites, he had opened his first American martial arts studio in Seattle's International District.

Back at home, I put the video on the coffee table and took out a scrap of loose-leaf paper, one that still had some white space on it and filled it with a half dozen tasks. Election night priorities. The first was a television set. We were going to have our election night party at Re-bar, and Steve the owner had assured me he wouldn't double-book us with any more truculent heavy metal DJs but neither could he provide us with a working television. So I had to come up with one on my own.

Of course I couldn't borrow the set in our common area—belonged to Seth. Doug had thrown out the previous one to make room for Seth's newer, bigger TV. I had an old set of my own, an '80s-era Zenith. The screen needed a good ten minutes to warm up, and if that didn't work another ten minutes of vigorous massaging across its top would sometimes bring the image to life. I would need a volunteer to stay by the set all night to make sure it didn't break down. Maybe Hal Colombo would do the honors.

I put the set on the dining room table, plugged it in, and started to play with the knobs and switches, some of which had already broken off. I started rubbing it as if it suffered from overwrought muscles. Doug came downstairs and paused to observe my efforts.

"What are you doing?" he asked. A lighter was in his hand and a cigarette was perched in the ridge of his ear. He was clearly heading for the porch, but he leaned against a wall, to chat.

"Trying to make this old TV work."

"For what?"

"Tomorrow's election night. We've got a party. We have to watch the results come in on the news."

"Oh. Where'd you get that TV?"

"Downstairs. You know, in that basement that I haven't cleaned up."

"Looks old, huh?" he said.

I stopped massaging the set and started hitting it. Now that I had an audience, I didn't want to look so effete. The result was the same.

"Are you going to win?"

I considered the question. "I don't know," I said truthfully.

"You wanna borrow my TV?"

"Your TV?" I said. "*Your* TV?" Doug's giant television was a critical part of his entertainment system, second only to his speakers. It was hard to imagine him lending it to anyone.

"Yeah, sure," he said.

"Well," I said. I looked my Zenith. Not even the sound was working. "OK. If it's all right with you. But you don't have to. That's a really nice set, and I would be taking it to a bar. I'd have to get someone to look after it all night."

Doug shrugged. "It's no problem."

"Well, then great. Thanks!"

He took off upstairs, and I followed. Before I reached his room, he had disconnected the wires connecting his TV to the rest of his entertainment system. I helped him haul the massive machine out onto the second-floor landing. It was heavy and too big for my arms. I would have to find someone tomorrow afternoon to help me get it into my car.

"Thanks again! We'll take good care of it."

"You want a beer?" Doug asked. He didn't seem to want our exchange to end.

"Well—" I hesitated. "Sure. Why not? Just one, I guess."

He went into his room again. I stood on the landing and

watched. He got a bottle out of the refrigerator. Back on the landing, he handed it to me. It was a Budweiser.

Doug didn't drink Bud, I did. I drank it for a variety of reasons, mostly because it was cheap. By buying Budweiser, Doug must have been trying to signal a truce between us. Whatever power struggles had obsessed him before, he was officially renouncing them now.

"You don't drink Bud," I said.

Doug twisted his lips. We both knew what the beer meant. He didn't want to explain it.

"Thanks," I said.

I opened the beer and took a swig. Doug opened a Corona and drank from that. Tipping my beer toward his, I walked off.

Back downstairs, I was overcome with fatigue. There were still more tasks to do but I no longer felt like doing them. I had a beer and a Bruce Lee video. Only a bag of fresh popcorn falling onto the porch straight from heaven would have offered a clearer sign of what I should do next. I popped the movie in and threw myself on the couch. A couple of hours of mindless entertainment couldn't hurt anything.

The phone rang. I didn't need caller ID to tell me who it was. I wanted to ignore it, but couldn't bring myself to do it. I reached for the phone. "Hey it's me," Grant said. "I know it's getting late, but I want us to make a couple more signs for tomorrow."

"We made signs already," I said. "We made them a few days ago. Remember—you hurt your back making them? They're right here, sitting in my living room."

"I know, but I want a really good sign for the volunteers to wave around Westlake Mall at lunchtime. And maybe one more sign to put up on a bridge." He wanted the first sign to read, rhetorically 'Tired of Traffic?' We would surround the sign with several Grant Cogswell volunteers wearing Grant Cogswell T-shirts and wielding Grant Cogswell posters, to intimate how voters could get this problem fixed.

I wanted to be the gung ho campaign manager, up to and beyond the official results, but I had absolutely nothing left.

"Oh, c'mon!" I said. "No."

"Why not?"

"Because I'm tired and it's late. Because I'm terrible at making signs; I have zero artistic skills. Because we've already made signs, like you wanted. We've done everything we could. Everything you wanted. And we both know this won't make any difference!"

Grant sighed. It was like listening to a punctured balloon. "Phil, I'm asking you," he said. "Please."

The blinds on the front porch were open. I could see that the porch light was off. I thought that our resident house sentry would be out there, standing guard and smoking his cigarette like a world-weary soldier. But Doug was nowhere to be seen. Traffic slogged by, the headlights a weak defense against the murky darkness.

"Who do you want me to call?" I said. "I don't even have the volunteer list anymore."

"Please, Phil," he said. "My back—"

Worn, irritated, guilty, I relented. "I'll get somebody. I'll get somebody." I hung up before he could say anything more.

A few phone calls later, I had someone, a woman named Megan. She had played a big role in Ralph Nader's campaign in Washington State in the 2000 election. She told me she'd come over after her soccer game, or after her shower after her game, or something like that. I mustered the energy to thank her and hung up.

Back to the movie. There's never been a movie star like Bruce Lee since Bruce Lee. His rage was something to marvel over. He probably wasn't acting. From the very beginning of the movie you could tell he wanted to kill someone, and by the movie's end he was going to get his wish, perhaps many times over. Seattle needed more icons like him. I made a mental note to visit his grave on the north side of Capitol Hill after the election was over.

That's when Merlin showed up. He was pale with fear.

"Doug pulled his gun on me," he said.

I stared at him.

"I was filling out my absentee ballot, and Doug was in my room, and I started joking around with him that I wrote him in for the mayor's race since I didn't like any of the candidates. And he says he's got a record with the police department and he doesn't want any trouble. And then he pulls this gun out of his pants and he starts waving it around and he says, 'Don't fuck with me, man.' "

To defuse the situation, Merlin had hastily added the German-sounding suffix "-enheimer" to distort Doug's last name. Doug was appeased. He had put his gun away and lurched back into his room.

"Goddammit!" I said. And leaped for the stairs.

"I don't think—" I thought I heard Merlin say. In that instant, Doug became everything I was campaigning against. Apathy. Fear. Neurotic addictions. The selfish, impossible desire to shut out the world as if nobody else existed. It didn't matter anymore if Richard McIver was defeated or not. Doug had to be stopped.

I composed a speech in my head as I ran up the stairs but it dissolved just as quickly. It didn't matter. Everything had crystallized for me into a single moment. After such a long period of feeling powerless, it was exhilarating to have something to actually respond to. I could put an end to a real problem, right here and now.

I hammered at Doug's door. When he answered, I was curt and loud.

"Did you pull a gun on Merlin?" I shouted.

He attempted a quizzical look by screwing up his face and giving his eyelids a quarter-close squint. Boozy sweat covered his forehead.

He said he hadn't, then pretended not to understand the question. His voice was small, an enormous child fearing the paddle. "No, no," he repeated. He wasn't even really speaking. He was mouthing the words and I was reading his lips.

"Did you pull a gun on Merlin?" I shouted again. Again, anxious denial.

In a funny, third person sort of way, I realized that Doug's right hand was bent behind his back. What was it doing back there? I felt a part of my body pulling away from itself as I struggled to come up with an answer that didn't end with my own death. I should have run back downstairs. I should have led Merlin outside and called the police from my cell phone. But I got even louder.

"What did you think you were doing?"

"You don't understand—" he said.

"Doug, you scared me a little, that's all." *Did I say that? No, I hadn't.* Merlin had followed me up the stairs. What an idiot. Why did twenty-two-year-olds believe themselves immortal?

Doug gave a half-hearted apology without admitting blame. I shouted at him more. His hand stayed behind his back. Instead of growing more aggressive he slowly retreated into his room. I let him move backward until he had closed the door.

Merlin and I went downstairs. Merlin went outside to get some air. I turned back to Bruce Lee, who was reaching his own climax, a primordial scream that used all of the muscles of his taut upper body. I turned the movie off and paced the room until I was dizzy. It was like the feeling I got the moment after a big car accident— amped up and terrified.

Doug came down. He shuddered past me. He went out on the porch to talk to Merlin. After a few minutes he came in and sat on the couch.

"Do you want my gun? You can keep it in your room if you want," he said weakly. "I guess I shouldn't have it."

I paced. "If I take that gun from you, the only way you're getting it back is if you take it with you to a gun range, sober and in the middle of a Saturday afternoon. And *then,* after you get back, you're giving it right back to me."

I took his silence as hesitation. Where the hell was the gun now, anyway?

"Why'd you pull the gun on Merlin?"

"I thought he was threatening me—" Doug said. He muttered something else. I think it had to do with dirty dishes.

"Threatening you?! How was he threatening you! He's only twenty-two! He's your housemate! He's a good guy!"

More long pauses. He wasn't going to answer.

Then, more quietly, Doug said, "The threat isn't over yet."

I was beside myself. "What threat? What threat?!"

Doug muttered something to himself, sunk deeper into the couch, and stared sullenly at the ceiling.

"I don't get it," I said. "As house manager, I have to ask you to think about what you're doing to the rest of us. Because as soon as everyone else finds out about what happened tonight everyone's going to be afraid to even talk to you now. Even SnowWolf won't go near you."

I turned my back and headed for the porch. Doug got up from the couch and raced up the stairs.

"You can't borrow my TV!" he shouted down from the landing.

"That's fucking fine with me!" I shouted back. I could hear him hauling his twenty-seven-inch set back into his room, its hard plastic bottom scraping the floor as he dragged it. Then he slammed the door.

I put Bruce Lee back on and waited for my volunteer to arrive. It was getting late.

23

Marion Zioncheck's funeral was one of the largest ever held in Seattle. Two thousand people packed the auditorium where the ceremony took place, thousands more jammed the streets outside. Traffic came to a halt. Reverend Fred W. Shorter of the Church of the People read Zioncheck's suicide note—the part that made sense, at least—during his eulogy. "Marion Zioncheck died fighting to the very last for the poor and dispossessed," Shorter proclaimed. Everyone who knew Zioncheck had to agree.

He was succeeded in Congress by Warren G. Magnuson, an old friend. Magnuson was a professional politician who was later appointed to the Senate, serving for more than three decades on some of the most important legislative committees in Congress and making his constituents proud by bringing home plenty of pork barrel money and benefits. Compared to Zioncheck, Magnuson was polished and agile, a shrewd back room dealer. Compared to Zioncheck, he was also a tremendous bore.

In time, people forgot about Marion Anthony Zioncheck. It's likely that Grant was the only person to visit his grave in years, maybe decades.

At Re-bar, election night 2001, I crouched in Steve's miniature office with Grant and a volunteer and waited for the last numbers of the night to appear on the Internet. Eyes dared not blink. Sweat refused to flow. Teeth crushed thumbs. The crowd waited outside.

Grant's numbers improved throughout the night. From an initial 44 percent they inched up to 45 percent. And from 45 percent they jumped to a little below 47 percent. It was maddening;

depending on which voter precincts were counted next, we could conceivably creep past McIver into the majority.

The last update for the night came around eleven o'clock. I saw the web page change, and I let out my breath. "Forty-seven point seven-nine," I said, turning to Grant. "It's not enough."

There were still thousands, perhaps tens of thousands of uncounted absentee votes, and the official, final count would not be posted for about a week, but I knew that we were not going to pull off an upset. Absentee voters tended to be more conservative voters; if anything, the late ballots would chip away at the progress we had made in the past couple hours, not improve our standing.

Grant leaned against a wall. "It's not over yet," he said, even though it was.

I staggered out into the smoky bar with the sole intention of getting drunk. I was wearing a dark maroon suit that I had bought for eighty dollars in Memphis at a store where Elvis Presley had once bought his suits. Emily had painted my fingernails light purple. Steve, the owner of Re-bar, was at the bar. He gave me free beer the rest of the night.

Around me, the bar filled up. There were people who had supported the campaign from the beginning. There were people who had jumped onto the bandwagon when they thought it might go somewhere. And there were people entering the bar late who, having feared political repercussions, had not raised a finger to help Grant but wanted to show their support now. There were some other failed challenger candidates from other races showing up, too; not a single incumbent on the Seattle city council lost that year.

I didn't care about any of them. I kept drinking and circulating. I didn't want to sit still and I didn't want to get stuck in a booth with anybody. As a reflex, I kept the banter going, talking about anything I could think of, telling anyone who would listen that Grant met Richard McIver for a drink right before the election returns had come in, and how McIver, not me, had driven Grant to his polling place. A DJ played.

Soon enough, Grant was on stage, saying he wouldn't concede until the final ballot was made official. He said some things about mass transit, and then some things about the nature of teamwork on political campaigns. And then he tried to name everybody on the campaign who had helped out.

Except he couldn't remember everybody. His pauses grew longer. He was beginning to drift off. Adrenaline and defeat make a strange cocktail.

Bryan Miller, one of our volunteers, started whispering names in my ear. "Cleve Stockmeyer," he said.

"Cleve Stockmeyer!" I shouted up at Grant.

"—Cleve Stockmeyer," said Grant, "who provided us with key advice at critical times during the campaign, and who spoke on my behalf at the Forty-sixth District Democrats—"

"Evan Sult," Bryan Miller said to me.

"Evan Sult," I dutifully shouted.

"—Evan Sult, for his incredible graphic designs skills that went into one of our campaign mail-outs. Thanks to Evan, our veteran printer said we had one of the best pieces of campaign literature that he had ever seen!"

"Katie Kurtz," said Bryan.

"Katie Kurtz!" I said.

"—Katie Kurtz, for her tremendous organizational—aw, hell," Grant said. "I can't remember everybody. Phil, you come up and do the rest.

"Sure!" I said. Three steps later I was in front of the microphone.

I looked out at the crowd. My mind was as blank as a freshly cut piece of limestone and about as deep as shale. And, as at the campaign kickoff party, I hadn't prepared a speech.

But I was drunk. So I winged it.

"Ladies and gentleman," I said. "I have traveled four thousand miles with this man right here." I let that sink in, raising four digits in the air. "Four thousand miles of driving within city limits. I clocked it on my odometer."

A murmur of respect rippled through the crowd.

"Given that," I said, "I will now do some Grant Cogswell imitations."

"Oh my God!" Grant said.

"Why don't you use your signal!" I barked into the mic, making a quick, jabby movement with my hand.

Turning to my left, like Grant turning to me as I drove, I said, in a flat, angry voice, "Let me tell you something—if people see you driving this way, they're not going to vote for me!"

I paused. There was more, but I had suddenly had enough. I gave a gesture to indicate I was done. A ripple of applause moved through the crowd. As I stumbled off-stage, someone shouted "funny!" Others would comment later on how bitter I sounded.

I went back to the bar, where I found a new group of people to tell my Doug story to. Grant grabbed me just as I was getting to the part about the gun. Pulling me close, he whispered in my ear, "This campaign really deepened our friendship. I can't tell you how grateful I am to you."

I recoiled. Four thousand miles of driving with this man and I no longer knew what to think. We had come within a few percentage points of beating an incumbent who campaigned half as hard with more than twice the money ($118,000 to our $50,000). We had survived each other's mistakes, indiosyncrasies, and outbursts. We had not been able to prove that the system didn't always protect the status quo. We had *lost*.

But, tonight, Grant was a changed man. He was in control of himself. He had, at the very end, survived with grace and maturity. He had even shared a (nonalcoholic) drink with his opponent and had come to terms with himself on some level. He looked more self-assured than I had ever seen him.

And I had made an ass of myself on stage, at Grant's expense.

I turned away, small and embarrassed, eager for escape. I've never been very good at expressing my emotions.

Epilogue

A house meeting was organized in Emily's basement suite. Doug was not invited.

We wrote a letter to the landlady outlining our problems with Doug and threatening to move out. Even SnowWolf signed it. The day after she received the letter, the landlady offered Doug a five-hundred-dollar bribe to move out of the house. He accepted. His brother came and helped him move his stuff—his toys, his fish, his mattress, and his TV—to a house not too far away. He and I exchanged peace offerings as he left—he gave me an expensive leather office chair with wheels and adjustable levers, I gave him my copy of *Lonesome Crowded West,* explaining defensively that track number four, his favorite song, was scratched beyond repair. After he left, I changed the locks.

I saw Doug only once after that. One afternoon he pulled into the parking lot of the grocery store next to Grant's apartment, just as I was about to cross the street to Victrola. Doug was stuffed inside a battered Camry, a stout arm hanging out the driver's side window. He got out and saw me. He grinned, patted me on the shoulder, and kept walking. He looked happy. Perhaps he had found a new obsession to pursue. I hoped it was a harmless one.

My girlfriend and I spent a lot of time catching up—I made wild promises to take her somewhere exotic as soon as I had a job and some money. A month and a half after the election, we decided to get married. When we had recovered from our hangovers the next day, we decided it was still a good idea, so we set a date the following year. Grant gave us a fine wedding toast, quipping that *he* was going to write a book about *me,* to compete with the book I was writing about him.

Despite his defeat, Grant drew comfort from the fact that plans to build the monorail have progressed, though he's gotten just as upset that Sound Transit's light rail plans have, too. And there have been other changes in the city to fret over ("I'm telling you," he said one afternoon in Victrola, "If they widen the 520 bridge, this city is going to fall apart. If they do it, I might get my tattoo removed!") His most recent cause has involved a proposal to avoid rebuilding a highway along the waterfront. This time, Grant said, he wouldn't let himself be overwhelmed by his political passions. "I'm not trying to kill myself over this one," was how he put it.

Grant also became obsessed with Marion Zioncheck's story again, deciding in 2002 to rewrite his entire poem. He wanted to work on the poem until it was perfect, he said.

My Geo Prizm met a tragic fate, a true martyr's demise. My girlfriend—by then my wife—and I were in downtown Vancouver, B.C., one January night, waiting at a stop light, when a full-size, gas-guzzling, environment-eroding, second world-constructed, SUV came tearing around the corner. The driver was trying to outrun police after blowing through a DUI checkpoint. He turned the SUV onto our street too fast, broadsiding the sedan in front of me and tossing it almost to the sidewalk, as if it were a toy. He would have come to a stop if he had not been accelerating and maneuvering so wildly. A monstrous, bony grille filled our vision, and my car crumpled like a piece of paper. We escaped injury, but Canadian police declared the Geo dead at the scene and had it towed away within a matter of minutes (dozens of Grant Cogswell campaign posters and other paraphernalia were still in the trunk). They never caught the driver of the SUV.

The murder of the Geo sped our decision to leave Seattle, something we had contemplated for more than a year. We wanted a new start, in a bigger city. Since we had already traveled to the very edge of the continental United States, we decided to turn back around. For a dozen reasons, we chose New York, where my wife had grown up. As our plane took off from Seattle, the mountains of the Pacific Northwest loomed before us in their full grandeur, doubtless a metaphor for some unmoving, ageless tranquility that exists just beyond man's pathetic neuroses and petty conficts. The gray, silent city that I had never fully understood slipped into the clouds, disappearing as if it had never been. At least I assume that happened; I had an aisle seat. I spent the first hour after takeoff preoccupied with with thoughts about Doug, Grant, and Marion Zioncheck. How was a story like that supposed to end?

August 2004

My new cell phone rang while I was in Central Park. It turned out to be a woman from one of the five temporary employment agencies I had registered with. Eight weeks in New York and neither my wife nor I had a job. My skills were so specific that I wasn't even qualified to answer an office phone, and nobody was hiring anyway.

"How would you like to work in collections?" she said.

Collections. I saw myself on the phone with little old ladies on fixed incomes in Newark, demanding they pay thirty-five dollars or face the possibility of having their cars repossessed and their credit ratings ruined. I would grow surly and depressed and become estranged from my wife. Despite my asthma I would take up smoking because all my colleagues were doing it to soothe their jangled nerves. Out of apathy I would keep the job for thirty years, leaving it only when I died of emphysema.

But I was broke. "Well, sure," I said. "I guess I could do that."

"It's at Fox," she said.

I groaned, loudly. *Fox.* Home of hyperpatriotic pro-conservative rhetoric as led by Bill O'Reilly. One of the most hated corporations a liberal could name, on par with only Halliburton and Enron. I would be badgering old people in Newark so that Rupert Murdoch could make more money.

But I had to tell my temp agent something. My most recent credit card statement told me what to do. "I can interview with them, at least," I said.

The interview was the next day, and when it was over I walked forty blocks back to the apartment where we were couch surfing and considered my options. Unable to think clearly, I sat down at my computer and made a list:

> • *The poor sometimes have no choice. They have to take the economic opportunities offered them.*
> • *This isn't Fox News—it's a collection of small cable corporations owned by the same parent . . . Globalism means never being able to avoid the companies that make you uneasy. Am I supposed to boycott* The Simpsons *because I don't like Joe Scarborough?*
> • *The left has to adjust to the new realities of the post-9/11 world (Question: Has it?). The kind of ideological purity favored by West Coast anarchists has never been, nor will it ever be, achievable.*
> • *Marion Zioncheck is dead.*

I took the job.

I was assigned to a desk in a cube farm in Fox's New York headquarters, an office building as modern and ugly as all the other prestigious office buildings around Rockefeller Center. The Republicans came for their national convention and clogged the hotels and the streets with ridiculous cowboy hats and fake Purple Hearts that made light of John Kerry's war record. Police with machine guns and bomb sniffing dogs wandered the city, blocking off random Midtown streets every morning. I kept to myself in my cubicle and did my data entry.

Someone asked me: "Are you coming to the Shut-up-a-thon?"

"The *what?*" I said, turning in my chair, blinking violently from the computer screen's relentless glare.

"C'mon!"

Curious, I piled into the elevator with half a dozen people. I had no idea what was going on until one of the full-time employees, a young woman, joyfully exclaimed, "I've never been to a street protest before!"

Outside, a platoon of liberals had surrounded the building. They had signs and were shouting, in a rhapsodic chant/scream, "*Shut! Up! Fox!*" Taking a swipe at O'Reilly's signature talk show rebuttal, no doubt. It wasn't a large crowd—a few hundred at best. They clung to the sidewalk, aware that New York Police would arrest anyone who dared step onto the street. They pressed and swayed against the makeshift guardrails that corporate security had thrown up. A phalanx of police and private guards formed a second barrier separating the employees from the protesters.

Don't you see? *They were screaming at us.*

I felt a nauseated rush to my head and ducked behind a burly man in a suit. But I was exposed when he moved closer for a better view, holding up his cell phone to take a picture. This was an amusing spectacle for him, a late afternoon diversion before the 6 P.M. train to Westchester. Not so for me.

With what dignity I had left, I straightened up and studied the crowd. In that moment I was seized by a vision. They appeared as ghosts to me, I did not know their names, but I recognized all of them, all at once. There was a dreadlocked young man who was only there because his hippie girlfriend had dragged him; there was an anxious woman from Portland who really did believe that world peace could be achieved if everyone engaged in a simultaneous, transcendental moment of yoga; there was a gay Midwesterner who couldn't get over the fact that African-Americans in general had never embraced gay rights, who would only petition government again in middle age when his local parks department wanted to rezone a hiking trail too close to his backyard; there was a social worker whose own self-worth only improved when she was telling other people how to get their lives in order; and there was a dour-faced anarchist waiting for television news to arrive so that they could tape him getting in a fight with a police officer (who, for the record, would much rather have been at home scrubbing the linoleum tiles on his kitchen floor).

I saw through them all. I could tell which ones would be patiently dedicated to social progress for the rest of their lives, which ones would gradually learn to incorporate pragmatism and compromise into their activism, which ones would betray their ideological colleagues as soon as they realized they were getting old and would one day die, and which ones would drive themselves to isolation and madness—most madnesses petty and harmless, one not—by their self-important efforts.

Then my vision vanished, and all that remained was me and the faceless crowd. Their chanting took on the force of a drumbeat. Every word was charged with accusation and reprobation. Every one of their flimsy cardboard signs held me in contempt. I knew what they were saying, and I didn't disagree with it. The only question left was which way I would run if the tear gas grenades began to fall.

Acknowledgments

If I had any outrage left in my system, I would be appalled at the recent rise of narcissism in book acknowledgments. The more people you thank, the less it really means.

I would like to thank my wife Emily Hall, my agent Leslie Falk, Deb Kim, Paula Gilovich, Rick Levin, Nate Lippens, Bruce Reid, Evan Sult, and David Wise.

Thanks to everyone who let themselves be interviewed or gave me information for this endeavor, and a special thanks to Grant Cogswell for being such a sport.